CERTIFICATE
BIOLOGY

n accordance with the latest syllabus prescribed by the Council for the Indian School Certificate Examination, New Delhi.

CERTIFICATE
BIOLOGY

CLASS IX

Author

Dominic Nicholas
C.I.D.T.T. (Cambridge)
Don Bosco School
Siliguri

Susmita Guha
M.Sc. (Botany)
J. D. Public School
Jaipur

Edited by
E. Anna Purna
M.Sc., B.Ed.

OSWAL PUBLISHERS
1/12, Sahitya Kunj, M. G. Road, Agra-282 002

No Part of this book can be reproduced in any form or by any means without the prior written permission of the publishers.

Edition : 2019

ISBN : 978-93-87660-71-7

OSWAL PUBLISHERS

Head office : 1/12, Sahitya Kunj, M.G. Road, Agra-282 002
Phone   : (0562) 2527771- 4, +91 75340 77222
E-mail   : contact@oswalpublishers.com, sales@oswalpublishers.com
Website   : www.oswalpublishers.com
Facebook link : https://www.facebook.com/oswalpublishersindia
Available at : amazon.in, Flipkart, snapdeal

Preface

It is a matter of great satisfaction and pride to present, Certificate Biology textbook for Class X students, from **Oswal Publishers** for the ICSE curriculum. Oswal Publishers take pride in the fact that all of their school textbooks published are widely accepted by the students and teachers.

This latest and current edition is in a completely new format, and is in strict conformity with the latest syllabus and it follows the curriculum laid down by the Council for Indian School Certificate Examination. Great care has been taken to present the subject matter and chapters in a simple and easy-to-understand manner, which is appealing and has high retention value. All topics have been adequately illustrated with detailed diagrams and illustrations, which add to the effectiveness of the text. Scientific concepts that might otherwise seem dull have been presented in a vital, compelling and in a meaningful manner.

Salient Features of the Book

- 'Chapter Highlights' at the beginning of each chapter provides an outline of the concepts discussed in that chapter, giving a step-by-step guide of the chapter content to the students.
- Hyperlinks to useful internet resources have been provided for relevant topics within the chapters.
- Questions have been provided at vital stages within each chapter after each topic, in order to help the students to recapitulate what they have learned so far.
- Diagrams, charts and tables have been incorporated in the text adequately, making the learning process easier and more interesting.
- Each part of this book has been designed and presented in a student friendly manner.
- Exercises at the end of each chapter will go a long way in helping the student assess their preparation for the examinations, and will help them to fine tune their study schedule.
- Interesting facts and questions have been provided to broaden the scope of learning.

Lastly, we wish to express our gratitude and sincere thanks to **Oswal Publishers**, for their complete co-operation in bringing out this book to the entire satisfaction. We sincerely hope that this book will deepen the students understanding in biological science and consequently help them being better prepared for their examination.

All constructive suggestions for the further improvement of the book are welcome and we shall try to incorporate as many of such suggestions as possible in the future editions.

Authors

SYLLABUS CLASS X
SCIENCE (52) : BIOLOGY
SCIENCE Paper - 3

There will be one paper of **two hours** duration of 80 marks and Internal Assessment of practical work carrying 20 marks.

The paper will be divided into **two** sections, Section I (40 marks) and Section II (40 marks).

Section I (compulsory) will contain short answer questions on the entire syllabus.

Section II will contain **six** questions. Candidates will be required to answer any **four** of these **six** questions.

1. **Basic Biology**

   (i) Cell Cycle and Cell Division :

   Cell cycle – Interphase (G1, S, G2) and Mphase

   Cell Division : Mitosis and its stages. A basic understanding of Meiosis as a reduction division (stages not required). Significance and major differences between mitotic and meiotic division.

   (ii) Structure of chromosome :

   Basic structure of chromosome with elementary understanding of terms such as chromatin, chromatid, gene structure of DNA and centromere.

   (iii) Genetics: Mendel's laws of inheritance and sex linked inheritance of diseases.

   Monohybrid cross, dihybrid cross. The following terms to be covered: gene, allele, heterozygous, homozygous, dominant, recessive, mutation, variation, phenotype, genotype. Sex determination in human beings.

   Sex linked inheritance of diseases to include haemophilia and colour blindness (only criss cross inheritance).

2. **Plant Physiology**

   (i) Absorption by roots, imbibition; diffusion and osmosis; osmotic pressure, root pressure; turgidity and flaccidity; plasmolysis and deplasmolysis,; the absorption of water and minerals, active and passive transport (in brief) ; the importance of root hair.

   Characteristics of roots, which make them suitable for absorbing water, should be discussed with the process of absorption. Structure of a single full-grown root hair should be explained.

   (ii) The rise of water up to the xylem; a general idea of Cohesive, Adhesive forces and transpirational pull) ; demonstrated by the use of dyes.

   Experiments to show the conduction of water through the xylem should be discussed. Mention of the causative forces must be made for better understanding but as per the syllabus.

   Transpiration, process and significance; experimental work includes the loss in weight of a potted plant or a leafy shoot in a test tube, the use of cobalt chloride paper. Ganong's potometer and its limitations. The effect of external conditions on the rate of water loss should be stressed.

   Mechanism of stomatal transpiration must be explained so that concept of the process is clear. Adaptations in plants to reduce transpiration to be discussed. A brief idea of guttation and bleeding should be given.

   (iii) Photosynthesis: the nature of the process itself and the great importance of photosynthesis to life in general; experiments to show the necessity of light, carbon dioxide & chlorophyll and also the formation of starch and the output of oxygen; carbon cycle.

   The internal structure of chloroplast should be explained to give an idea of the site of light and dark reaction. Opening and closing of stomata should be explained. Teachers should stress upon the importance of a correct balanced chemical equation. The terms "photochemical" for light phase and "biosynthetic" for dark phase must be introduced. In the light reaction, activation of chlorophyll molecule followed by photolysis of water, release of O_2, formation of ATP and NADPH should be taught. In the dark reaction (detailed equations are not required), only combination of hydrogen released by NADP with CO_2 to form glucose o be discussed. Adaptations in a plant for photosynthesis and experiments with regard to the factors essential for the process should be discussed.

3. **Human Anatomy and Physiology**

    (i) Circulatory System: Main features; the structure and working of the heart, blood vessels, structure and functions of blood and circulation of blood (only names of the main blood vessels entering and leaving the heart, liver and kidney will be required).

    Composition of blood (Structure and functions of RBC, WBC and platelets). Brief idea of tissue fluid and lymph. Increase in efficiency of mammalian red blood cells due to absence of certain organelles should be explained with reasons. A brief idea of blood coagulation. Structure of vein, artery and capillary should be explained with the help of diagrams to bring out clearly the relationship between their structure and function. ABO blood group system, Rh factor; concept of double circulation; concept systole and diastole; blood pressure. Reference to portal system should be made. Working of the heart along with names of the main blood vessels entering and leaving the heart, the liver and the kidney must be taught. Examination of a blood smear under a microscope.

    (ii) Excretory System: Elementary treatment of the structure and function of the kidneys; the kidneys treated as comprising cortex and medulla and consisting of a branched system of tubules well supplied with blood vessels leading to the ureter (details of the courses of the tubules and their blood vessels not required).

    External and internal structure of the kidney; parts of the excretory system along with the blood vessels entering and leaving it should be taught with the help of charts or models. Students should be able to draw the diagrams with correct labelling and know the functions of various parts. A general idea of the structure of a kidney tubule nephron should be given. A brief idea of ultra filtration, selective reabsorption and tubular secretion in relation to the composition of blood plasma and urine formed.

    (iii) Nervous System: Structure of Neuron; central, autonomous and peripheral nervous system (in brief); brain and spinal cord; reflex action and how it differs from voluntary reflex.

    Sense organs – Eye and ear; Eye defects and corrective measures (myopia, hypermetropia, presbiopia, astigmatism and cataract).

    Various parts of the external structure of the brain and its parts (Medulla Oblongata, Cerebrum, Cerebellum, Thalamus, Hypothalamus) and their functions; reference should be made to the distribution of white and gray matter internally. Diagrammatic explanation of the reflex arc, showing the pathway from receptor to effector, differences between natural and acquired reflex should be taught. Structure and function of the Eye and Ear and their various parts. The external and V.S. of the eye must be taught with a brief idea of stereoscopic vision. The course of perception of sound in human ear. Role of ear in maintaining balance.

    (iv) Endocrine System: General study of the following glands: Adrenal, Pancreas, Thyroid and Pituitary. Difference in Endocrine and Exocrine glands.

    Correct location and shape of the gland in the human body should be discussed along with the hormones they secrete (Pancreas: insulin and glucagon to be taught; Thyroid: only thyroxin to be taught). Effects of hypo secretion and hyper secretion of hormones must be discussed. The term tropic hormones should be explained in the study of pituitary. Brief idea of feedback mechanism must be given.

    (v) The Reproductive System: Organs, fertilisation and a general outline of nutrition and respiration of the embryo. Menstrual cycle, outline of menstrual cycle.

    Functions of organs and accessory glands must be discussed. An idea of secondary sexual characters, structure and functions of the various parts of the sperm and an egg. Fertilization, implantation, placenta, foetal membranes, gestation and parturition identical and fraternal twins to be explained briefly.

    (vi) Population: Problems posed by the increase in population in India; need for adopting control measures - population control.

    Main reasons for the sharp rise in human population in India and in the world. The terms demography, population density, birth rate, death rate and growth rate of population should be explained. With population growth, increased consumption and urbanization, there is a need to keep a check on demands of urban areas over rural areas, of exploitative use of resources rather than sustainable use. Methods of population control to be taught.

4. **Physical Health and Hygiene**

    (i) Aids to health: an understanding of the use and action of the following - vaccination; immunisation; antitoxin; serum; antiseptics; disinfectants; penicillin; sulphonamide drugs; First Aid.

An idea of local defense system and their merits, active and passive immunity, difference between antiseptics and disinfectants to be discussed. Basic principles of first aid to be taught.

(ii) Health organisations: Red Cross, WHO; common health problems in India.

Major activities of Red Cross and WHO should be discussed. Common health problems in India.

5. Pollution

(i) Types of pollution - air, water, (fresh and marine) soil, radiation and noise.

Self explanatory.

(ii) Sources of pollution and major pollutant:

Air : *Vehicular, industrial, burning garbage, brick kilns.*

Water: *Household detergents, sewage, industrial waste, oil spills, thermal pollution.*

Soil : *Industrial waste, urban commercial and domestic waste, chemical fertilizers, biomedical waste, like needles, syringes, soiled dressings etc, biodegradable waste, like paper, vegetable peels, etc; Non biodegradable waste like plastics, glass, Styrofoam etc.; Pesticides like DDT etc.*

Radiation : *X-rays; radioactive fallout from nuclear plants.*

(iii) Effects of pollution on climate, environment, human health and other organisms and its abatement.

Greenhouse effect and global warming, Acid rain, Ozone layer depletion.

Meaning of the terms, causes, effect on life on earth, idea about setting standards - Euro/Bharat stage vehicular standards.

INTERNAL ASSESSMENT OF PRACTICAL WORK

The practical work will be designed to test the ability of the candidates to make accurate observation from specimens of plants and animals. For this, the candidates should be familiar with the use of a hand lens of not less than x6 magnification. Candidates should be trained to make simple and accurate drawings and brief notes as a means of recording their observations.

The practical examiners will assume that candidates would have carried out the practical work outlined below.

PLANT LIFE

(i) Observation of permanent slides of mitosis.

Self-explanatory.

(ii) Experiments indicating osmosis, diffusion and absorption.

The teacher should give a demonstration and then the students should perform the experiments in order to have a better understanding of the processes.

(iii) Physiological experiments on transpiration to be set up by the teacher and the pupils to identify the products, draw and label the apparatus.

The teacher should set up the experiment stepwise so that the student gets a clear idea of the aim, apparatus, procedure and result of the experiment. For transpiration experiments the $CoCl_2$ paper should be kept in a dessicator and its importance should be explained. Limitations for the use of Ganong's potometer should be given.

(iv) Experiments to show the necessity of light, carbon dioxide and chlorophyll essential for photosynthesis; release of O_2 during photosynthesis. Candidates to write down their observations and draw and label the apparatus.

Importance of destarching the plant before the experiment should be discussed. Diagrams should be drawn with the correct labelling. Pupils should be able to analyse the result.

ANIMAL LIFE

(i) Identification of the structure of the urinary system, heart (internal structure) and brain (external view) through models and charts

(ii) The identification of different types of blood cells under a microscope.

Different types of WBCs should be observed. Teacher should point out the differences between red blood cells and white blood cells. Ratio of red blood cells to white blood cells should be discussed.

(iii) The structure of the Ear and an Eye (candidates will be required to identify each structure in the models of these organs).

Models should be shown and students should draw correct labelled diagrams.

(iv) Identification and location of selected endocrine glands (Adrenal, Pancreas, Thyroid and Pituitary glands) with the help of a model or chart.

Correct labelled diagram to be drawn.

(v) Compiling material for a First Aid box.

Self-explanatory.

EVALUATION

The practical work/project work are to be evaluated by the subject teacher and by an External Examiner. (The External Examiner may be a teacher nominated by the Head of the school, who could be from the faculty, **but not teaching the subject in the relevant section/class**. For example, a teacher of Biology of Class VIII may be deputed to be an External Examiner for Class X, Biology projects.)

The Internal Examiner and the External Examiner will assess the practical work/project work independently.

Award of Marks (20 Marks)

Subject Teacher (Internal Examiner)	10 marks
External Examiner	10 marks

The total marks obtained out of 20 are to be sent to the Council by the Head of the school.

The Head of the school will be responsible for the entry of marks on the mark sheets provided by the Council.

INTERNAL ASSESSMENT IN SCIENCE - GUIDELINES FOR MARKING WITH GRADES

Criteria	Preparation	Procedure/Testing	Observation	Inference/Results	Presentation
Grade I (4 marks)	Follows instructions (written, oral, diagrammatic with understanding; modifies if needed. Familiarity with and safe use of apparatus, materials, techniques.	Analyses problem systematically. Recognises a number of variables and attempt to control them to build a logical plan of investigation.	Records data/observations without being given a format. Comments upon, recognises use of instruments, degree of accuracy. Recording is systematic.	Processes data without format. Recognises and comments upon sources of error. Can deal with unexpected results, suggesting modifications.	Presentation is accurate and good. Appropriate techniques are well used.
Grade II (3 marks)	Follows instructions to perform experiment with step-by-step operations. Awareness of safety. Familiarity with apparatus, materials and techniques.	Specifies sequence of operation; gives reasons for any change in procedure. Can deal with two variables, controlling one.	Makes relevant observations. No assistance is needed for recording format that is appropriate.	Processes data appropriately as per a given format. Draws qualitative conclusions consistent with required results.	Presentation is adequate. Appropriate techniques are used.
Grade III (2 marks)	Follws instructions to perform a single operation at a time. Safety awareness. Familiarity with apparatus & materials.	Develops simple experimental stratery. Trial and error modifications made to proceed with the experiment.	Detailed instructions needed to record observations. Format required to record results.	Processes data approximately with a detailed format provided. Draws observations qualitative conclusions as required	Presentation is reasonable, but disorganised in some places. Overwriting; rough work is untidy.
Grade IV (1 mark)	Follows some instructions to perform a single practical operation. Casual about safety. Manages to use apparatus & materials.	Struggles through the experiment. Follows very obvious experimental strategy.	Format required to record observations/readings, but tends to make mistakes in recording.	Even when detailed format is provided, struggle or makes errors while processing data. Reaches conclusions with help.	Presentation is poor and disorganised but follows an acceptable sequence. Rough work missing or untidy.
Grade V (0 marks)	Not able to follow instructions or proceed with practical work without full assistance. Unaware of safety.	Cannot proceed with the experiment without help from time to time.	Even when format is given, recording is faulty or irrelevant.	Cannot process results, nor draw conclusions, even with considerable help.	Presentation unacceptable; disorganised, untidy/poor. Rough work missing.

CONTENTS

1. Cell : The Unit of Life — 13–25
2. Cell : Cycle, Division and Structure of Chromosomes — 26–38
3. Genetics — 39–49
4. Absorption by Roots — 50–59
5. Transpiration — 60–69
6. Photosynthesis — 70–79
7. The Circulatory System — 80–92
8. Excretory System — 93–100
9. Nervous System — 101–119
10. Endocrine Glands — 120–131
11. The Reproductive System — 132–140
12. Population : The Increasing Numbers and Rising Problems — 141–145
13. Aids to Health — 146–155
14. Health and Health Organizations — 156–159
15. Pollution : An Increasing Environmental Hazard — 160–168

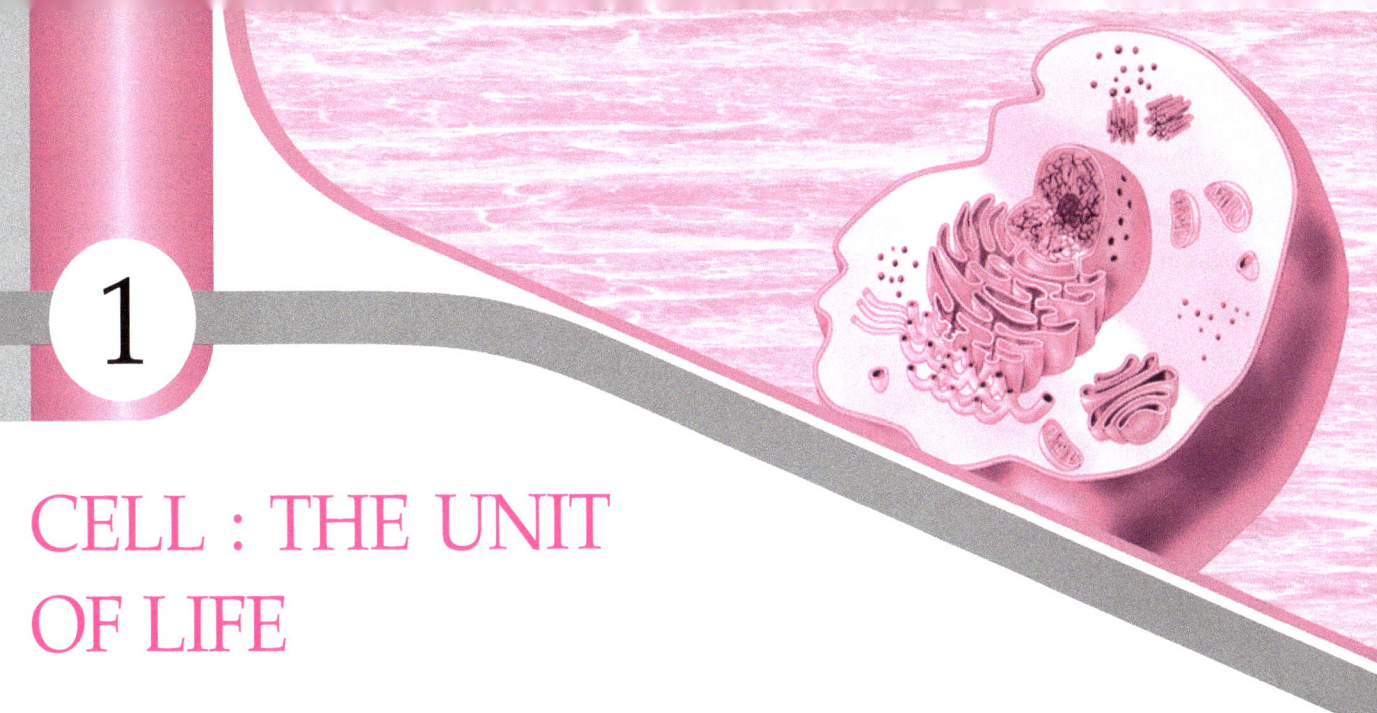

1

CELL : THE UNIT OF LIFE

CHAPTER HIGHLIGHTS
1.1. Basic Study of Cell
1.2. Discovery of Cell – Cell Theory
1.3. Characteristics of Cells
    1.3.1. Cell - its Abundance
    1.3.2. Cell Size
    1.3.3. Cell Shapes
1.4. Cell Structure and Functions
1.5. Structure of Cell : Cell Organelles
    1.5.1. Cell Organelles, their Characteristics and Functions
1.6. Microscopic Examination
    (a) Onion Peel (Plant Cell) and (b) Cells of Cheek Lining (Animal Cell)
1.7 Cellular Activity Results in Activities of Living Beings
1.8. Nucleus: Key Performer of the Cell

The *Cell*, (from Latin cella, meaning "small room"), is the basic structural and functional unit of all living organisms. Cells are the fundamental biological units of all known life forms and are often called the *'building blocks of life'*. Before moving on to more advanced study of the cell, it is important to refresh what you have already studied about cell structure and functions in class IX.

1.1. BASIC STUDY OF CELL

Cell is the fundamental structural and functional unit of all living beings. The study of cells is called cell biology.

It is important to remember some fundamental facts about cells :

(a) It is the *basic unit of life*, present within all living beings, animals and plants.

(b) New cells are formed from *pre-existing cells*.

(c) Each cell is the *structural* and *the functional unit* of all living organisms.

(d) Cells of all organisms have close similarities in structure, molecular organisation and biological activities.

1.2. DISCOVERY OF CELL

(a) The cell was first discovered by **Robert Hooke** in 1665. He examined (under a coarse, compound microscope) very thin slices of bottle cork and saw a multitude of tiny pores that he remarked looked like the walled compartments a monk would live in. Because of this association, Hooke called them cells, the name they still bear. Hooke's description of cells was published in the book, *Micrographia*. The cells observed by Hooke gave no indication of the nucleus and other organelles found in most living cells.

(b) The first man to witness a living cell under a microscope was **Antony van Leeuwenhoek**, who in 1674 described the algae *Spirogyra*. **Van Leeuwenhoek** probably also saw bacteria.

(c) In 1833, botanist **Robert Brown** coined the term "nucleus" while studying fertilization in orchids. He identified the nucleus as a dark, opaque spot that was seen in germ cells.

(d) **Schleiden and Theodor Schwann** (1810-1882) was the first to recognize that all plants and animals are composed of cells. In 1839, they defined their *"cell theory"* in which they also stated that nuclei and cell membranes are common to all cells and recognized the presence of unicellular (single-celled) and multicellular (many-celled) organisms.

1.3. CHARACTERISTICS OF CELL

1.3.1. Cell - its Abundance

The growth of the living organism is the result of the growth of cell.

Not all living organisms are made up of an identical number of cells. Living organisms could be either:

(i) Single celled : Made up of just one cell. They are called unicellular organisms.

Examples : *Paramecium, euglena,* diatoms, leucocytes, yeast (Fig. 1.1) etc. as shown below.

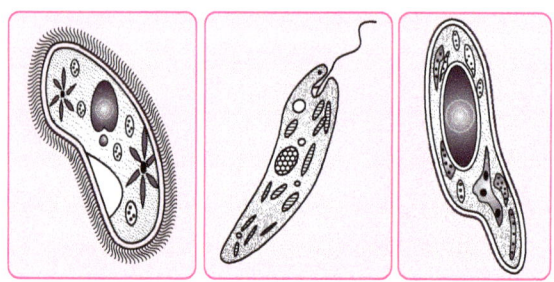

Fig. 1.1 : (A) Paramecium, (B) Euglena, (C) Yeast single celled organisms

(ii) Few-celled : Made up of few cells, may be a hundred or a few thousand.

Examples : *Spirogyra, Volvox* (Fig. 1.2), as shown in picture below :

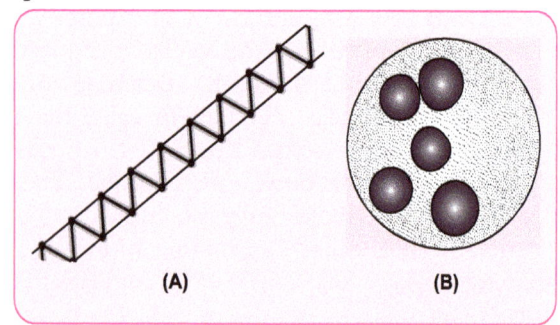

Fig. 1.2 : Few-celled organisms (A) Spirogyra (B) Volvox

(iii) Multi-celled : Made up of millions and billions of cells. They are called multicellular.

Example : Human, coral reef, mango, etc.

1.3.2. Cell Size

Cells are the smallest component of an organism, and are microscopic in size. Even so, they tend to vary in size from 1/10th of a millimetre to 1/10,000th of a millimetre.

(a) Smallest cells : Bacteria and red blood cells in the human body are the smallest known cells.

(b) Longest cells : Nerve cells in the human body extend from the finger tips to the spinal cord in the backbone and are the longest cells known. In mammals the nerve cells may reach a length of more than a metre.

(c) Largest cells : Bird eggs, especially the yellow yolk part, is the largest single cell known to man. The egg of an ostrich is the largest cell in the world, which is about 176 mm in diameter.

1.3.3. Cell Shapes

Cells though small in size but vary vastly in shapes. They can be disc-like, polygonal, rectangular, cuboid, thread-like, branched or even irregular depending upon functions they perform (Fig. 1.3).

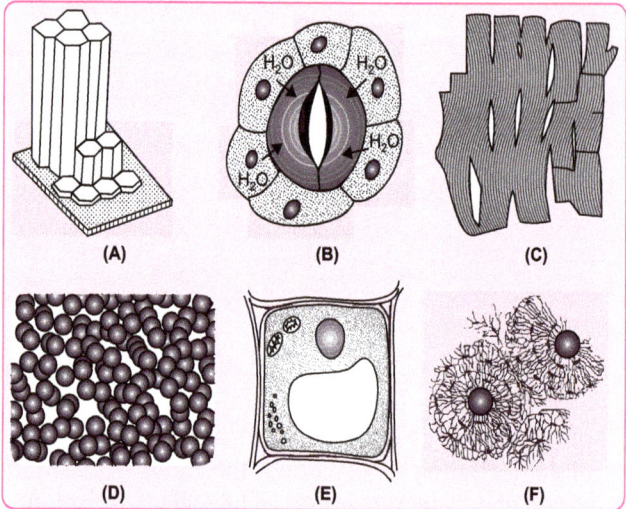

Fig. 1.3 : (A) Epithelial cells, (B) Guard cells, (C) Striated muscle fibre, (D) Red blood cells, (E) Plant cells, (F) Bone cells

(a) The human red *blood cells* are circular and biconcave, which helps in the easy passage of blood through the narrow capillaries and helps in the transmission of oxygen. Red blood cells are devoid of nuclei so that they can bind to maximum amount of oxygen.

(b) The *white blood cells* or WBC are amoeboid in shape and movement. They can thus easily squeeze out through capillary walls and protect our body from attacks by disease causing germs (pathogens).

(c) *Nerve cells* are long cells, connecting one part of the body to another and are specially adapted to carry 'impulses' over large distances across the

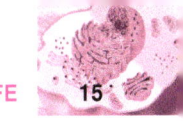

CELL : THE UNIT OF LIFE

body rapidly. In humans, nerve cells are connected, from the tip of the finger to the spinal cord in the backbone and serve to transmit impulses to and fro from one region to another.

(d) *Muscle cells* are long and contractile, which help to pull or squeeze parts and thus allow movement of body parts.

(e) *Guard cells* of the stomatal pores in the leaves of plants are bean-shaped, which help in the opening and closing of the pore by becoming turgid or flaccid, thus changing their shape. This enables gaseous exchange in leaves.

(f) Fat cells are the fat repository of the body, for its energy requirements.

(g) Bone cells are the cells which vary in shape depending upon their function.

(h) Sieve cells are with sieves or pores, allowing nutrient supply, intake and processing in plants.

Smaller the cell–Greater the efficiency.

The small size of the cells is an advantage for two reasons :

(i) The small dimension of the cell helps in rapid communication with the other cells of the body, thus helping to perform the cell activities effectively and efficiently.

(ii) Small cells with large surface area result in a higher surface to volume ratio, thus allowing the following activities to occur more efficiently:

(1) Greater diffusion of nutrient intake into the cell.
(2) Greater ability to expel water from the cell.
(3) Greater diffusion of oxygen into the cell and carbon dioxide out of it.
(4) Greater ability to repair damaged cells.

PROGRESS CHECK

TRUE OR FALSE

1. Humans and plants are few celled. (T/F)
2. Ostrich eggs termed as the longest cell on earth. (T/F)
3. White blood cells are amoeboid and move around in an amoeboid form. (T/F)
4. Cells are composed of highly independent and randomly interacting components.

1.4. CELL STRUCTURE (FIG. 1.4 AND FIG. 1.5) AND FUNCTIONS

Animation for Cell Structure
http://www.youtube.com/watch?v=o1GQyciJaTA
http://www.youtube.com/watch?v=MD5kvqO96Os

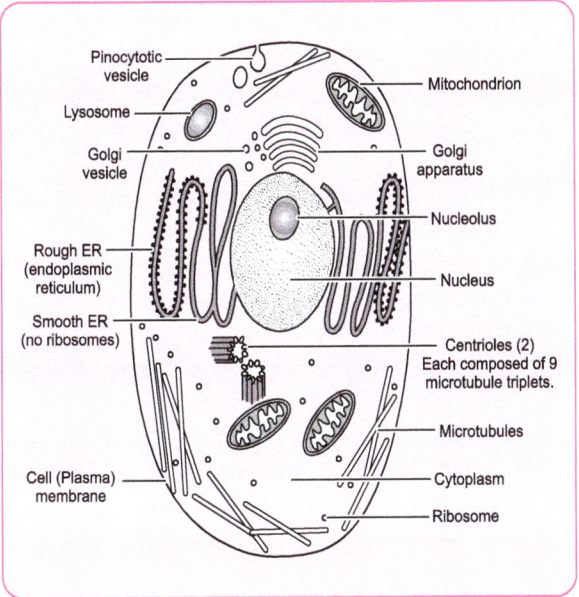

Fig. 1.4 : Generalised view of animal cell under the compound microscope

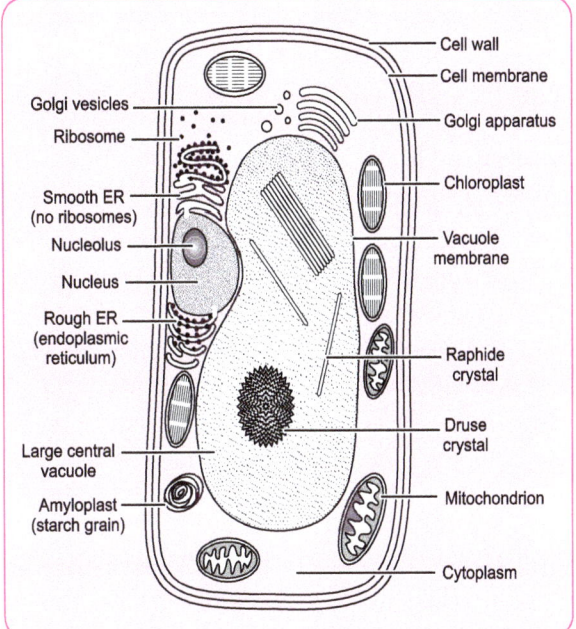

Fig. 1.5 : Generalised view of plant cell under the compound microscope

Essential parts of the Cell

All cells have following the essential parts :

(a) Cell membrane, (b) Cell wall (plant cell), (c) Cytoplasm, (d) Nucleus.

(a) Cell membrane

(i) Found in the both animal and plant cells.

(ii) They have fine pores, whose function is to allow substances to enter or leave the cell.

(iii) Cell membranes are selectively *semi permeable*, allowing only certain substances to enter or leave the cell and preventing others (Fig. 1.6).

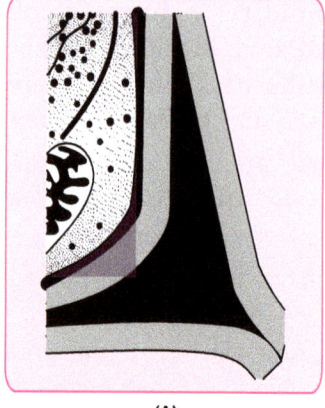

(A)

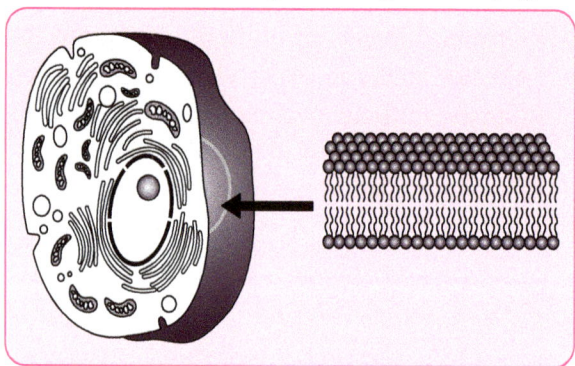

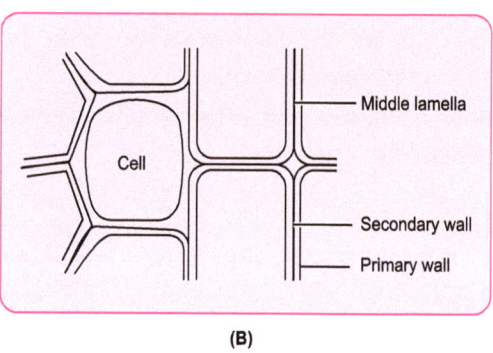

(B)

Fig. 1.6 : Cell membrane which is found in both animal and plant cell regulates the entry and exit of substances from the cell

Fig. 1.7 : Structure of cell wall

(iv) This part of the cell is the outermost layer in animal cell; in plant cell, an additional outer, rigid, protective and non-living semi permeable layer called cell wall surrounds the cell membrane. The cell wall is made up of cellulose.

(v) It separates protoplasm from the environment.

(vi) It controls cell form and activity.

(vii) Flexible and living, they are made up of lipoproteins.

(b) Cell wall

(i) Cell wall is non-living, made up of cellulose and provides protection to plant cells (Fig. 1.7 A). In fungi, cell wall is composed of chitin.

(ii) Cell wall provides shape and the rigidity to the plant cell but does not interfere with the functioning of the cell membrane.

(iii) Cell wall is permeable due to the presence of microscopic channels called *plasmodesmata* that allows the entry and exit of substances from the cell.

(iv) Cell wall protects the cell organelles and is attached to the cell membrane via thin layer.

(v) Cell wall is composed of three layers, middle lamella, primary wall and secondary wall (Fig.1.7B).

(c) Cytoplasm

(i) Cytoplasm is colourless part within the cell membrane and all the cell organelles are embedded in it.

(ii) It is a jelly like semi-liquid substance which appears colourless and transparent under the compound microscope.

(iii) Most of the chemical reactions in the cell occur in the cytoplasm. Cytoplasm is in a perpetual state of dynamic motion.

(iv) Living cell organelles are contained in the cytoplasm, viz., *mitochondria, golgi bodies, ribosomes,* etc.

(v) Other than the organelles, the rest of the cytoplasm is known *as cytosol*.

(vi) Cytoplasm contains mixtures of soluble organic and inorganic compounds along with water and different organelles.

(vii) The constituents of cytoplasm vary from cell to cell and with the age of the cell.

(viii) Cytoplasm participates in intracellular distribution of nutrients, metabolites and enzyme.

Many enzyme catalysed chemical reactions occur in the cytoplasm.

(d) Nucleus

In the centre of the cytoplasm lies a small round mass called *nucleus* (Fig. 1.8). Discovered by **Robert**

Brown in 1833, it is often described as the brain of the cell, being responsible for regulating all the metabolic and hereditary activities of the cell. The nucleus is made up of the following :

(i) Nuclear membrane : Within the nucleus lies the nuclear membrane, a selectively permeable envelope-like structure, which contains the somewhat denser nucleoplasm. The nuclear membrane separates the nucleoplasm from cytoplasm and provides a pathway for the transport of material between nucleus and cytoplasm.

(ii) Nucleoplasm : The nuclear envelope has an empty space which is filled with a transparent semi-solid, granular substance called nucleoplasm. All nuclear components are suspended in the nucleoplasm. Nucleoplasm contains a variety of chemical substances such as iron, protein etc. The nucleoplasm contains fibre like structures called chromatin fibres which get thicker during the process of cell division and are then called chromosomes.

(iii) Nucleolus : It is a conspicuous rounded structure within the nucleus. Every nucleus must contain at least one nucleolus, which helps in the synthesis of proteins. Some cells may contain more than one nucleolus, but each cell has a fixed number of nucleoli. It is dense and typically spherical in shape and its size is related to the level of synthetic activity in the cell. It takes stains intensely because of large amount of DNA and RNA it contains. They are responsible for the production of ribosomes. They also participate in the production of protein, which

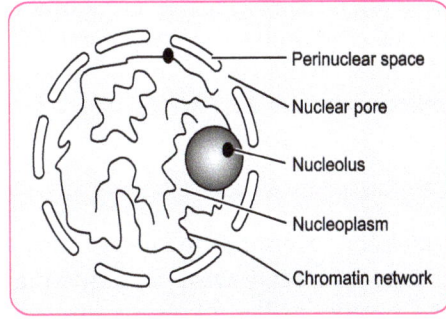

Fig.1.8 : Structure of nucleus

leads to the formation and storing of RNA.

1.5. FINER STRUCTURE OF CELL : THE ORGANELLES

In cell biology, an organelle is a specialized subunit within a cell that has a specific function, and it is usually separately enclosed within its own *lipid bilayer*. These structures are to the cell what individual organs are to the body and hence the name organelle.

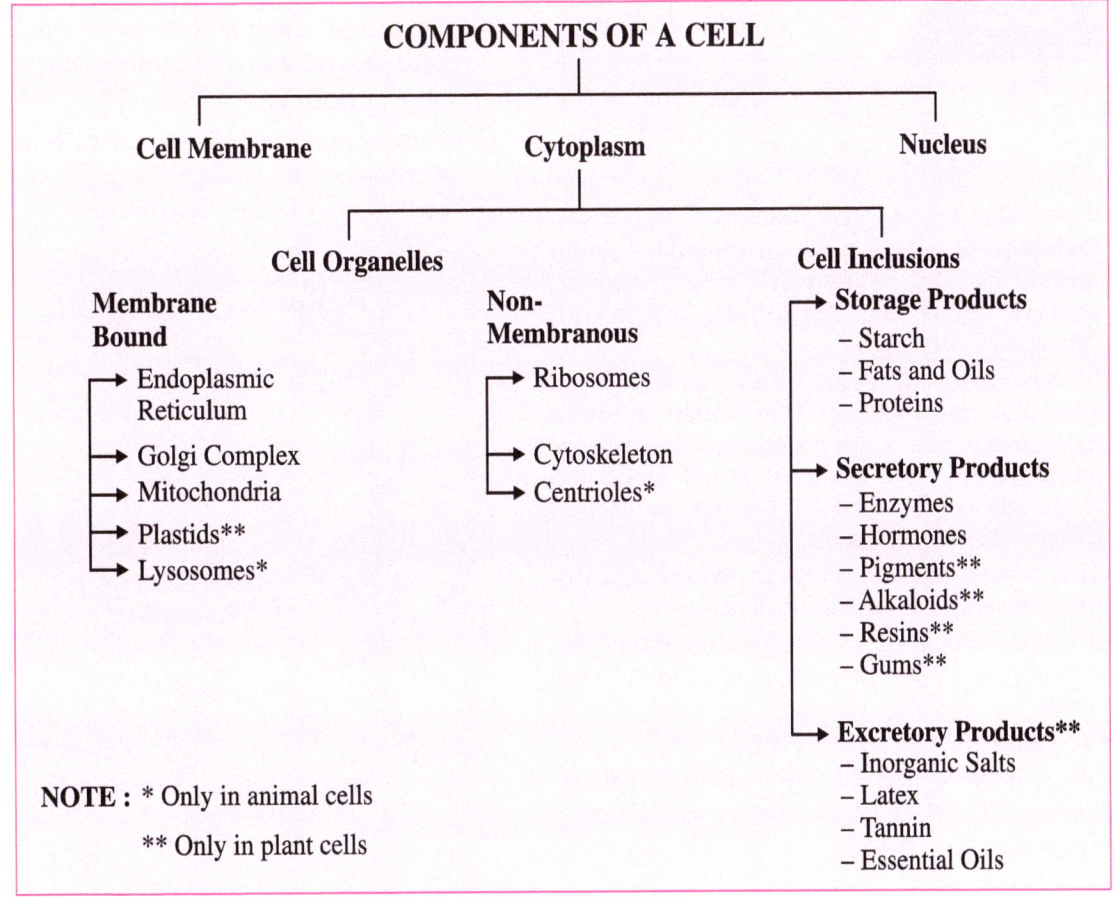

Protoplasm is the living substance of the cell, including the cytoplasm, nucleus and other living bodies within the cell. It is a semi-transparent fluid, mostly colourless, grey or brown. It is known as protoplast in plant cells after the cell wall is removed from them. Both the plant and the animal cells have similar living bodies except for the additional cell wall in plant cells and centrosomes with centrioles in animal cells. All these living bodies are collectively termed as organelles.

1.5.1. Cell Organelles, their Characteristics and Functions

Besides the exterior structures of the cell like cell membrane and cell wall described above, the cytoplasm contains the following organelles that are vital for all cell functions :

(a) Endoplasmic reticulum
  (i) Endoplasmic reticulum (Fig. 1.9), named by **Porter.** due to its reticulate form.

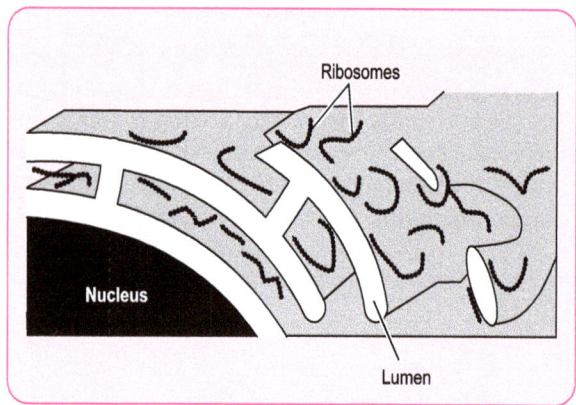

Fig. 1.9 : Structure of endoplasmic reticulum

  (ii) It provides a supportive framework to the cell.
  (iii) Endoplasmic reticulum is an irregular tubular double membrane network which may be smooth (without ribosomes) or rough (ribosomes attached).
  (iv) It has ribosomes attached to it. When ribosomes are attached they impart a rough appearance and known as *rough endoplasmic reticulum*. In some cases ER is not associated with ribosomes and is known as *smooth endoplasmic reticulum*.
  (v) This tubular network helps in the transport of proteins and fats to the nucleus.
  (vi) It is continuous with the cell membrane on the outside and the nuclear membrane on the inside.

(b) Mitochondria
  (i) Mitochondria are double-walled structure, sausage like in shape and are the cell's energy producers (Fig. 1.10).

  (ii) Its inner walls are thrown into folds called *cristae*.

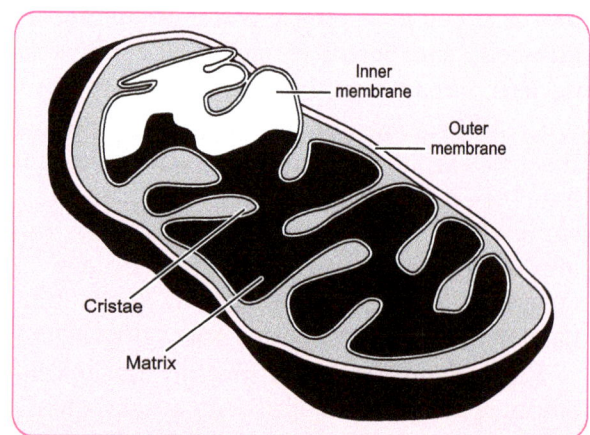

Fig.1.10 : Sausage like mitochondria structure

  (iii) They allow molecular oxygen from the air to oxidize fats and carbohydrates existing in the cell. They are called the *powerhouse of the cell*.
  (iv) In plants, energy is released during photosynthesis thus, justifying the lack of mitochondria in plant cells.
  (v) They release energy into the cytoplasm through pyruvic acid in the form of ATP (adenosine triphosphate), an energy rich compound.
  (vi) Mitochondria have their own DNA containing several genes and hence are self-duplicating units.
  (vii) They also contain their own ribosomes and help to synthesize respiratory enzymes.

(c) Golgi apparatus
  (i) Golgi apparatus in animal cells is flattened membrane sacs stacked like a pile of coins; they consist of *tubules, vesicles* and *vacuoles* (Fig. 1.11).

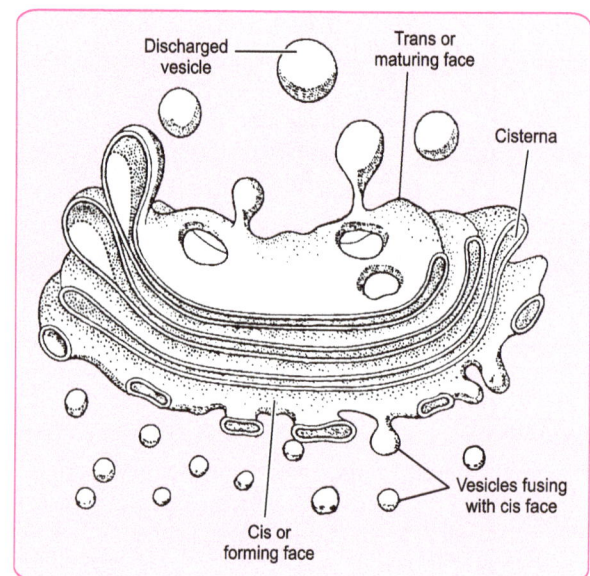

Fig.1.11 : Structure of golgi apparatus

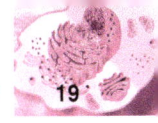

CELL : THE UNIT OF LIFE

(ii) In plant cells these are distributed throughout the cytoplasm and are called *dicytosomes*.

(iii) In animal cells they are larger and may be one or two in number.

(iv) In plant cells, they are smaller and more numerous.

(v) Their main functions are synthesis and secretion of glycoproteins, formation of yolk and formation of acrosome of sperm.

(d) Ribosomes

(i) They are single walled, dense bodies, spherical in shape, which mainly consist of the RNA (ribo nucleic acid).

(ii) Ribosomes are termed as protein factories of the cell, since they help in the manufacture and synthesis of proteins.

(iii) Ribosomes occur either scattered in the cytoplasm or attached to the endoplasmic reticulum (Fig. 1.12).

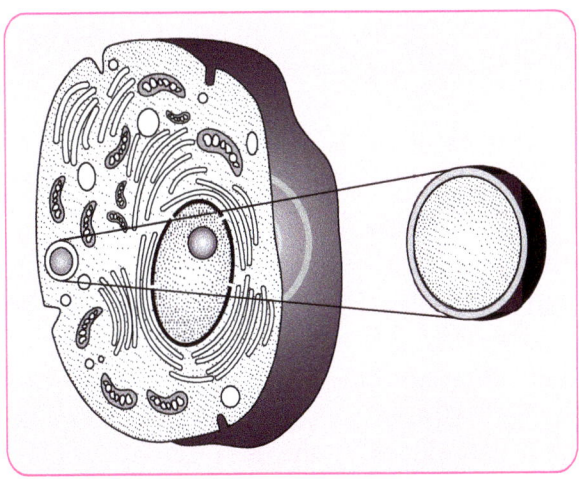

Fig. 1.13 : Lysosomes

(v) These digestive centres tend to digest the stored food during starvation period of the cell.

When the cells are damaged or old, they are mostly destroyed by their own lysosomes thus, they are also termed as suicide bags.

(f) Centrosomes

(i) Centrosomes are only found in animal cells. Centriole is an oval or rounded structure, which lies near the nucleus (Fig. 1.14). Each centriole is made up of nine triplets of microtubules.

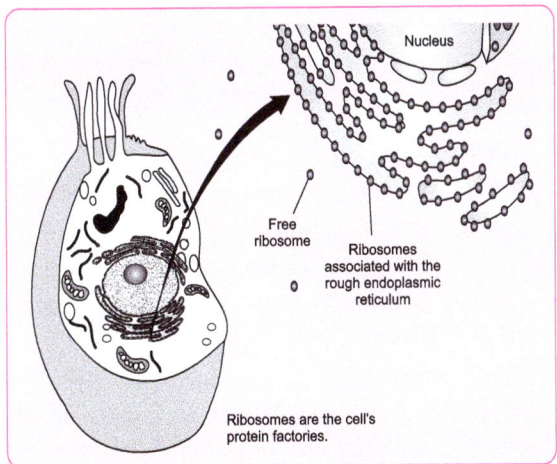

Fig.1.12 : Ribosomes attached to the endoplasmic recticulum

(iv) They are single walled, dense and spherical in shape and are composed mainly of RNA.

(v) Ribosomes found in clusters are known as *polysomes or polyribosomes*.

(e) Lysosomes

(i) Lysosomes (Fig. 1.13) are found in most eukaryotic cells, but are abundant in animal cells showing phagocytic activity.

(ii) They are minute vesicles or granules which contain 40 different types of enzymes.

(iii) These enzymes aid intracellular digestion. Lysomes also destroy foreign bodies that enter the cell.

(iv) They bud out from the Golgi bodies and are also known as the intracellular digestive centres.

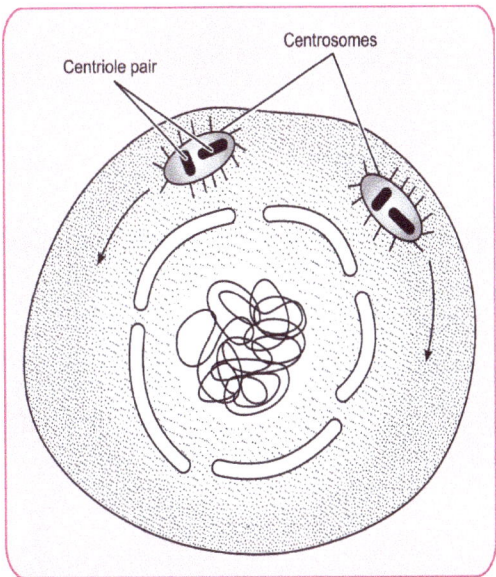

Fig.1.14 : Centrosomes is located mostly near the nucleus

(ii) They help in the initiating and controlling the cell division. Centrioles are also involved in the organisation and development of cilia and flagella.

(g) Peroxisomes

(i) Peroxisomes are micro bodies that are found mostly in kidney and liver cells and leaf parenchyma cells.

(ii) They contain powerful oxidative enzymes such as uric acid, adenine and guanine, for the purpose of photorespiration, hydrogen peroxide metabolism and purine metabolism. This is the reason they help in the removal of toxic substances.

(h) Centrioles
(i) Centrioles (Fig. 1.15) are only found in animal cells.
(ii) They are bundles of *microtubules*, which are structured in a right angle form and are surrounded by the centrosomes.

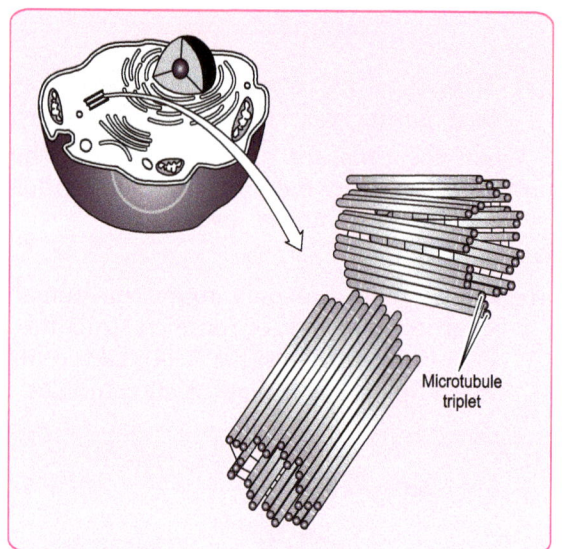

Fig.1.15 : Microscopic view of centrioles

(iii) They initiate cell division by facilitating spindle formation.

(i) Plastids
(i) Plastids are found in plant cells only (Fig. 1.16).

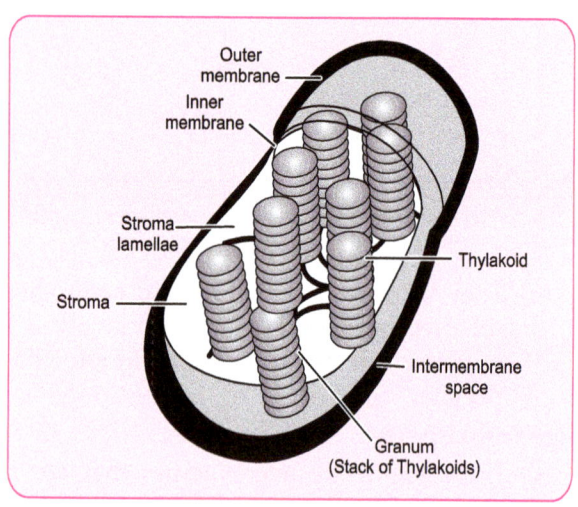

Fig. 1.16 : Plastids only found in plant cells

(ii) They come in different shapes: oval, spherical, or disc-like and contain the thylakoids known as chlorophyll.
(iii) Plastids have double membranous wall with protein matrix which contains the DNA.
(iv) Plastids have the power to divide and replicate themselves.
(v) Plastids are categorized into *leucoplast*, *chromoplast* and *chloroplast* (Fig. 1.17).
(vi) Plastids are involved in the synthesis and storage of carbohydrates.

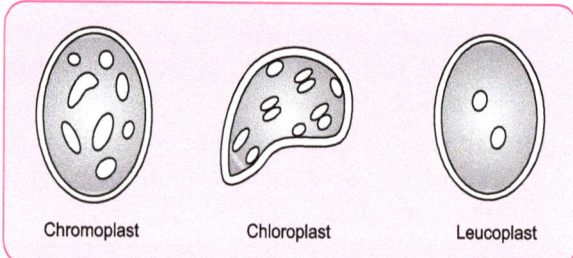

Fig.1.17 : Plastids in three forms: Chromoplast, Chloroplast and Leucoplast

1. **Leucoplast**
   - The word 'leuco' means white, which signifies no involvement of colour or pigment.
   - Leucoplasts help in the storage of starch and are found in potato cells. When they store starch they are known as *amyloplasts*.
   - They store food in the form of carbohydrates, lipids and proteins. When they store oil, they are known as *elaioplasts* and *proteinoplasts* when they store proteins.
   - They are typically found in ground tissue of certain roots and stems, in meristematic cells and seeds.

2. **Chromoplast**
   - The word 'chromo' means colour.
   - It includes coloured plastids such as yellow, orange, and red which are usually found in the petals of flowers or in fruits.
   - The pigments which give these colours are known as xanthophylls (yellow) and carotene (orange-red).
   - Pigments associated with colours such as blue, violet, or purple are known as *anthocyanins*.
   - These colours help attract insects for pollination.

3. **Chloroplasts**
   - The word chloro means green. The pigment associated with this color is chlorophyll.

- It is typically present in green algae and higher plants and is bounded by a double membrane of lipo protein which is known as stroma.
- The function of chlorophyll is to take in carbon dioxide and solar energy to produce starch and sugar. Since chlorophyll is a green pigment, it is mostly found in leaves.
- It contains DNA and also has the capacity to divide.

Example of fruit Ripening

A raw tomato is green and as it ripens, it turns red. This is because during the process of ripening chlorophyll disintegrates and red carotene takes its place.

(j) Chromatin fibres

(i) Chromatin fibres are thread-like structures present in nucleoplasm. They are made up of DNA. They are not clearly visible in the nucleus but become distinct during cell division.

(ii) During cell division these threads tend to swell up and form ribbon like structures. These ribbons like threads are then known as chromosomes.

(iii) Chromosomes carry the hereditary information on genes.

Besides the living organelles described above, the cell also includes non-living structures such as :

1. Vacuoles
- Present in both plant as well as animal cells.
- They are clear spaces which are either filled with water or solutions of other substances.
- Vacuoles are large in size in plant cells and smaller in animal cells.
- Vacuoles function in regulation of the water and solute content of the cell, i.e. in osmoregulation, storage and digestion.
- They are pressed against the cell wall in plant cell thus, providing turgidity to the cell.
- They help in storage of water, food substances, and waste products.
- They have an outer covering called tonoplast which covers the vacuole (Fig. 1.18).
- They occupy more than 90% of the volume of most mature plant cells.

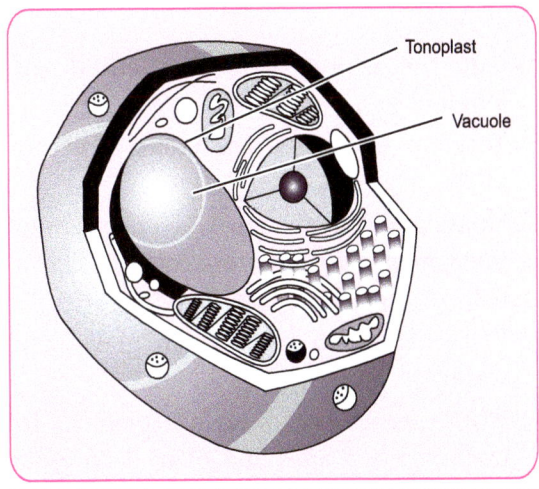

Fig.1.18 : A vacuole with an outer covering tonoplast

2. Granules
- These are non-living cytoplasmic inclusions. These are small particles, crystals or droplets.
- Starch (in plant cell), glycogen (in animal cell) and fat containing granules serve as food for the cell (Fig. 1.19).

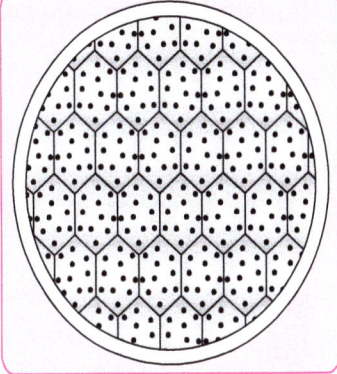

Fig. 1.19 : Microscopic view of granules present in plant cell

1.6. MICROSCOPIC EXAMINATION OF PLANT & ANIMAL CELL

Microscopic Examination of Onion Peel

Following the procedure given below, one can easily prepare the epidermal peel from an onion (Fig. 1.20).

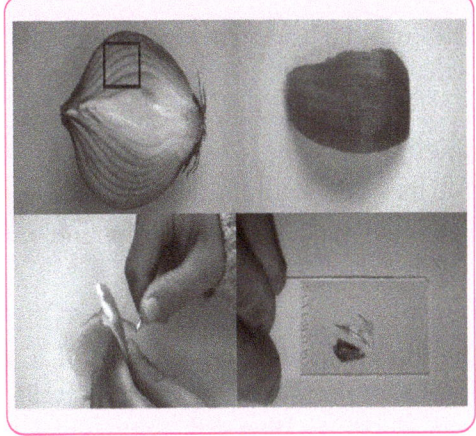

Fig.1.20 : A pictorial representation of the procedure to prepare the epidermal peel of an onion

Procedure

(a) Cut the onion into four equal quarters, lengthwise.
(b) Tear one thick scale leaf (inner layer) from one of the quarters.
(c) Holding the fleshy inner layer, carefully tear a transparent strip from the concave side with the help of forceps or tweezers.
(d) Place this strip in a watch glass containing water.
(e) Now carefully cut a square piece of this peel (approx 5 x 5 mm) and place it on a slide.
(f) To avoid the wrinkling of the tissues, cover the peel with cover slip carefully.
(g) Now examine the slide under a low power microscope.
(h) Staining the material with iodine or eosin solution will give a clearer view of the nucleus.
(i) For a detailed structure of the cell examine the preparation under a high power microscope.

Observations

Cells are strongly bound together and the nucleus is located on a one side which is common in plant cells.

(a) Onion peel cells are regular shaped, linear and rectangular (Fig. 1.21).

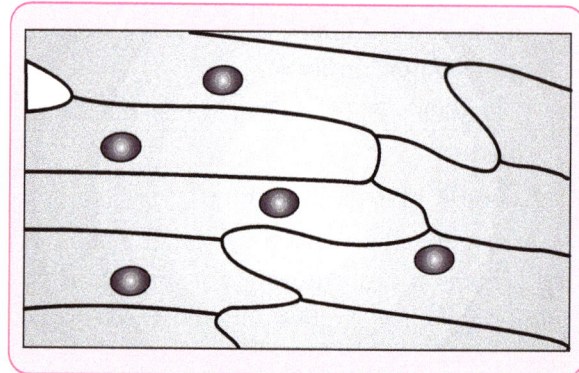

Fig.1.21 : Onion peel cells under low power

(b) They have a definite cell wall with cytoplasm surrounding one or two large vacuoles and a well-defined nucleus.
(c) Greater details such as the thickness of the cell wall can be observed under a high power microscope.

PROGRESS CHECK

FILL IN THE BLANKS

1. Cell membrane separates ....
2. Nucleus was discovered by ....
3. Nucleoplasm contains fiber like structures called ....
4. .... is the power house of the cell.
5. .... help in controlling of cell division.
6. The chloroplast is where .... occur.

Microscopic Examination of Animal Cell

Procedure

(a) Using a blunt knife, scrape the inner side of the cheek.
(b) The mass collected should then be placed on a slide.
(c) To observe the nucleus better, use methylene blue for staining.
(d) Tilt the slide to drain out the extra stain.
(e) Place the slide under a compound microscope for studying.

Observations

The cheek cells are a single layer of flat, thin scale like cells with prominent nuclei. Cheek cells are often studied in school laboratory settings because they can be easily obtained through a mouth rinse or simple swab. Yet, though the individual cells appear very simple under the microscope, they each contain the genetic make-up of the entire body.

1.7. ALL ACTIVITIES OF LIVING BEINGS ARE DUE TO CELLULAR ACTIVITY; BUT EVERY CELL OR A GROUP OF CELLS HAVE A SPECIFIC FUNCTION

Various cellular activities are responsible for the daily activities of living beings. Some of them are listed below :

(a) Growth : Cells multiply and divide at regular intervals. These cell divisions lead to the growth in the body of the living organism. Of the two types of cell division, *Mitosis is* responsible for the growth and development of the body while *Meiosis or* reduction division occurs in the reproductive cells and gives rise to the male and female gametes.

Example : Growth seen in the body of a man, animal, or parts of plant from the time of birth is due to the multiplication of cells.

(b) Repair : Repairing is the process of regaining a part or region lost due to injury. This occurs due to cell activity.

Example : Whenever we are hurt or injured, the wound tends to heal with time. Cell division and cell activity plays an important role in the healing process.

(c) Movement : Movement of various body parts of an organism is due to the contraction and relaxation of the muscle cells in the body.

Example : Movement in our bodies as we walk, run, jump or fly are all due to intense and organ specific cell activity.

(d) Nutrition : Nutrition in all living beings is also the result of cellular activity. Without cells, tissues and organs, living beings will not be able to feed and generate energy for themselves and would soon die.

The tongue contains *sensory cells* which help in tasting food. Muscle cells present in the jaws help in chewing the food; even the *digestive glands* have cells that secrete enzymes to digest the food. Because of the presence of cells in digestive tract food is able to move in digestive system.

(e) Blood circulation : The circulation of blood in our body, through blood vessels like arteries and veins is made possible by the contraction of muscles cells of the heart and various other parts. Presence of white blood and red blood cells and platelets help in fighting infection, transport of O_2 and blood clotting.

(f) Respiration : The transportation of gases from the lungs to the different parts of the body is taken care by the blood cells of the body.

(g) Protection : The white blood cells in our body act as safeguards against any germs that enter our body. They even give out certain enzymes or antitoxins that could prevent these germs from causing any harm thus leading to complete protection.

(h) Sensation and response : Cells play a very significant role in responding to any stimulus and responding accordingly with the help of *nerve cells*.

Sensation is the pickup of information by our *sensory receptors*, for example the eyes, skin, nostrils, and tongue. The difference between sensation and perception is that sensations are the passive process of bringing information from the outside into the body and to the brain. *Perception*, on the other hand, is the active process of selecting, organizing, and interpreting the information brought to the brain by the senses.

Functions such as sight, hearing, sensation etc. are all performed by the *sensory cells*. Muscle cells receive signals from the brain for secretion or contraction. Even memory function of the brain and the capacity to solve problems is the result of cell activity.

(i) Homeostasis or maintenance of body temperature : Our body sweats when we feel hot. This is done by the skin gland cells which help to maintain body temperature.

(j) Reproduction : All mammals reproduce due to cell activity. All life starts as a single cell. Gamete cell are produced in mammals during reproduction which fuse to form *zygote*.

Example : In animals to produce babies or lay eggs, Humans too.

(k) Cell activities in plant : Cells activity is responsible for various life activities in plants too.

Example : Absorption of water through the root cells, trapping of solar energy or light by the green leaf cells and attracting of insect via cells on the petals, transportation of water, minerals and food by xylem and phloem cells etc. are all activities conducted by the cells in plant tissues.

(l) Inheritance : It is the cells in the body of a living organism that are responsible for the transmission of genetic characteristics from the parents to their offspring.

Example : Apple seed produces apple plant.

1.8. NUCLEUS : THE KEY PERFORMER OF THE CELL

Nucleus is the most important part of the cell. It constitutes life of the cell. Though other parts are also significantly important, the nucleus is the most prominent as the key performer of the cell. The example taken in this case is shown with an experiment done on a single celled organism, Amoeba (Fig. 1.22).

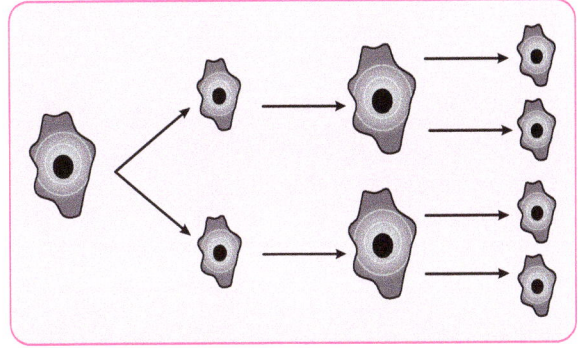

Fig.1.22 : A single celled organism amoeba grows and divides itself by binary fission into two amoebae which further after growth repeats the same process. Thus, one nucleus gets divided into two

Table 1 : Differences between Plant and Animal Cell

Plant Cell	Animal Cell
1. Plant cells have cell wall made of cellulose.	1. Animal cells contain only the cell membrane, no cell wall present.
2. Centrosomes are not present in plant cell.	2. Centrosomes are present in.
3. Plastids are present.	3. Plastids are absent.
4. Cytoplasm is not as dense as compared to the animal cell.	4. Cytoplasm is very dense and also granular.
5. Cytoplasm lining is thin and is pushed mostly towards the border of the cell.	5. The animal cell is entirely filled with cytoplasm.
6. Plant cells are usually large and are distinctively outlined.	6. Animal cells are usually smaller and are not distinctively outlined.
7. Vacuoles are present and prominent and can be more than one.	7. Vacuoles may or may not be present and if they are, they may be minute and temporary.
8. Subunits of Golgi Apparatus called dictyosomes are present.	8. Highly complex Golgi Apparatus are present near the nucleus.
9. Plant cells reserve food in the form of starch.	9. Animal cells reserve food in the form of glycogen.

EXERCISE

A. VERY SHORT ANSWER TYPE

(I) Give One Word for the Following

1. It is the structural and the fundamental unit of the body.
2. Made up of just few or thousands of cells.
3. Nerve cells.
4. Bean shaped cells.
5. Semi permeable and have fine pores.
6. It gives shape and rigidity to the cell.
7. The part of the cytoplasm other than organelles.
8. Nucleoplasm contains a network of dark coloured fibers.
9. Membrane bound compartments.
10. Supportive framework for the cell.
11. Factories of protein, that helps in the formation or synthesis of proteins.
12. Termed as suicide bags.
13. A covering that covers vacuoles.
14. Key performer of the cell.
15. Freely permeable.
16. Cell without nuclei.
17. Two cell organelles with their own genes.
18. Suicidal bags of the cell.
19. Part of cell responsible for breaking down and digesting food.
20. DNA is stored in these organelles.

(II) Define the Following Terms

1. Cells
2. Cell wall
3. Nucleus
4. Organelles
5. Chromosomes
6. Dictyosomes
7. Polysomes
8. Centrosome

B. SHORT ANSWER TYPE

(I) Answer these Questions

1. State the fundamental characteristics of cells?
2. Cells are of different shapes. Explain with examples.
3. Explain the function of cell wall.
4. Explain the function of the nucleus.
5. What are chromosomes?
6. Give an example of cells containing two nuclei.
7. Why are lysosomes called digestive bags or suicide bags of the cell.
8. Why are mitochondria called power-house of cell.
9. There would be no plant life if chloroplast did not exist. Justify.
10. Why is the golgi apparatus called the secretory organelle of the cell?

(II) Distinguish between

1. Plant cell and Animal cell
2. Cell membrane and cell wall
3. Rough E. R. and Smooth E.R.

C. LONG ANSWER TYPE

1. Explain the exterior cell structures in detail.

CELL : THE UNIT OF LIFE

2. Explain any 5 interior cell structures in detail.
3. Explain the function of plastids. State its categories and explain each category.
4. Describe briefly the microscopic structure either of a plant or animal cell.

D. STRUCTURED/APPLICATION BASED

1. Answer the questions based on the figure alongside :
   (a) Name a, b, c, d, e, and f as marked in the diagram above.
   (b) Identifying the diagram above, explain the function of part a.
   (c) What is part e also termed as and what do they consist of?
   (d) Is part f of great importance? Give a reason for your answer.
   (e) Parts c and d are present in both plant as well as animal cell. (T/F)

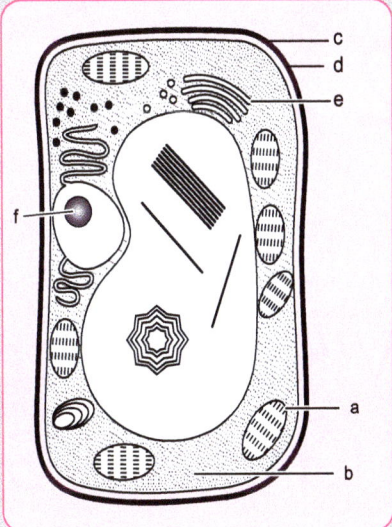

DO YOU KNOW?

➢ The largest cell in the human body is the female egg and the smallest is the male sperm.
➢ The nucleus within a cell is so tiny it could easily fit on the head of a sewing pin.
➢ It is believed that there are more nerve cells in your brain than stars in the Milky Way.
➢ About 8 million blood cells die in the human body every second, and the same number are born each second.
➢ It takes about 20 seconds for a red blood cell to circle the whole body.
➢ Unlike other body cells, brain cells cannot regenerate. Once brain cells are damaged they are not replaced.
➢ The human brain cell can hold 5 times more information as the Encyclopedia Britannica.
➢ White blood cells, or leukocytes, make up about 1% of blood. This number can double within a day when a body responds to infection.
➢ Unlike other cells, which contain an individual's full DNA, the egg and sperm each contain only half of the DNA required to create a new human. Both halves must be combined for humans to reproduce.
➢ Tears and mucus contain an enzyme (lysozyme) that breaks down the cell wall of many bacteria.

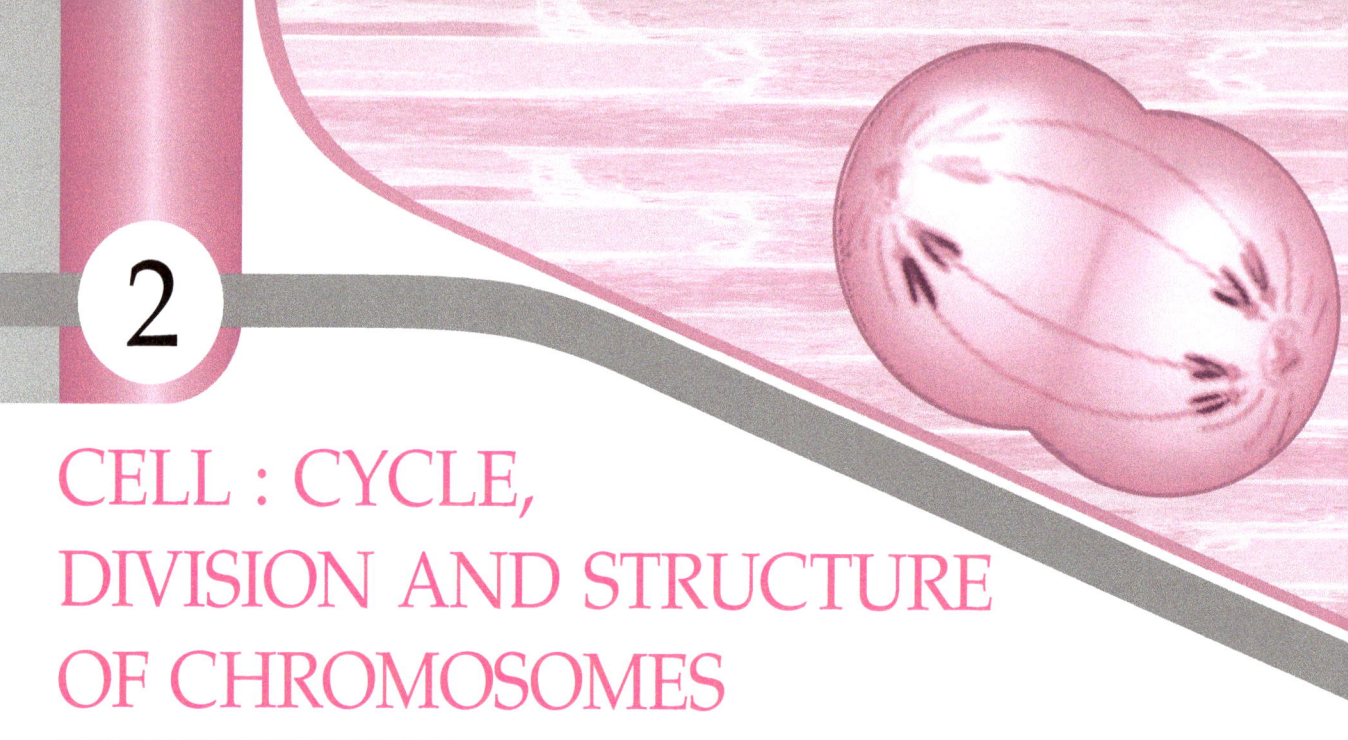

2

CELL : CYCLE, DIVISION AND STRUCTURE OF CHROMOSOMES

CHAPTER HIGHLIGHTS
- **2.1. Cell Division**
  - 2.1.1. *Production of New Cells from Pre-existing Cells*
- **2.2. Kinds of Cell Division**
  - 2.2.1. *Mitosis and its Significance*
  - 2.2.2. *Meiosis and its Significance*
- **2.3. Stages of Meiosis**
- **2.4. Cell Cycle**
- **2.5. Chromosomes**
  - 2.5.1. *Introduction*
  - 2.5.2. *Discovery of Chromosomes*
  - 2.5.3. *Structure of Chromosomes*
  - 2.5.4. *Shapes and Types of Chromosomes*
- **2.6. DNA – Brief Discussion of Structure and Function**
- **2.7. Genes**

2.1. CELL DIVISION

Every organism begins life as a single cell. The cell divides repeatedly to produce a cluster of cells. This cluster of cells forms tissues and organs to perform the different activities of life. Cell division is essential for growth. There is constant degeneration and generation of cells during normal body functions. These worn-out cells are replaced by new cells, which are produced by pre-existing cells themselves. This process, called cell division, is a fundamental characteristic of life itself. After attaining maximum size the cell begins to divide (Fig. 2.1).

Cell division is vital for the perpetuation of life on earth generation after generation. It occurs in all life forms on earth, from the simplest – the single celled amoeba to the most complex – the human race.

To be able to understand the cell cycle, it is important to first understand cell division.

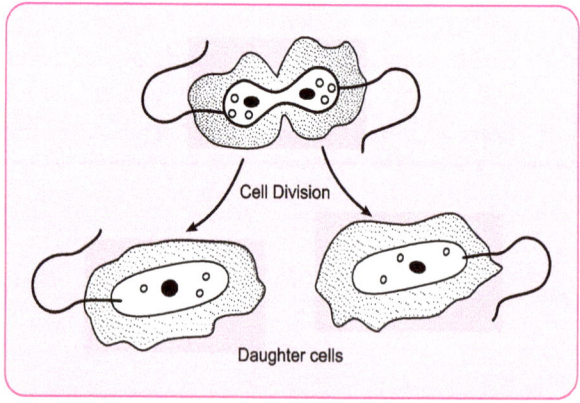

Fig. 2.1 : Cell division leads to the production of two identical daughter cells

2.1.1. Production of New Cells From Pre-existing Cells

Production of new cells is important for the following reasons :

(a) Growth, (b) Replacement, (c) Repair, (d) Reproduction

(a) Growth : Growth means increase in mass and multiplication in number of individuals (Fig. 2.2) of every species. Every organism, animal or plant, starts life as a single cell or a fertilised egg. These cells divide and re-divide repeatedly, further forming a cluster, which then starts shaping and growing

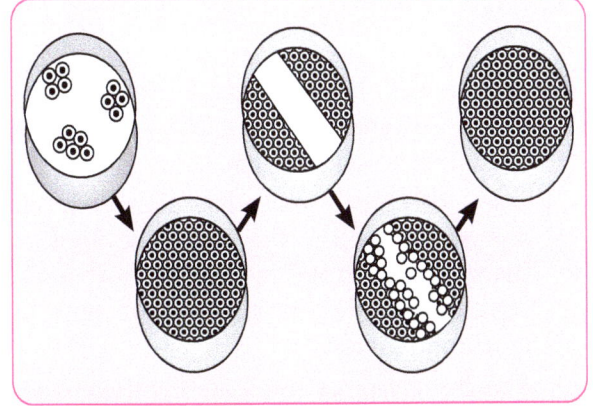

Fig. 2.2 : Cells in a petri dish continue to grow until they come in contact with other cells

for various functions, eventually forming tissues and organs. Thus, cell division is essential for proper cell growth. Increase in size in organisms is due to increase in the number of cells as a result of repeated cell division.

In our body about 3 billion cells die every minute and are replaced by cell division.

(b) Replacement : Worn out cells are replaced by new cells formed in the bone marrow through the process of cell division. Cells in different parts of body have different life spans, after which they die and need replacement. In plants too, old and dried up leaves and stems fall off and are soon replaced.

(c) Repair : There are situations when sudden injury tends to occur. In such situations the cells divide and re-divide at the site of the injury, repairing the injured tissue or organ.

In the case of a cut in our skin or fracture in the bone, the cells rapidly divide, cover up the gaps and join the broken ends.

(d) Reproduction : Reproduction refers to the production of progeny possessing features more or less similar to those of parents.

Single celled organisms like amoeba or bacteria use the process of *mitosis* to divide, themselves producing two similar independent cells.

In more complex life forms like humans, animals and plants, the reproductive organs of the body go through a specialised form of cell division called *meiosis* or *reduction division*, which leads to the production of sperms and eggs with half the number of somatic chromosomes. By this process, the sperms and eggs produced possess half the number of chromosomes of their parent cells, or one chromosome from each pair. This distribution is very important for maintaining the normal chromosome number in the resulting organism.

> **NOTE**
>
> In reproduction as read above, the chromosomes get partly distributed, but the case is not same in cell division for growth, replacement, and repair. The chromosomes distributed to the daughter cells in such cases are same as the parent cell. The chromosomes received by the daughter cells are equally distributed and duplicate. This kind of cell division, mitosis, occurs in all body cells except the reproductive organs, the ovaries that produce eggs and testes that produce sperms.

2.2. KINDS OF CELL DIVISION

Cell division is of two kinds :

(a) Mitosis : Mitosis means thread (chromatin fibre). This kind of cell division leads to growth and development.

(b) Meiosis : Meiosis (Fig. 2.3) means diminution (reduction). This kind of cell division leads to gamete formation or sex cells production.

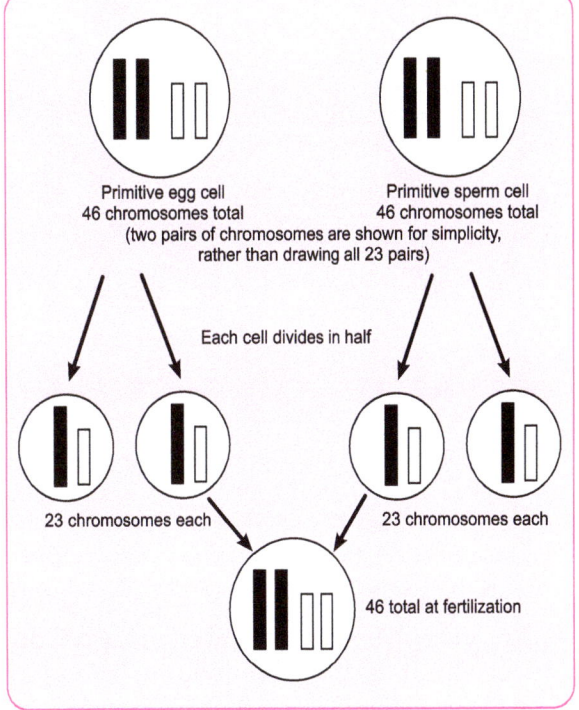

Fig.2.3 : Image showing the process of meiosis

2.2.1. Mitosis and Its Significance

(a) Introduction : Mitosis is the division of a cell into two identical daughter cells which have the same number of chromosomes that is present in the parent cells.

In this kind of cell division, the most significant factor is that the chromosomes get equally distributed and the same chromosome count is maintained at each cell division. Thus, in mitosis, two identical daughter cells are produced by the division of one parent cell. Mitosis occurs in the somatic cells of both plants and animals.

(b) Phases of mitosis : Mitosis is described as a process having four distinct phases, though each phase merges into the next phase, thus forming one continuous process. The major phases of mitosis are :

(i) Prophase   (ii) Metaphase
(iii) Anaphase   (iv) Telophase

The cell prepares itself for mitosis by doubling the quantity of DNA in the cell. This resting phase is known as Interphase, even though synthesis of DNA occurs during this phase.

The four phases of mitosis are similar to quite an extent in both plant and animal cells.

The start of the prophase is preceded by a resting phase known *as interphase* (Fig. 2.4) (mentioned

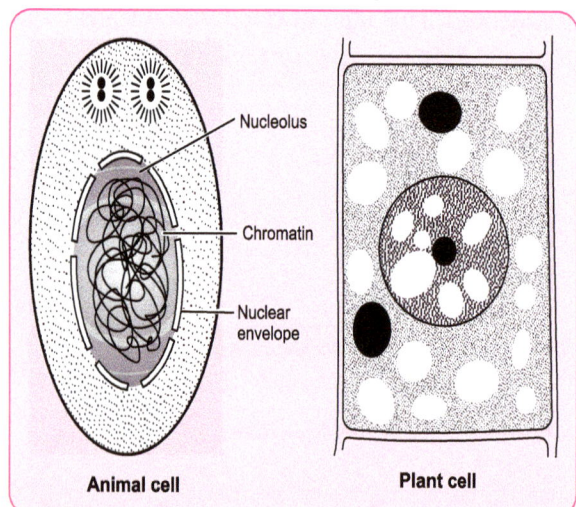

Fig. 2.4 : Interphase is shown in animal cell and plant cell. It is a resting stage, where variations take place internally, and not externally. Chromosomes multiply in both the cells and additional centrosomes containing centrioles are formed in the animal cell

above). This phase starts even before the cell division can occur. It is the non-dividing phase or the preparatory phase. Though it is known *as resting phase*, it is a phase of active metabolism in which the chromosomes (DNA) get doubled internally and starts to multiply for the further stages of cell division. No external changes take place during Interphase. Centrosomes containing centrioles get formed in the animal cell. Interphase can be subdivided into three distinct phases: G_1-phase, S-phase and G_2-phase

(i) Prophase

(1) Prophase is the initial phase of the process of mitosis, where pro means first, which marks the beginning of cell division.

(2) Since the chromosomes had started developing and swelling up in the interphase itself, in this phase they become visible as short and thick structures in the nucleus and are now known as chromosomes.

(3) The chromosomes duplicate themselves to form two sister chromatids.

(4) These two sister chromatids are attached to each other by a thin, small region known as the centromere.

(5) In animal cell the centrosome splits into two along with simultaneous duplication of the centrioles contained in it (Fig.2.5).

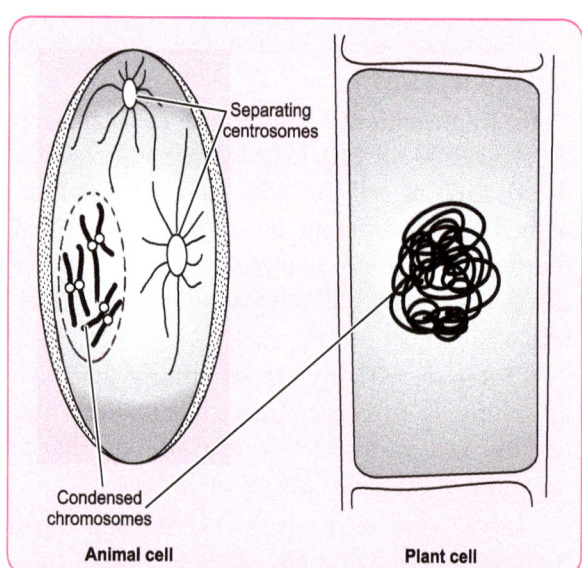

Fig. 2.5 : Prophase is shown in animal and plant cell. The chromatin gets thicker to form chromosomes. Additional centrosomes get divided into identical centrioles, which are not found in plant cells

➢ These daughter centrioles move away from each other, securing themselves to the extreme axis or poles of the cell.

➢ Each of these centrioles has radiating rays surrounding them called *aster rays* (aster: star). The centriole with its astral rays forms an aster.

CELL : CYCLE, DIVISION AND STRUCTURE OF CHROMOSOMES

➤ There may be one or more centrioles present in an animal cell.
➤ After the parting of the two daughter centrioles, the cell moves into the late prophase stage where number of fibres, called *spindle fibres,* start appearing between the two daughter centrioles.
➤ The nuclear membrane and the nucleolus disappear during this stage.
➤ The chromosomes start moving towards the equator of the cell.

(ii) Metaphase

(1) After the late prophase stage the cell enters the next stage, metaphase (Fig. 2.6), where Meta means after.
(2) In this stage the chromosomes get arranged on the equator and can be easily counted.
(3) These chromosomes get connected to the spindle fibres via a centromere.
(4) Chromosomes are the shortest and thickest in metaphase.

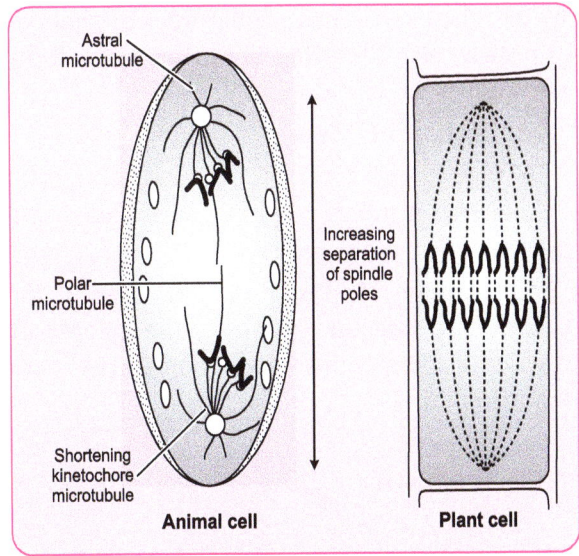

Fig. 2.7 : Anaphase where sister chromatids separate and move towards opposite poles on account of contraction of spindle fibres

(iv) Telophase

Telophase is the last major phase of the process of mitosis.

(1) A network of chromatin threads is formed where each chromatid or daughter chromosome elongates and becomes thinner.
(2) The nuclear membrane reappears and uncoiling and unwinding of chromosomes takes place (Fig.2.8).

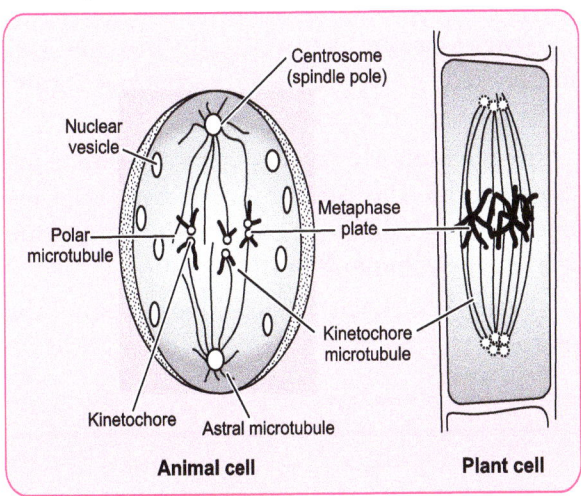

Fig.2.6 : Metaphase where the chromosomes lie along the equatorial plane of the cell

(iii) Anaphase

(1) Metaphase is followed by anaphase where 'Ana' means away. This is the shortest phase in which the centromere divides and the two sister chromatids of each chromosome separate and are drawn apart towards the opposite poles (Fig. 2.7).
(2) The action of moving apart is due to the contraction of the spindle fibres, which pulls or drags them away from the equator.

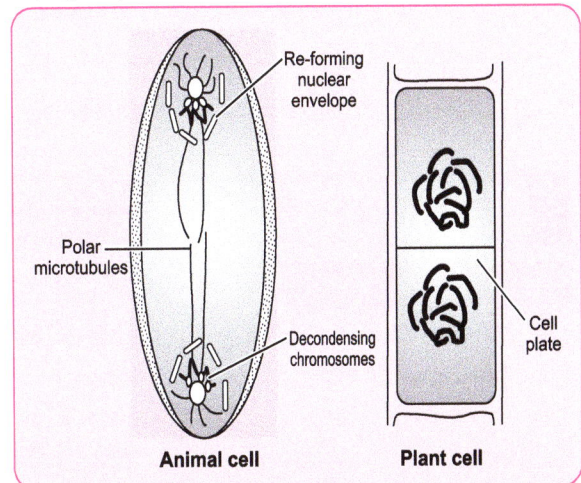

Fig.2.8 : Telophase where cell plate is laid down in the cytoplasm at the equatorial plane

(3) Nucleolus gets reformed in each daughter nucleus.
(4) Spindle and astral rays disappear.

All the substances in the cytoplasm get randomly distributed in the daughter cells during karyokinesis, including mitochondria as well as the chloroplast in the plant cell. Thus all the nuclear changes that appear in the cell during the process of cell division are known as *karyokineisis*.

Animation of Mitosis

https://highered.mcgraw-hill.com/sites/0072495855/student_view0 chapter2animation__ mitosis_and_ cytokinesis.html

Cytokinesis : Cytokinesis takes place at the end of the telophase. In this stage, the cytoplasm gets divided leading to the production of two new cells (Fig. 2.9).

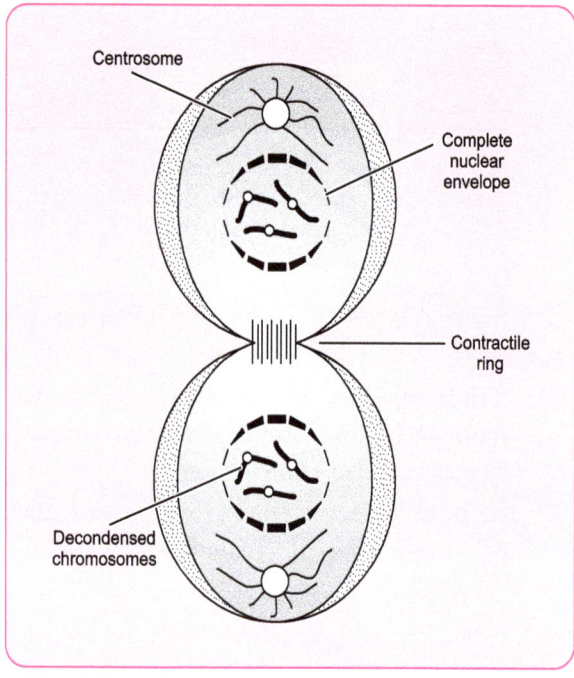

Fig. 2.9 : Begining of cytokinesis begins

This division happens due to the formation of cleavage furrow at the middle which deepens, and then finally splits the cytoplasm. In animal cells, cytoplasm divides by constriction which begins on the equator and gradually deepens but in plant cells, a cell plate is formed at the equator which begins from the middle and proceeds towards periphery. Thus, two new daughter cells are formed.

(c) Importance of mitosis : The process of mitosis is vital for the following reasons:

Growth : Mitosis leads to the growth or increase in body size as new cells are formed in this tissue.

Repair : It helps in the repairing of damaged or wounded cells.

Replacement : Replacement of old or dead cells, e.g. blood cells and epidermal cells of the skin is possible by mitosis only.

Asexual reproduction : This process helps in the cell division of unicellular organisms into two new cells, e.g., amoeba and yeast cell.

Maintenance of chromosomes : Equal count of chromosomes to the two divided daughter cells.

Uncontrolled growth : If mitosis remains unchecked, it may result in uncontrolled growth of cells leading to cancer.

Regeneration : Some organisms can regenerate body parts. The production of new cells in such instances is achieved by mitosis. It restores the surface to volume ratio of the cell.

Example : Starfish regenerate lost arms through mitosis.

PROGRESS CHECK

FILL IN THE BLANKS

1. Amoeba uses the process of .... to divide.
2. Meiosis leads to the .... production.
3. Prophase is preceded by a resting phase known as ....
4. Centrioles are surrounded by .... rays.
5. .... is the last phase of mitosis.
6. Cytokinesis takes place at the end of ....

2.2.2. Meiosis and Its Significance

(a) Introduction : The cell division which leads to the production of sex cells or gametes is known as meiosis. It takes place.

In human reproductive organs

(i) Testes (males) to produce sperms

(ii) Ovaries (female) to produce ova

In flowering plants

(i) *Anthers* (male reproductive organ) to produce *pollen grains*

(ii) *Ovary* (female reproductive organs) to produce *ovules*

The most important fact about meiosis is that the numbers of chromosomes in the sex cells are halved in this process and this division is critical.

In this process the chromosomes re-condense and the spindle fibres are re-formed and get re-attached. The chromosomes then form pairs of two being close together but not attached, they later split forming a pair of four. Then the two divisions take place, firstly the reduction division where the chromosomes pairs split up (sister chromatids separate) finally the second cell division where the centromere separates forming four individual haploid daughters (Fig. 2.10).

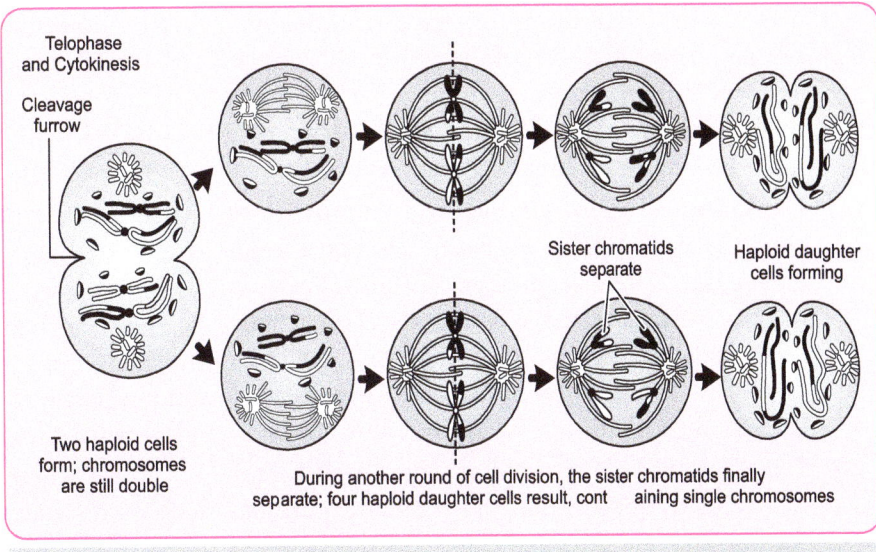

Fig. 2.10 : The process of meiosis

Example : There are 23 pairs of chromosomes in humans from which one chromosome, or one member from each pair (haploid expressed as "n") is passed onto the sex cells. This is important because when the male and female gametes fuse during fertilization, thus diploid number of chromosomes restored.

2.3. STAGES OF MEIOSIS

These are not included in the syllabus but are mentioned below to meet personal learning objectives. Meiosis is a process that completes in two divisions :

(a) Reduction division (Meiosis I). (b) Equational division (Meiosis II).

The diagram given above explains in detail the process of meiosis.

(a) Stages in Meiosis : The stages in meiosis can broadly be divided into two parts :

(i) Division I (Haploid or reduction division)- Consisting of the following four stages :

(1) Prophase I (2) Metaphase I (3) Anaphase I (4) Telophase I

(ii) Division II (Diploid or Mitotic division). Consisting of the following for stages :

(1) Prophase II (2) Metaphase II (3) Anaphase II (4) Telophase II

The above are discussed below in greater detail for better understanding.

(i) Division I (Haploid or Reduction division)

(1) Prophase I : This stage consists of the following steps :

- **Leptotene (Leptonema) :** In this process, definite thread-like structures called chromosomes are formed from the condensation and shortening of the *chromatic reticulum* which is rolled up and tightly packed in the nucleolus. The number of chromosomes gets doubled during interface, the nucleus increases in volume while the centrioles double and move towards the poles. Each chromosome is made up of only one chromonema; half of the total chromosomes are paternal, half maternal. For every paternal chromosome there is a corresponding maternal chromosome similar in size, shape and nature. These are called *homologous chromosomes*.

- **Zygotene (zygonema) :** These homologous chromosomes, one from the male parent and the other from the female parent, come together and associate laterally. This is not a fusion of chromosomes, but simply a pairing resulting from the attraction between them. This pairing process is called synapsis and the paired chromosomes are called *bivalent*. Soon after, the paired chromosomes shorten and thicken. Pairing takes place not only between homologous chromosomes, but also between homologous regions of the chromosomes.

- **Pachytene (pachynema) :** At this stage, the chromosomes split longitudinally forming four chromatids (two from each homologue). This is termed *as tetrad*. The non-sister chromatids twist around each other while the homologous chromosomes remain connected at points called chiasmata. This is called crossing over or chiasmata formation. A series of exchanges of genetic material occurs by breakage and re-joining.

- **Diplotene (Diplonema)** : The homologous chromosomes develop a *repulsive force* and begin to separate from each other. This cytogenetic activity results in the crossing over of genetic traits and the recombination of genetic material. Nucleolus though diminished, still persists. No nuclear membrane can be seen at this stage.
- **Diakinesis** : The nuclear membrane and nucleolus disappear, the chromosome condenses further and the centrioles move to the poles to initiate spindle formation. It is easy to count the number of chromosomes at this stage.

(2) **Metaphase I** : The chromosomes gather at the centre of the spindle while the four chromatids attach themselves to the spindle fibres by two centromeres while facing opposite poles. Chromosomes are more condensed.

(3) **Anaphase I** : The four chromatids (in 2 pairs) now separate and start moving towards the opposite poles of the spindle.

(4) **Telophase I** : The chromatids now come close to each other and from a group at each pole. The resulting two daughter nuclei contain haploid or (n) chromosomes.

(ii) **Division II (Diploid or mitotic division)**

(1) **Prophase II**
1. The nucleolus resurfaces in each nucleus.
2. The two chromatids stay connected at the chiasma yet remain separate.

(2) **Metaphase II**
- The chromosomes attach themselves to the centre of the spindle.
- The chromatids are paired, yet separated.
- This phase is of very short duration.

(3) **Anaphase II**
- The chromatids move towards the opposite poles of the spindle. Centromere divides into two.

(4) **Telophase II**
- During the process of *cytokinesis*, four nuclei are formed.
- Each nucleus has chromosomes reorganised in it.
- Nuclear membrane, nucleoli are reconstituted.

(i) **Importance of meiosis**

(i) It maintains the same chromosome number in the sexually reproducing organisms. From a diploid cell, haploid gametes are produced which in turn fuse to form a diploid cell.

(ii) It leads to the mixing up of genes in two ways :

(ii) **Mixing up of maternal and paternal chromosomes** : In the first division (reduction), the *maternal* and the *paternal* chromosomes get mixed up when they separate from the homologous pairs and introduces variations in a population. This is also called crossing over (Fig. 2.11).

(2) **Genetic recombination** : The exchange of the chromatid material between the two members of the homologous pair, during the separation of the maternal and the paternal chromosomes, leads to genetic *recombination*.

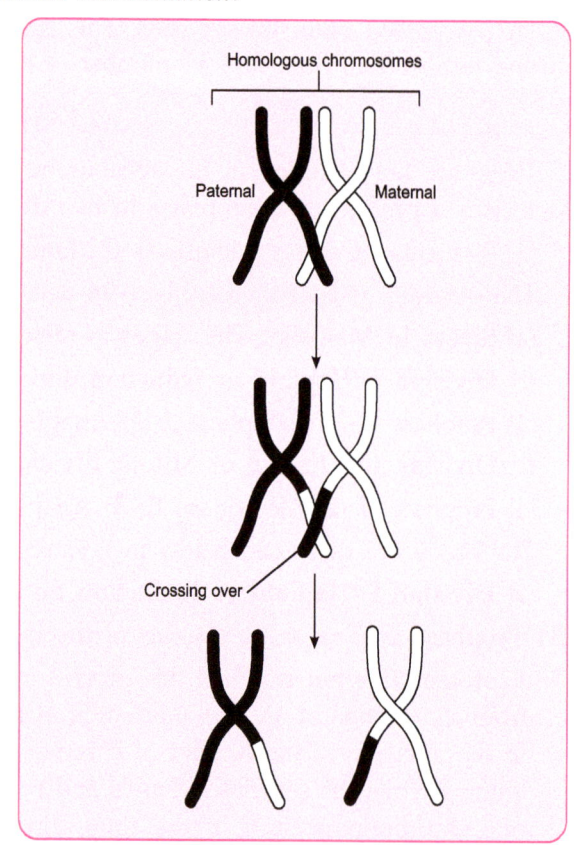

Fig.2.11 : The process of meiosis where maternal and paternal chromatids cross-over to produce a new combination of genes

These above specified exchanging and combining of the chromosomes leads to various dissimilarities in the offspring. Thus, children of the same parent tend to be different in various aspects. This evolution is the result of these variations. Because of variations all the children from the same parents are not identical.

It restricts the multiplication of chromosome number and maintains the stability of the species.

All the four chromatids of a homologous pair of chromosomes segregate and go over separately to four different daughter cells. This leads to variation in the daughter cells genetically.

Animation of meiosis

https://highered.mcgraw-hill.com/sites/0072495855/student_view0/chapter28/animation__how_meiosis_works.html

2.4. CELL CYCLE : THE PHASE OF GROWTH AND DIVISION

The cell cycle or cell-division cycle, (Fig. 2.12), is the series of events that take place in a cell leading to its division and duplication (replication) that produces two daughter cells. After the process of mitosis, the cells formed are relatively small. They have a large nucleus surrounded by comparatively less cytoplasm. Thus, cells during the process of cell division undergo the interphase stage and regain the size of the mother cell. The sequence of events that occur from the end of one cell division to the start of second represents one *cell cycle*.

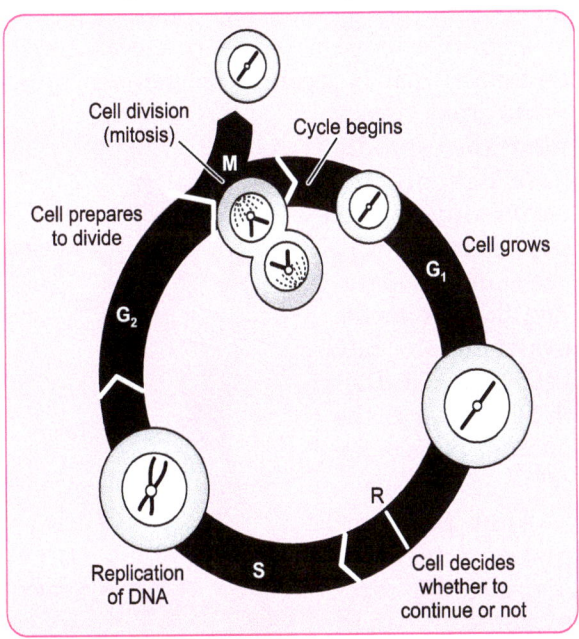

Fig.2.12 : A simplified description of cell cycle

There are three major phases of the cell cycle (Fig.2.13) :

(a) First growth phase (G_1)
(b) Synthesis phase (S)
(c) Second growth phase (G_2)

(a) First Growth Phase (G_1) : This is the initial phase where the cellular content such as cytoplasm duplicates and proteins are produced. Cell organelles such as mitochondria and chloroplasts in the animal and plant cell respectively, having their own DNA, divide. This phase in the later stage provides two choices to the cells. They can either enter the *resting stage* (G_0) or move on to the next syn*thesis phase* (S). This phase is the phase of active growth. This phase occupies 30-50% of the cell cycle.

(b) Synthesis phase : When the cells move on to the next phase, they enter the synthesis phase where more DNA is produced and chromosomes are multiplied. In this phase replication of DNA and synthesis of histones is completed.

(c) Second growth phase (G_2) : Synthesis phase is followed by a comparatively shorter second gap phase or G_2. RNA and proteins continue to synthesise in this phase which are necessary for further cell division. The cell is now ready for the next division, i.e. mitosis.

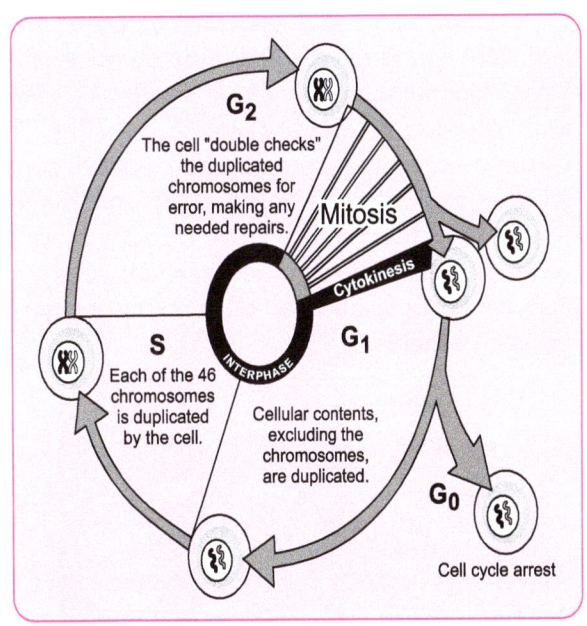

Fig.2.13 : A generalized Eukaryotic cell cycle

To access an animation of the cell cycle, please click here

http://www.cellsalive.com/cell_cycle.htm

Is there an end to this cell cycle?

Yes, cell cycle may sometimes stop depending on the conditions prevailing for the organism. It may stop completely in some cases and might temporarily be halted.

Some examples are given below for better understanding :

(i) The brain and nerve cells in our body, once formed in the embryo cannot be formed again if they become dead.

(ii) The cells found in our liver divide every one or two years replacing damaged or dead cells.

(iii) The cells found on the surface of the skin destroy or die continuously. Household dust usually contains large portions of dead cells.

(iv) In plants, *Meristem* which is the growing point, multiplies at a rapid speed leading to the production of new leaves, buds, flowers etc.

(v) Specialized germinal cells found in the ovary and testis in humans and in the anthers and ovary in the plants produce sex cells after undergoing certain kind of cell division.

(vi) Uncontrollable running of cell cycles can become *symptomatic* or malignant tumours.

2.5. CHROMOSOMES

2.5.1. Introduction

A chromosome is a structure of DNA, protein, and RNA found in cells. It is a single piece of coiled DNA containing many genes, regulatory elements and other nucleotide sequences (Fig. 2.14). Chromosomes also contain DNA-bound proteins, which serve to package the DNA and control its functions. Chromosomal DNA encodes most or all of an organism's genetic information; some species also contain plasmids or other extra-chromosomal genetic elements.

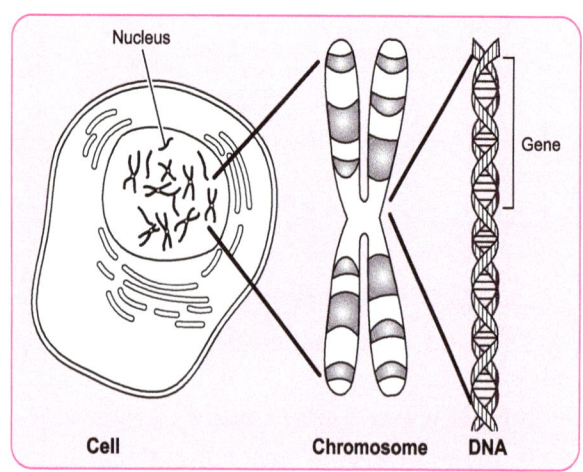

Fig.2.14 : Location of chromosomes inside the cell

Chromosomes are highly compressed coiled chromatin fibres which play a very significant role in the process of cell division. These chromosomes duplicate, multiply and divide during the process of mitosis, ensuring the proper functioning of the cell. At the metaphase stage, they become distinct, connected together at the centromere, and can be counted. Individual chromosomes can be distinguished by their shape and size, position of centromere and pattern of banding.

Where are chromosomes found in a living cell?

Chromosomes are the gene carrying structure that consist of one very long DNA molecule and associated proteins and, is found in the nucleus of a cell. Chromosomes easily get stained with certain dyes and get coloured, thus the name *chroma* which means colour and *soma* which means body.

2.5.2. Discovery of Chromosomes

In 1882, **Walter Fleming**, a German scientist was the first one to observe chromosomes. He observed them rapidly dividing in the larvae of salamander. The threads like structures were called chromosomes, a term coined by **W. Waldeyer** in 1888.

2.5.3. Structure of Chromosomes

Before cell division takes place, the chromosomes are already visible in their condensed form with twin chromatids joined together. The constricted point at which these chromatids join is known as centromere (Fig. 2.15). This point later attaches to the spindle fibres during cell division. Each centromere is located at a specific location for every chromosome. The centromere may be terminal, sub-terminal or median in position. Every time the spindle fibre tightens, the chromatids get pulled away from each other separating them from the centromere. They thus move individually towards the opposite poles of the cell.

After the completion of cell division, the chromosomes (then chromatids) go back to the initial chromatin fibre form and are similar in number to the chromosomes seen in a nucleus.

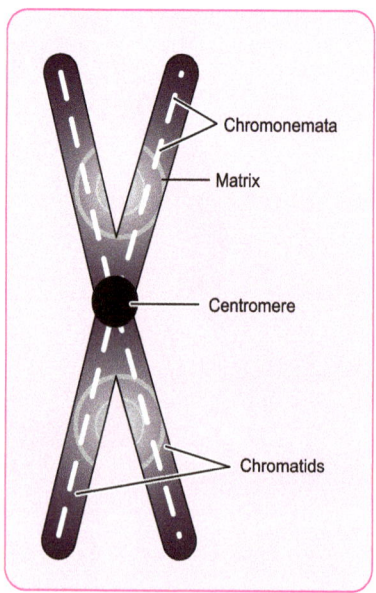

Fig.2.15 : Structure of chromosome

2.5.4. Shapes and types of chromosomes

As already discussed, before mitosis, each chromosome duplicates or doubles and condenses into short chromatids. The ends of chromosomes are called telomeres and the sister chromatids are held together by the centromere, which splits the chromosome into two chromosome arms. The location of the centromere varies between different chromosomes arms to have varying shapes (Fig.2.16). Some are described below :

(a) *Acrocentric*, where the centromere is situated more towards one end, resulting in one very short arm and one very long arm. These are rod shaped.
(b) *Telocentric*, where the centromere is situated on the proximal end of the rod-shaped chromosome. These chromosomes appear 'J' shaped.
(c) *Metacentric*, where the rod-shaped chromosome, resulting in the formation of almost equal arms, giving the chromosome a 'V' shape.
(d) *Submetacentric*, where the centromere is situated near the centre of the chromosome, resulting in unequal arms giving the chromosome a 'L' shape.

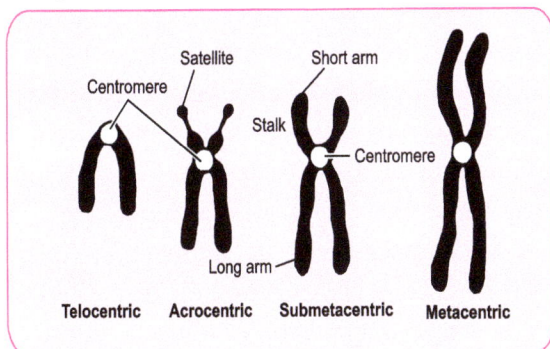

Fig.2.16 : Different types of chromosome

Centromere

(i) Monocentric : Most organisms have only one centromere in their chromosomes which are thus called monocentric chromosomes.

(ii) Dicentric/Polycentric : Chromosomes which have two or more centromeres are called dicentric and polycentric respectively.

Nuclear chromosomes : The point where the arms of the split chromosome meet is called primary constriction. It is the narrow, constricted and light coloured region of the chromosome. In this region lies a granula like *centromere or kinetochore*. Sometimes however, there is a secondary constriction which might play an important role in the formation of the nucleolus, thus also giving it the name of a *nucleolar organizer region* (NOR). Only two chromosomes possess such nucleolar zone in a nucleus and are thus called nucleolar chromosomes.

Sat-chromosomes : At times, chromosomes have round, knob like or elongated appendages called satellites. A thin chromatin filament connects this satellite to the rest of the chromosome. Chromosomes which have satellites are called *sat-chromosomes*.

2.6. DNA

The chromatin material that constitutes the chromatin fibre is made up of two substances :

(a) DNA (deoxyribonucleic acid) which constitutes about 40% of the chromatic fibre.
(b) Histones, a particular type of protein, constitute about 60% of the chromatin fibre.

A DNA strand is a coiled, double helical structure composed of two polynucleotide strands around a core of eight histone molecules. Each such complex is called nucleosome.

For example, a single human chromosome is actually made up of more than a million nucleosomes.

The DNA molecule is a single large molecule, often described as macromolecule, and is made up of two complementary strands wound around each other in a double helix.

Each DNA macromolecule strand is made up of repeating nucleotides which are, in turn, made up of the following three components:

(i) Phosphate (ii) Pentose sugar (iii) Nitrogenous base

In each DNA strand, the pentose is arranged lengthwise while the nitrogenous base attaches to the sugar inwards. This extends to join the nitrogenous base of the other stand. Bound together by a hydrogen bond, the two strands together making a ladder-like arrangement, with the nitrogenous bases serving as rungs of the ladder.

During the interphase of the cell cycle, each DNA molecule duplicates to ready itself for mitosis so as to allow equitable distribution of chromosomes to the two daughter cells. During replication, the DNA double helix opens at one end, and the strands thus freed form new strands by base pairing and the process continues in specific sequence for the length of the DNA strand.

Nitrogenous bases found in DNA : There are four types of nitrogenous bases found in DNA. These are adenine (A), guanine (G), cytosine (C) and thymine (T).

The base pairing is specific. Adenine always pairs with thymine and guanine pairs with cytosine.

There are three kinds of DNA :
(1) **Nuclear DNA** which is found in chromosomes.
(2) **Mitochondrial DNA** which is contained in the mitochondria of both plant and animal cells.
(3) **Chloroplast DNA** which is contained in the chloroplast of plant cells.

2.7. GENES

A gene is a segment of DNA having specific sequences of nucleotides that encode a particular protein. The sequences of three nitrogenous bases are called codons. Encoded protein is expressed in the form of certain features of our physical appearance.

PROGRESS CHECK

TRUE / FALSE

1. The ends of the chromosomes are called centromere.
2. Acrocentric chromosomes are J-shaped.
3. DNA is made up of phosphate, pentose and nitrogen.
4. Mitochondrial DNA is found in plants only.

Table 1 : Difference between Mitosis and Meiosis

Mitosis	Meiosis
1. It takes place in all somatic cells.	1. It takes place either in reproductive cells or gametes.
2. Cells which go through the process of mitosis may be either haploid or diploid.	2. Cells which go through the process of meiosis are always diploid.
3. Before cell division takes place, a chromosome replicates in the interphase.	3. In this process, cell division takes place only once, before interphase takes place prior to Meiosis I. It does not take place before Meiosis II.
4. Chromatids occur in the form of dyads.	4. Chromatids occur as tetrads.
5. It occurs in four steps.	5. It occurs in two successive steps.
6. Two daughter cells are formed.	6. Four daughter cells are formed.
7. The numbers of chromosomes remain constant.	7. The numbers of chromosomes are reduced to half.
8. Genes are not transferred. As a result, genetic variation does not take place.	8. Genes are transferred. As a result, genetic variation takes place.
9. The chromosomes in the daughter cells and the parent cells are similar.	9. The chromosomes in the daughter cells have chromosomal material extracted from each parent cell. So, they are dissimilar.
10. 10Participates in the repair of damaged cells, body growth and regeneration.	10. Participates in the build-up of gametes and the preservation of the chromosome number of the race.
11. There is no synapsis, chiasma formation and crossing over between homologous chromosomes.	11. Synapsis, chiasma formation and crossing over occur between homologous chromosomes.

Table 2 : Difference between Plant and Animal Mitosis

Plant Mitosis	Animal Mitosis
1. This takes place in the meristematic area.	1. This takes place in many places in the body.
2. There is no alteration in the cell structure before cell division occurs.	2. There is alteration in the cell structure before cell division. It takes in a spherical shape.
3. Centrioles are absent.	3. Centrioles are present.
4. Plates are formed and cytokinesis takes place.	4. Cytokinesis takes place by the process of cleavage

There is centrifugal growth of the cell plate.	or furrowing. There is centripetal growth of the cell plate.
5. The daughter cells are fused together by the cell plate or middle lamella.	5. The daughter cells have intercellular spaces between them.
6. Asters are not formed.	6. Asters are formed.

EXERCISE

A. VERY SHORT ANSWER TYPE

(I) Fill in the Blanks

1. Approximately .... red blood cells die every minute.
2. Chromosomes are the .... in a cell.
3. Mitosis leads to the .... and .... of a cell.
4. Meiosis is a form of cell division which results in the production of .... or ....
5. In cytokinesis, the cytoplasm is .... and .... new cells are produced.
6. Chromosomes are the vehicles of ....
7. No of chromosomes in our somatic cells is ....
8. Mitosis occurs in ....

(II) Name the Following

1. The first phase of meiosis.
2. The process in which cytoplasm gets divided and two new cells are produced.
3. The male reproductive organ which produces pollen grains.
4. The proteins or an organised structure of DNA that occur in a cell.
5. The nuclear changes appearing in the cell when the process of cell division is underway.
6. Membrane that disappears during late prophase.
7. Chromosomes can be counted best at the stage of ....
8. The stage in which daughter chromosomes move toward the poles of the spindle is .....
9. Chiasmata are first seen in ....
10. Cell plate grows from ......
11. Centromere splits and chromatids separate ....
12. Chromosomes are moved to spindle equator ....
13. Pairing between homologous chromosomes takes place during .....
14. The kind of division that takes place in the reproductive tissues ......
15. A region of plant body where cell division occurs very actively ......
16. The type of cell division that occurs during :

    (a) Growth of shoot
    (b) Formation of pollen grains
    (c) Repair of worn out tissues.

B. SHORT ANSWER TYPE

1. What is cell division?
2. What are chromosomes?
3. What is interphase?
4. What are genes?
5. Distinguish cytokinesis and karyokinesis.
6. Why is mitosis called equational division?
7. How many daughter cells are formed at the end of mitosis and at the end of meiosis?
8. Between a prokaryote and a eukaryote, which cell has a shorter cell division time?
9. Name a stain commonly used to colour chromosomes.
10. Which tissue of animals and plants exhibits meiosis?
11. If a tissue has at a given time 1024 cells, how many cycles of mitosis had the original parental single cell undergone?
12. An anther has 1200 pollen grains. How many pollen mother cells must have been there to produce them?

C. LONG ANSWER TYPE

(I) Answer these Questions

1. Distinguish anaphase of mitosis from anaphase I of meiosis.
2. List the main differences between mitosis and meiosis.
3. How are the productions of new cells important for growth of the organism?
4. What is the importance of mitosis?
5. What are the three major phases of the cell cycle?

(II) Explain

(1) Cell cycle (2) Chromosome number
(3) Synapsis (4) Crossing over
(5) SAT-chromosome (6) Haploid
(7) Bivalent (8) Chiasmata

D. STRUCTURED/APPLICATION BASED

1. Observe the given figure which represents meiotic division in a human cell. What will be the correct chromosome number in the cells 1 & 2?

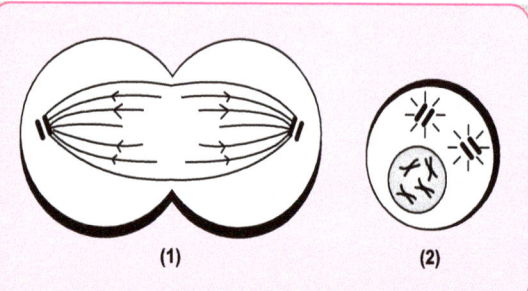

(1)   (2)

2. The diagram given along side represents a stage during mitotic cell division in an animal cell :
   (a) Identify the stage. Give a reason to support your answer.
   (b) Name the parts labelled 1, 2 and 3.
   (c) What is the chromosome number of the cell?
   (d) Draw a neat, labelled diagram of the cell as it would appear in the next stage. Name the stage.

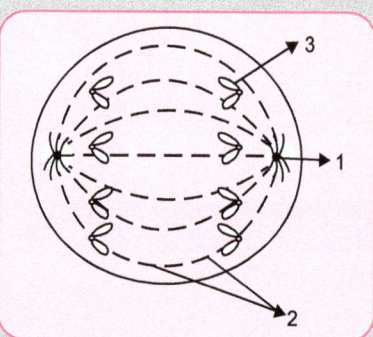

3. With the help of a diagram, write about different types of chromosomes based on the position of centromere.

DO YOU KNOW?

- Mitosis is the division of somatic cells into two daughter cells that are completely identical to the parent cell.
- Brain cells never complete mitosis once the organism is mature.
- Liver cells act like brain cells. If a piece of liver is damaged (or removed) then liver cells will engage in mitosis until the liver is repaired.
- The same thing happens with lizard tails.
- If you were to stretch out the 46 chromosomes in one cell and lay them end to end, they will be over 2 yards in length.
- If the total DNA in one person were laid in a straight line, it would stretch to the sun and back over 30 times.
- Humans are 99.8% genetically identical, only 0.2% of our genetic make-up differs.

3

GENETICS

CHAPTER HIGHLIGHTS

3.1. Genetics – Definition and Scope
3.2. Population Variation
3.3. Chromosomes
3.4. Sex Determination
3.5. Genes
3.6. Alleles
3.7. Genotype and Phenotype
3.8. Sex-linked Inheritance
3.9. Mendel's Experiments
3.10. Mendel's Laws of Inheritance
3.11. Mutation
3.12. Cloning
3.13. The Future of Genetics

3.1. GENETICS

Genetics deals with the genes, heredity and variation in living beings. It is the science of trait, inheritance from parents to offspring.

When an organism reproduces, the offspring produced will resemble the parents but will never be identical to them. Differences from the parents, however small, will always be observed. This is due to the remarkable twin phenomena of *heredity* and *variation*. Heredity is the transmission of biological trait or characteristics from parent to offspring while *variation* is manifested as differences among individuals of a species.

Genetics is a branch of biology that deals with the study and understanding of the phenomenon of heredity and variation from parents to offspring and the related transmission laws. Genetics term was coined by **William Bateson** in 1906. The word genetics is derived from the Greek word 'genesis', meaning to grow into or become.

Gregor Johann Mendel (Fig. 3.1) (1822-1884), the Father of Genetics was born in a peasant family in Austria. After receiving basic education in a monastery, Mendel joined the University of Vienna to study Mathematics and Science. He returned to the monastery and continued to be an abbot for the rest of his life. The monastery's garden served as a natural laboratory for Mendel's keenly probing mind. He studied how particular characteristics in the garden pea plant were passed on in succeeding generations and his findings are now known as Mendel's Laws of Inheritance. Modern genetics is based on his findings regarding inheritance that remain relevant to this day. Mendel's work was, however, ignored during his time due to the following reasons :

Fig. 3.1 : Gregor Mendel

(a) He published his work in an obscure journal.
(b) Scientists did not notice his work because at that time the scientific world was busy with Darwin's theory of Origin of Species.

(c) His idea was ahead of his time as ignorance prevailed in that period.

Mendel discovered that certain hitherto unknown 'factor' was present in the gametes of parents and this new 'factor' was responsible for the presence of certain characteristics in the offspring. This is known as the Mendelian factor.

Modern applications of genetics

(i) Genetic engineering : Using genetic engineering, new genes are introduced into the chromosomes of an organism and its genetic configuration is altered. The *genetically-modified organism* (GMO) is then left to grow and multiply and large quantities of gene product are obtained. Genetic engineering was first employed for the generation of insulin. *Insulin* can be generated by introducing the insulin producing mammalian gene in certain bacteria which were made to produce it.

(ii) Genetic counselling : This application of genetics, eliminates the possibility of the replication of undesirable genes that may lead to the transfer of genetic disorders from parents to their children. *Genetically transmitted diseases like haemophilia,* (bleeding disorder that slows the blood clotting process), *thalassaemia* and *sickle cell anaemia* (defective haemoglobin) can be avoided by genetic counselling.

Like begets like : It is due to heredity that we commonly observe the phenomenon of *"like begets like"*, i.e. a seed of mango develops into a mango tree, the offspring of a dog is a puppy and not a cat, and human beings reproduce to give birth to humans only.

3.2. POPULATION VARIATION

Humans belong to the genus *Homo sapiens*. But all humans do not look alike. They may differ in colour, height and various other attributes. People belonging to the same tribe or even family also have difference in features. Thus, differences among individuals of a species are called variation.

Similar is the case of animals. This is clearly evident in the several breeds of cats and dogs that are remarkably different from each other.

In humans, the various external characteristics and traits that are inherited by offspring from the parents are :

(a) Colour of eyes – Brown, Black, Blue, etc.
(b) Hair – Curly, Straight, Wavy, etc.
(c) Natural hair colour – Brown, black.
(d) Shape and size of nose.
(e) Hand Use – Either left-handed or right-handed.
(f) Ear lobe – Free or attached.
(g) Lips – Thick or thin.
(h) Rh Blood Group – Rh positive or Rh negative.
(i) Skin colour – Normal (Wheatish, fair, dark) or Albinism (Total absence of pigment).
(j) Colour Vision – Normal or red-green colour blindness.
(k) Thumb – Non-flexible, straight/flexible, curved.

Character is defined as any heritable feature and the alternative forms of character are called traits. Height of a pea plant is a trait, which may be expressed as a plant being either tall or short.

PROGRESS CHECK

DEFINE THE FOLLOWING TERMS

1. Genetics   2. Heredity   3. Character   4. Trait.   5. Variation

3.3. CHROMOSOMES

Chromosomes are visible under a high powered microscope at the time of nuclear division during cell division. They are visible only when nucleus is in metaphase or anaphase stage. We use photographs to artificially put in order the complete set of chromosomes based on their sizes to get a chart called a Karyotype (Fig 3.2). Individuals of a certain species have a constant number of chromosomes, e.g., humans have a total of 46 chromosomes.

The numbers of chromosomes in other common animals are given below :

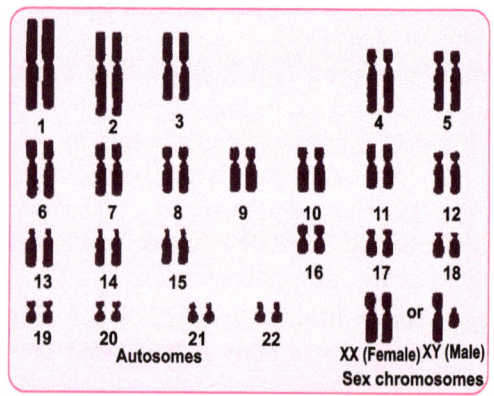

Fig. 3.2 : Human Karyotype

Cat	38
Chimpanzee	48
Elephant	56
Cow	60
Goat	60
Donkey	62
Chicken	78
Kangaroo	16

Chromosomes always occur in pairs. Hence, the total number of chromosomes in every organism is an even number.

These chromosomes are similar in size and shape. The two chromosomes that make up a pair are obtained one from each parent and are called *homologous chromosomes or autosomes*. Chromo-somes from numbers 1-22 are autosomes. The 23rd pair is composed of sex chromosomes and is dissimilar in male and female. These dissimilar chromosomes are designated as X and Y.

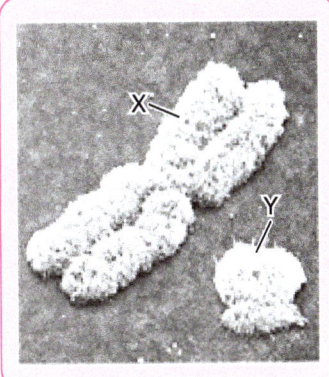

Fig. 3.3 : X and Y chromosome

In a male, the 23rd pair has X and Y chromosomes which are different. In females, the 23rd pair has two X chromosomes which are similar. The Y chromosome of males is much smaller than the X chromosome (Fig. 3.3).

3.4. SEX DETERMINATION

Female is homogametic sex having XX chromosome pair while male is heterogametic sex having XY chromosomes.

During fertilization, sperm from a male fertilizes the egg in a female. The sperm, and not the egg, determines the sex of the offspring. The egg is composed of only X chromosomes. But half of each of the X and Y bearing sperms are released into the female. The sex of the child depends on the type of sperm fusing with the egg.

A male child is born if the Y-bearing sperm fuses with the egg (X) leading to the formation of XY chromosomes.

A female child is born if the X-bearing sperm fuses with the egg (X) leading to the formation of XX chromosomes (Fig. 3.4).

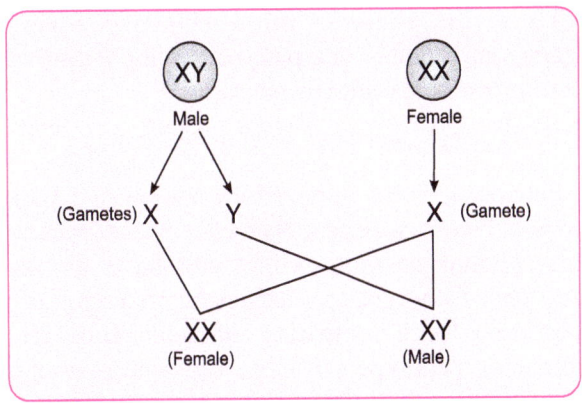

Fig. 3.4 : Sex Determination in human beings

3.5. GENES

The nucleus of a cell contains chromosomes that carry genetic information. Most body cells have the same number of chromosomes, but this varies between species. Human body cells, for example, each have 23 matching pairs of chromosomes. A gene is a shorter region of DNA that carries the genetic code for a particular characteristic or cell activity. Genes result in organisms of the same species differing from each other in colour, size, appearance, body, hand, behaviour etc. Human beings have nearly 30,000 genes, with the largest number (2968) present in Chromosomes No. 1 and the least (231) present in Chromosome Y. The full complement of DNA, including all genes and the intergenic regions is called a Genome of an organism.

3.6. ALLELES

A single gene determines the colour of a petal in a flower (rose). But, the colour and shades of the petals vary. The colour-producing gene is responsible for this phenomenon. *The alternative forms of gene for determining a character are called alleles.*

Alleles determine the same character but to a different degree. Alleles occupy the same position in both the homologous chromosomes of a pair.

Out of the two alleles of a gene, one is *dominant* or *super ruling* or *expressed* and the other is *recessive* or *submissive*.

Let us take the example of eye colour. If an individual inherits a blue allele and a brown allele from each of two parents, his or her eyes will be brown, because brown is a dominant genetic trait, requiring only one allele for expression. However, if that person had a child with someone who also carried a blue allele and both parents passed the blue trait down, the child would have blue eyes.

Thus, an allele is an alternative form of a gene (one member of a pair) occupying a particular position on a specific chromosome.

3.7. GENOTYPE AND PHENOTYPE

Phenotype is the outward expression of a pair of genes, which is seen as a character. Individuals with same phenotype may or may not have the same genotype. Genotype is the genetic make-up of an individual for a particular character. Individuals with same genotype can have the same phenotype.

There are three combinations possible with dominant and recessive alleles :

(a) Dominant with Dominant
(b) Dominant with Recessive
(c) Recessive with Recessive

Dominant alleles are represented by capital letters and recessive ones are represented by small letters.

Let us take the example of a colour of petal of a flower.

Assume that White (W) is dominant over the recessive Yellow (y). Thus, depending on the allele acquired by the flower, its colour could be:

(i) White when WW is present
(ii) White when Wy is present.
(iii) Yellow when yy is present.

Therefore, for the phenotype of white in the above example, the two genotypes are :

(1) homozygous dominant (homo means same and zygous means pair). Here, WW.
(2) heterozygous dominant (hetero means different). Here, Wy.

The homozygous recessive pair, here yy, is the only genotype for yellow phenotype.

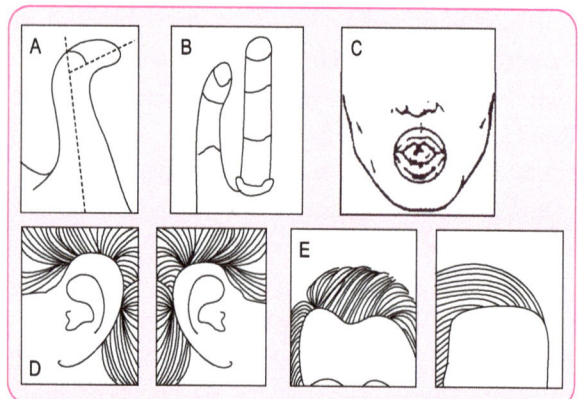

Fig. 3.5 : Phenotypic expression of single gene human trait

Referring to the above figure 3.5
➤ A shows hitchhiker's thumb.
➤ B shows bent index finger.
➤ C shows tongue rolling.
➤ d shows unattached versus attached ear lobes.
➤ E shows widow's peak versus straight hair line.

Example of inheritance : Consider the following example to understand the concept of inheritance.

The chart demonstrates how eye colour is inherited from parents by offspring. The brown eye has a dominant allele B that is responsible for brown colour phenotype and a recessive allele b responsible for blue colour phenotype (Fig. 3.6).

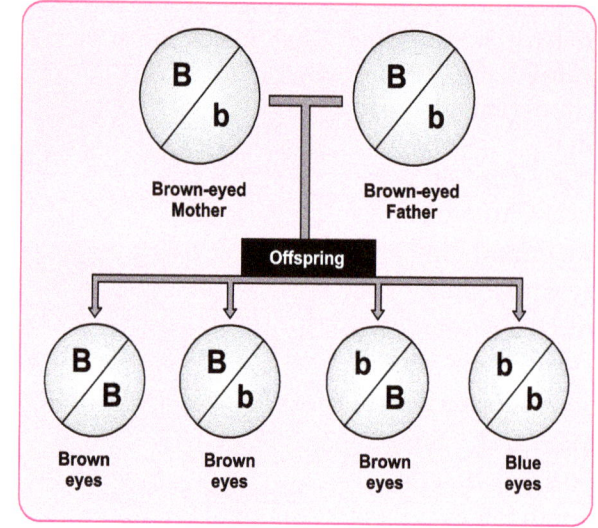

Fig. 3.6 : Inheritance of eye colour

Therefore, depending on the allele acquired, the offspring of brown colour eyed parents can have the following possible eye colour :

➤ Homozygous dominant (BB) giving brown-coloured eyes.
➤ Heterozygous dominant (Bb) giving brown-coloured eyes.
➤ Homozygous recessive (bb) giving blue-coloured eyes.

So, a parent can have brown-coloured eyes, but the offspring can have blue-coloured eyes.

The same example can be illustrated with the help of a Punnet Square, which is a simple diagrammatic method of depicting the possible combinations (genotypes) that can arise when two different gametes (sex cells with a specific trait) come together. The resulting phenotypes can also be known from this diagram. Let us plot and see.

How to draw a Punnett square (Fig. 3.7)
Step 1. Draw four boxes as shown in Fig. (i).

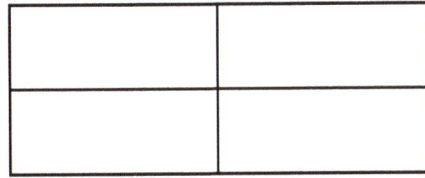

Fig. (i)

Step 2. Write down the alleles in gametes from each sex. Put the female gametes horizontally along the top one above each box. Place the male gametes along the left side. as in Fig. (ii).

A gametes	B	b
B		
b		

Fig. (ii)

Step 3. Write the products of fusion of these gametes in the appropriate boxes as in Fig. (iii).

A gametes	B	b
B	BB	Bb
b	Bb	bb

Fig. 3.7 : Steps to draw a punnet square

Step 4. Write down the phenotypic and genotypic ratio of the offspring.

3.8. SEX-LINKED INHERITANCE

Sex linked inheritance is the appearance of a trait because of the presence of an allele exclusively on either the X or Y chromosome. But they also carry some genes that control some body characters. The somatic characters whose genes are located on sex chromosomes are called sex linked characters. Some traits are found in males and not in females. Examples are baldness, hypertrichosis of the ears, etc.

'X'-linked inheritance : *Haemophilia* (a disease in which the blood does not clot) is caused by absence of a factor which is responsible for blood clotting (antihaemophilic globulin AHG) and colour blindness (not being able to differentiate between red and green colour) are disorders caused by the presence of recessive genes which are present on the X chromosomes. Hence, these kinds of diseases are called X-linked diseases. Female, who has two X chromosomes, may not be affected by colour vision or haemophilia as it is not possible that both the X chromosomes will carry the abnormal gene. One of the genes may be abnormal but due to the fact that it is recessive its effect will be eclipsed by the gene on the other X chromosome. Male, who has just one X chromosome, has just one gene for colour vision or clotting factor. In case that is the abnormal gene, the Y chromosome contains nothing to mask it and that causes colour blindness or haemophilia.

Usually, males are affected by X-linked diseases. As males have only one X chromosome, a single recessive gene on that X chromosome causes the disease.

Linkage : The phenomenon of two or more genes being closely linked during hereditary transmission is called linkage. Many sets of two or more genes are usually inherited. These genes make up a linkage group. An individual has many more hereditary characters than chromosomes. As an example we may cite the name of the fruit fly *Drosophila melanogaster* which contains eight chromosomes in each of its somatic cells but there are as many as 2,500 genes in each. It is also found that the gene responsible for body colour and the size of the wings are connected and are passed down the generations.

Crossing over or incomplete linkage : The process of exchange of genetic material between the non-sister chromatids of homologous chromosomes during diplotene stage of meiosis is called crossing over. Incomplete linkage is due to the breakage of chromosonal segments during crossing over. In this process, homologous pairs form synaptic pairs and then divide. Some sections of one partner of a homologous pair of chromosomes are interchanged with the corresponding sections of the other. Consequently, paternal and maternal characters inter-mix and the resultant offspring possess characters that are different from the parent. As a consequence, individuals experience variation. But, the variation may result from genetic or environmental factors too. For example, the height of a person may be a result of his diet and exercise; but his blood group cannot be environment dependent, but is genetically determined. We can state that incomplete linkage occurs when the genes for different characters are separated at the time of gamete formation due to breaking and exchange of chromosome during meiosis.

CASE–1

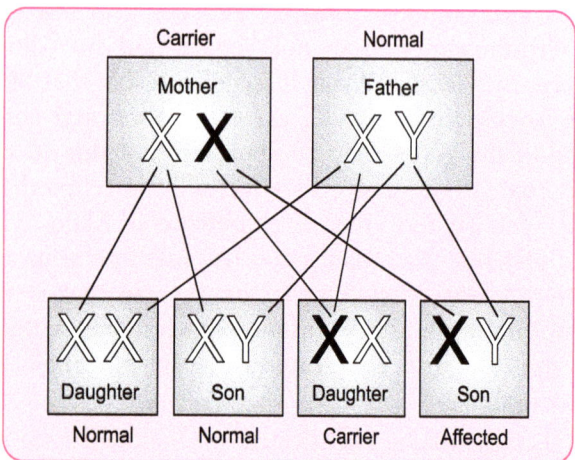

Fig. 3.8 : Pedigree Chart of inheritance of X linked disease from a carrier mother and normal father

If the mother is a carrier (only one abnormal X) and the father is normal then there is a (Fig. 3.8) :
(a) 25% chance of a normal boy
(b) 25% chance of a boy with disease
(c) 25% chance of a normal girl
(d) 25% chance of a carrier girl without disease

CASE–2

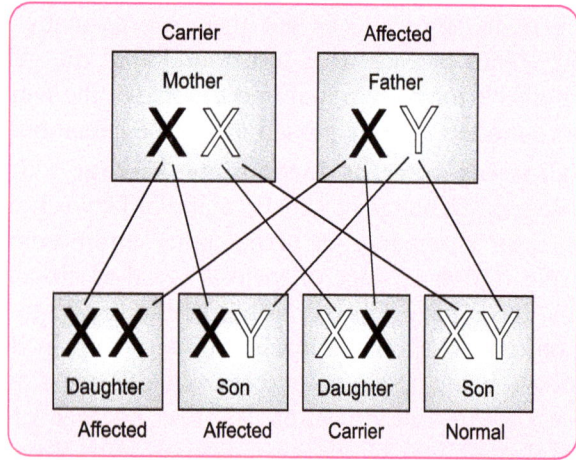

Fig. 3.9 : Pedigree Chart of inheritance of X linked disease from a carrier mother and affected father

If the mother is a carrier (only one abnormal X) and the father is affected with the disease then there is a (Fig. 3.9) :
(i) 25% chance of a healthy boy
(ii) 25% chance of a boy with the disease
(iii) 25% chance of a carrier girl
(iv) 25% chance of a girl with the disease

CASE–3

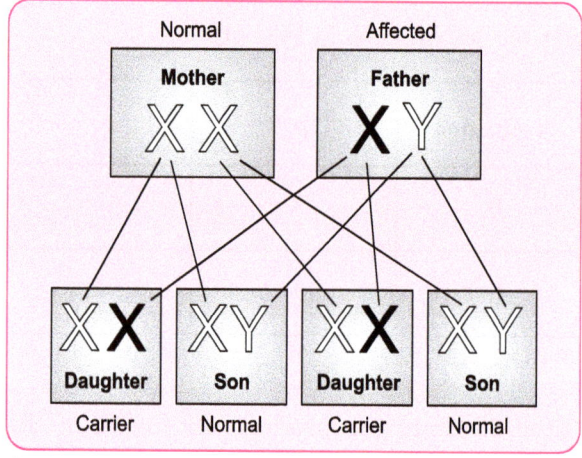

Fig. 3.10 : Pedigree chart of disease of X-linked inheritance from a normal mother and affected father

If the mother is normal and the father is affected with the disease then there is a (Fig. 3.10)
(i) 50% chance of a healthy boy
(ii) 50% chance of a carrier female.

X-linked inherited diseases are also called criss-cross inherited diseases. The son may get this disease from a carrier mother (refer case 2) and the daughter may get it from her father who is colour blind if the mother is a carrier (refer case 3).

Y-linked inheritance : Dominant genes on the Y-chromosomes cause diseases like hypertrichosis pinnae (growth of hair on ears), male infertility, pattern baldness, etc. However, females do not get these diseases since they do not have the Y chromosome. Y linked genes are called holandric genes. They are inherited by sons. Whether dominant or recessive, Y-linked genes express in all males.

PROGRESS CHECK

FILL IN THE BLANKS
1. Female is .... sex.
2. Human body has nearly .... genes.
3. Males are affected by .... linked disease.
4. Homologous pairs form .... pairs.

3.9. MENDEL'S EXPERIMENTS

Mendel is known as the 'Father of Genetics'. Mendel carried out cross-pollination of red white flowers of true breeding species of the garden pea (*pisum sativum*). For his experiments, he selected seven pairs of contrasting characters in the pea plant. This was called the parental generation and he depicted this by the symbol P. This parental generation led to the growth of the *first filial generation* (F_1). The plants in the first filial generation were self-pollinated and that led to the production of offspring of the *second filial generation* (F_2). It was found that the flowers in the F_1 generation contained both the characters of redness and whiteness even though just one characteristic was conspicuous. Mendel named these offspring hybrids. It is in the F_2 generation that the two characters are separated. George Mendel conducted various breeding experiments on the garden pea. His research work led to new and revolutionary findings in biology.

Why did Mendel select garden pea for his experiments?

Mendel selected garden pea due to the following reasons :

(a) Pea plants bear bisexual flowers and are self-pollinated.
(b) The structure of pea flower ensures self-pollination.
(c) Pea plants produce offspring of only one type generation after generation and so they maintain pure lines.
(d) Pea plants are annual. So, many generations could be studied within a short period.
(e) There are several varieties of pea plants, all with sharp contrasting characteristics such as color, shape of seeds etc.

Animations for Mendel's Experiments

(1) http://www.wiley.com/college/test/0471787159/biology_basics/animations/mendelianInheritance.swf
(2) http://www.learnerstv.com/animation/animation.php?ani=5&cat=Biology

Pea flowers contain both male and female parts, called stamen and stigma, and usually self-pollinate. Self-pollination happens before the flowers open, so progeny are produced from a single plant. Peas can also be cross pollinated by hand, *i.e.*, Removal of anthers from a bisexual flower is called emasculation. When the stigma of these flowers were fully mature, the pollens from the anthers of flowers were transferred.

Mendel took several varieties of the garden pea plant that had seven pairs of contrasting characters. Each pair had differing traits (Fig. 3.11).

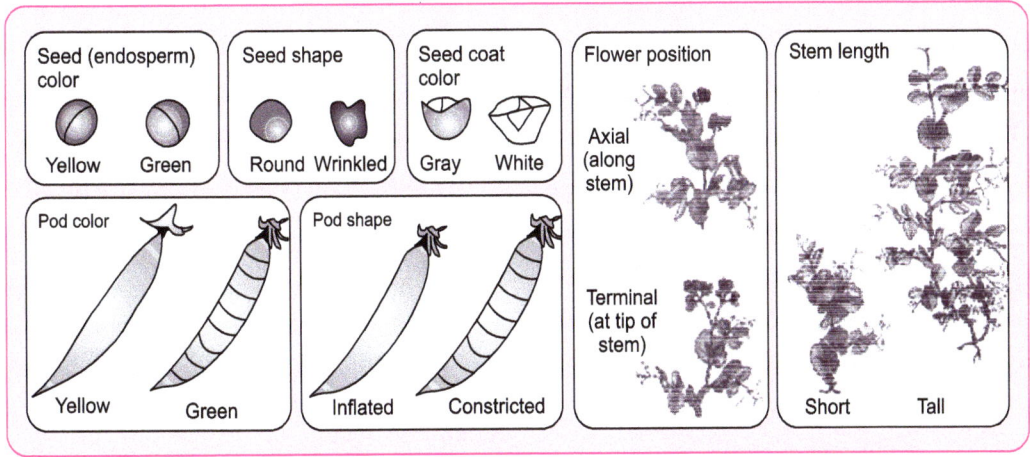

Fig. 3.11 : Seven pairs of contrasting features of garden pea studied by Mendel

Mendel cross pollinated the pure breeds of peas in two ways.

(i) Monohybrid cross.
(ii) Dihybrid cross.

(i) Monohybrid cross : It is a cross made to study the inheritance of only one pair of contrasting characters at one time.

CASE–1

A pure breeding tall (TT) pea plant is cross pollinated with a pure breeding dwarf (tt) pea plant (Fig. 3.12). Cross breeding in this manner leads to the first filial generation i.e. F_1 of hybrid tall (Tt) plants. Filial generation actually refers to a cross between off-springs. Self pollination of these hybrid tall pea plants leads to second filial generation i.e. F_2 of tall plants and dwarf plants in the ratio of 3:1. The tall plants generated are either pure tall (TT) or hybrid tall (Tt).

Thus, the phenotypic (visible feature) ratio is 3:1 in which 3 correspond to axial and 1 corresponds to terminal.

The genotypic (gene feature) ratio is 1:2:1 where 1 correspond to TT, 2 correspond to Tt and 1 correspond to tt.

The ratios are called monohybrid ratio which is obtained by crossing for two different traits of a single (mono) character.

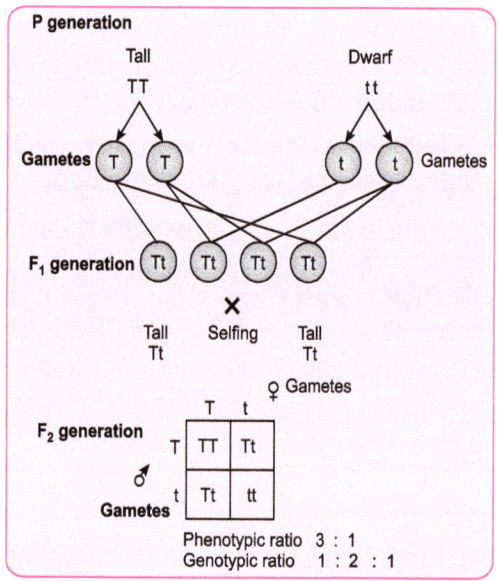

Fig. 3.12 : Cross pollination of pure tall (TT) pea plant and pure dwarf (tt) pea plant through two generations

CASE–2

A pure axial flowering (AA) pea plant is cross pollinated with a pure terminal flowering (aa) pea plant (Fig. 3.13). This kind of cross breeding only gives first filial generation i.e. F_1 of hybrid axial flowering (Aa) plants. Self-pollination of these hybrid axial flowering plants gives second filial generation i.e. F_2 of axial flowering plants and pure terminal flowering plants in the ratio of 3:1. The tall plants are either pure axial flowering plants (AA) or hybrid axial flowering plants (Aa).

Phenotypic Ratio = 3:1

Genotypic Ratio = 1:2:1

CASE–3

A pure round seed (RR) pea plant is cross pollinated with a pure wrinkled seed (rr) pea plant.

Like the cases mentioned above, this is also monohybrid cross pollination and the monohybrid ratios obtained are 3:1 (phenotypic ratio) and 1:2:1 (genotypic ratio)

The conclusions that can be drawn from the above experiments are :

(a) Determiners occur in pairs.

(b) Such genes are borne by every individual in duplicate.

(c) We all produce sex cells called gametes which contain just one member of the gene pair.

(d) The fertilisation of gametes leads to a restoration of duplicate condition of the genes.

(e) Sex cells get fertilized randomly based on the genes they contain.

(f) One of the contrasting features of a pair was not present in F_1 generation.

(ii) Dihybrid cross : In this type of cross, two pairs of contrasting characters are cross-pollinated. Mendel experimented with many combinations. We present here the crossing of green pods with yellow seeds and yellow pods with green seeds :

When hybrid green pods with yellow seeded pea plants are cross-pollinated, the second filial generation results i.e. F_2 are :

The phenotypic (visible feature) ratio is 9:3:3:1 where 9 corresponds to green pods with yellow seeds, 3 corresponds to green pods with green seeds, 3 corresponds to yellow pods with yellow seeds and 1 corresponds to yellow pod with green seed.

The genotypic ratio is very complex.

The two kinds of ratios in the two kinds of hybridisation in F_2 generations are :

Monohybrid Ratio	Phenotypic- 3:1 Genotypic- 1:2:1
Dihybrid Ratio	Phenotypic- 9:3:3:1 Genotypic- complex

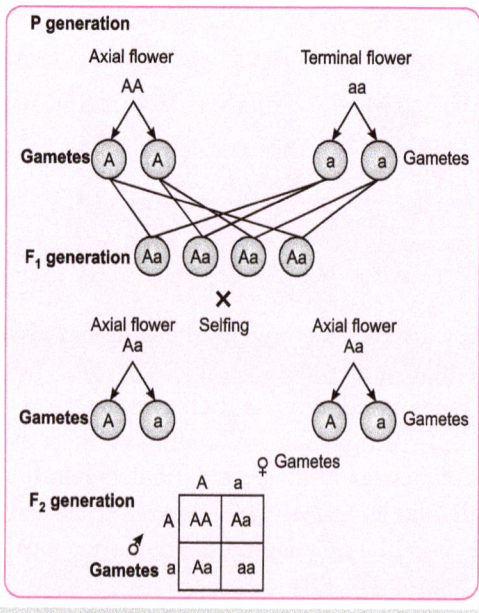

Fig. 3.13 : Cross pollination of pure axial flowering (AA) pea plant and pure terminal flowering (aa) pea plant through two generations

3.10. MENDEL'S LAWS OF INHERITANCE

Based on Mendel's breeding experiments and his observations, three laws of inheritance were formulated:

(a) Law of dominance : When two homozygous individuals with one or more sets of contrasting characters are crossed, only one character is able to manifest itself while the other remains suppressed.

The suppressed character is called the recessive character and the manifested one is called the dominant character. If the genotype is homozygous recessive, then the recessive character is manifested.

(b) Law of segregation : This law states that the two members of a pair of factors separate during gamete formation. This law is also called the *Law of Purity of Genes*. When the gametes fuse a zygote is formed. The characters do not mix i.e. the flowers either exists as red or white. In the F_2 generation, the differentiation of characters takes place in the ratio 1:2:1. The dominant in an allelomorph appears in both the homozygous and the heterozygous individual but the recessive characteristics can be evident in the homozygous when the recessive gene does not appear with the dominant. According to this law there is no blending of characters, that is, the plants are either tall or dwarf.

(c) The Law of independent assortment : This law states that when inheritance of two or more genes occurs at the same time, their distribution in the gametes is independent of each other. To prove this, Mendel did a dihybrid cross, a cross involving two pairs of contrasting characters or traits. He crossed homozygous dominant round and yellow seeded (YYRR) with homozygous recessive wrinkled and green seeded (yyrr) plants. All the plants produced in the F_1 generation were with round and yellow seeds, which were heterozygous for both the traits. The F_1 hybrid was self-pollinated and F_2 generation was obtained with the phenotypic ratio of 9 : 3 : 3 : 1 and genotypic ratio of 1 : 2 : 1 : 2 : 4 : 2 : 1 : 2 : 1.

Application of Mendel's Laws

(i) Mendel's Laws help us in getting to know about the new combination in the offspring of hybrids and also in calculating their frequency.
(ii) Those involved in the breeding of animal and plants make use of this information which leads to breeding of better and desired varieties of particular animals and plants.
(iii) Mendel's Laws aid in the production of new varieties of plants with new combinations of desired characters achieved through the process of hybridisation.
(iv) These laws have helped in the identification of several hereditary diseases in humans and in finding solutions for them.

3.11. MUTATION

A sudden, relatively permanent change in one or more genes, either in number or in structure of chromosomes, is called Mutation. It leads to the alteration of the hereditary characteristics of organisms thus permanently altering the gene pool. Some examples are:

(a) Cystic fibrosis (CF) is an inherited disease that causes the body to produce mucus that's extremely thick and sticky. The two organs most affected are the lungs and pancreas, where the thick mucus causes breathing and digestive problems. The thicker mucus has trouble moving out of the lungs, so bacteria can remain and cause infections. CF mucus affects digestion by obstructing the pancreas and stopping natural enzymes from helping the body to break down and absorb food.

(b) People directly exposed to radiation by the atomic-bomb detonations in Japan during the Second World War and by nuclear accidents at Chernobyl in Russia and Three Mile Island in the USA, develop increased risk of cancer. Exposure to radioactivity changes the gene structure permanently and this change is inherited down the generations.

(c) Sickle cell anaemia is a blood disease that is a result of gene mutation. It causes the DNA of the organism to change, causing the production of sickle-shaped RBCs, which decrease the ability to transport Oxygen.

(d) Down's syndrome is another genetic mutation where a person might be born with an extra chromosome or with an oversized one.

3.12. CLONING

Using genetic engineering, it is possible to isolate and clone single copy of a gene or a DNA segment into an infinite number of copies.

Cloning allows the creation of a genetically identical duplicate of an individual by means of sexual reproduction, either by stimulating a single cell or by taking cuttings from a plant. The resulting organism is called a clone.

Dolly, the sheep, was the first cloned mammal, and was cloned from a single adult cell. There are several ethical issues and controversies surround-ing cloning currently.

3.13. THE FUTURE OF GENETICS

There are several anticipated uses of genetics in the future. Some of them are:

(a) Disease identification : Doctors at clinical centres will put droplets of our genes onto a biochip to identify the diseases that are likely to befall us.

(b) Curative genes : When a problem occurs, doctors would 'turn on' specific genes in our bodies to cure the disease or problem.

(c) Cloning : Cloning of amputated or diseased body parts and organs can result in large scale alleviation of disease and injuries.

EXERCISE

A. VERY SHORT ANSWER TYPE

(I) Fill in the Blanks

1. .... are denoted with capital letters and .... are denoted with small letters.
2. Genetic engineering was first used in the production of ....
3. The phenotypic (visible feature) ratio of dihybrid cross is ....
4. Main cause of heritable variation is ....
5. Gametes are ....
6. Genetic composition of an organism represents its ....
7. Phenotype refers to the .... of an individual.
8. Human egg cell have .... Y chromosomes.
9. A woman receives her X-chromosome from ....
10. Each gene of a pair of genes controlling a character .... to the other.

(II) Answer the Following

1. For each of the genotypes below, determine the phenotype.
    (a) Purple flowers are dominant to white flowers
        PP ....
        Pp ....
        pp ....
    (b) Bobtails are recessive (long tails dominant)
        TT ....
        Tt ....
        tt ....
2. For each phenotype, list the genotypes. (Remember to use the letter of the dominant trait)
    (a) Straight hair is dominant to curly.
        .... straight
        .... straight
        .... curly
    (b) Pointed heads are dominant to round heads.
        .... pointed
        .... pointed
        .... round

(III) Name of the Following

1. Father of Genetics.
2. Collective information of genes and the intergenic region.
3. Alternative forms of character.
4. Examples of different animals with equal number of chromosomes.
5. Genetic constitution of an organism.
6. The chemical substance which constitutes the genes.
7. The sex chromosomes of a male.
8. Pair of genes responsible for a particular characteristic in an individual.
9. The structure that transmits characteristics from parent to offspring.
10. The type of gene, which in the presence of a contrasting allele is not expressed.
11. The Mendelian cross which is carried out by taking one pair of contrasting character.

B. SHORT ANSWER TYPE

1. Why are X linked inherited diseases also known as criss cross connected diseases?
2. Define Mutation. How does radioactive radiation cause mutation?
3. Explain with a pedigree chart the inheritance of X linked disease from a carrier mother and normal father.
4. What determines the sex of a child in humans?
5. Give examples of traits that are inherited from parents in the case of humans.
6. What is a monohybrid cross, and what are the genotypic and phenotypic ratios expected in the offspring of the cross?
7. What is a dihybrid cross, and what is the phenotypic ratio expected in the offspring of the cross?
8. The sex of a child depends upon his father. Explain.
9. What are genes? Where are they found in the cell? Mention their functions.
10. Differentiate between:
    (a) Genotype and Phenotype
    (b) Pure strain and hybrid strain

C. LONG ANSWER TYPE

1. What are the Mendel's Laws of Inheritance? Give the applications of the same.
2. Write a detailed note on (a) monohybrid cross between pure tall (TT) pea plant and pure dwarf (tt) pea plant. (b) dihybrid cross between green pods with yellow seeds (GGYY) pea plant and yellow pods with green seeds (ggyy) pea plants.
3. Define Genetics. Write a note on its applications.
4. Draw a chart of the traits observed in peas.
5. Explain why generally only the male child suffers from colour blindness and not the female?

D. STRUCTURED/APPLICATION BASED

1. Give the genotypes and phenotypes of the offspring produced during following crosses. Represent the results in the form of Punnett square.
   (a) Tt × Tt   (b) Tt × tt
   (c) AaBb × AaBb   (d) YYrr × yyRR
2. Set up the square for each of the crosses listed below. The trait being studied is round seeds (dominant) and wrinkled seeds (recessive)
   (a) Rr × rr
       What percentage of the offspring will be round?
   (b) Rr × Rr
       What percentage of the offspring will be round?
   (c) RR × Rr
       What percentage of the offspring will be round.

3. Cystic fibrosis, a genetic disease, is caused by a recessive allele (r), the normal condition (R) is dominant.

   Mummy is a carrier for cystic fibrosis, daddy has normal alleles

   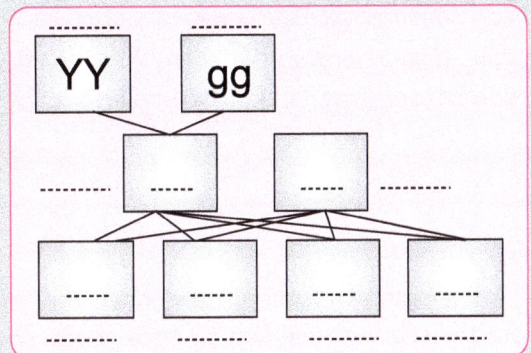

   (a) Complete the diagram to show possible children
   (b) Will any of their children have cystic fibrosis? Explain.
   (c) Complete the following chart for a monohybrid cross between a yellow colour (YY) seed pea plant and a green coloured (gg) seedpea plant. Calculate the monohybrid ratios for the same.

DO YOU KNOW?

➢ Human beings share 70% of genes with E. coli bacterium, 21% with worms, 90% with mice and 98% with chimpanzees.
➢ Humans are 99.9% genetically identical – only 0.1% of our genetic make-up differs.
➢ A genetic study is being done on an African ethnic group Yoruba. They have an unusually high birth rate of twins.
➢ Lion and Tiger have nineteen pairs of chromosomes only.

4

ABSORPTION BY ROOTS

CHAPTER HIGHLIGHTS
4.1. Absorption in Plants
4.2. Requirement of Water and Minerals in Plants
4.3. Absorption by Roots, Imbibition; Diffusion and Osmosis
4.4. Absorption and Conduction of Water and Minerals
4.5. Experiments 1 to 5 (Plasmolysis)
4.6. Transportation in Plants
4.7. Experiment 6 : Ringing or Girdling Experiment

4.1. ABSORPTION IN PLANTS

All terrestrial plants absorb water and minerals from the soil with the help of their roots. Roots are branched, mostly underground structures that perform three primary functions :

(a) Roots fix the plant firmly in the soil.
(b) Root hairs absorb water and dissolved mineral salts from soil.
(c) Roots transport water and dissolved salts upward to the stem and then to the leaves.

There are several modes of absorption and conduction of water in plants. For a better understanding of these physiological phenomena, we need to know why water and mineral salts are so essential for plants.

4.2. REQUIREMENT OF WATER AND MINERALS IN PLANTS

Water, besides being an important constituent of the protoplasm in plant cells, is also needed for the following processes :

(a) Photosynthesis : Water is used as a raw material during photosynthesis in the green leaves for making food.

(b) Transpiration : Water is emitted as water vapour by the plant during transpiration. This process cools the plant in hot weather conditions and also produces a suction force in the plant.

(c) Transportation : Mineral salts are carried upwards into the shoot as water solution during transportation. Also, substances like sugar are transported from the leaves to other parts of the plant in the downward direction.

(d) Mechanical function : Water provides much needed turgidity (fully distended state) to the plant, so vital to maintain stiffness of plant tissues.

(e) Opening and closing of stomata : Depending on the amount of water present, stomata open and close during transpiration.

(f) Germination of seeds : Seeds absorb water and saplings come out (germination).

We should bear in mind that water is a universal solvent and is involved in almost all the biochemical reactions that take place in cells.

Mineral nutrients are an essential constituent of the cell and cell organelles and help to synthesise many compounds or enzymes in the cell. The absorption of minerals from the soil is done by the roots only. Some minerals are absorbed as salts in the form of nitrates, phosphates and sulphates and others as ions like potassium, calcium, magnesium and chlorine. Nitrogen is needed for protein synthesis and growth. Calcium is required to maintain the semi-permeability of the cells. Chlorophyll is synthesized from magnesium and iron. Phosphorus aids nuclear and cell division. Cystine, an amino acid, contains calcium. Minerals help to maintain osmotic pressure within the cells and for exchange of other essential materials.

4.3. ABSORPTION OF WATER BY THE ROOTS

Roots absorb water from the soil. The amount of water that can be absorbed by the root is dependent on the following characteristics of roots :

(a) Large surface area : Large surface area of the root due to presence of rootlets and enormous numbers of root hairs allow for greater absorption. For example, in the balsam plant, root hairs if laid end to end, would extend for many kilometres.

(b) Root hairs with cell sap at higher concentration than that of the soil water around the root : The epidermal cells of the root grow out as root hairs. These contain vacuoles filled with *cell sap* (Fig. 4.1). The concentration of the cell sap is greater than the water around it the roots. This helps in *osmosis*, which affects the plants ability to draw in water.

(c) Root hairs have thin walls : All plant cells, including root hair, have two outer layers – a cell wall and a cell membrane. The cell wall is thin and permeable and allows the movement of substances in and out of the cell easily. The cell membrane is thinner than the cell wall and is semi-permeable, only allowing the partial movement of substances i.e., lets water molecules to pass through but stops the movement of larger molecules of dissolved salts.

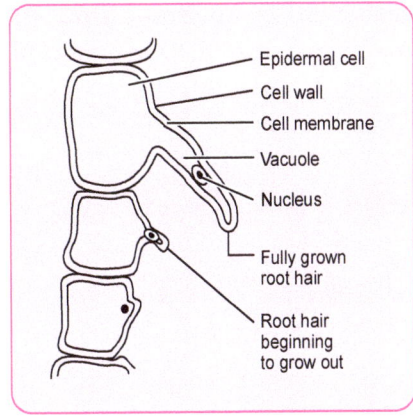

Fig. 4.1 : Structure of root growing from epidermal cells

4.4. ABSORPTION AND CONDUCTION OF WATER AND MINERALS

The entire process of the absorption and upward conduction of water and minerals from the soil through the roots in the plant is due to the following five physiological processes :

(a) Imbibition   (b) Diffusion
(c) Osmosis   (d) Active Transport
(e) Turgidity and Flaccidity (Plasmolysis)

(a) Imbibition : Imbibition is a process which involves the absorption of water molecules by living or dead plant cells through their hydrophilic surfaces (having strong affinity for water). Substances such as cellulose and proteins are strongly hydrophilic. When seeds germinate, the seed coat breaks due to the imbibition pressure. It also helps in ripening of ovules into seeds and is responsible for ascent of sap.

(b) Diffusion : During diffusion, molecules of a substance (solid, liquid, gas) move without inhibition from a region of higher concentration to a region of lower concentration (Fig. 4.2). This process takes place when the two are directly in contact with each other. Common examples are—(i) when perfume bottle is opened, its fragrance spreads to other corners of the room. (ii) Crystal of copper sulphate added to a beaker of water slowly disappear because its molecules spread uniformly in water by diffusion.

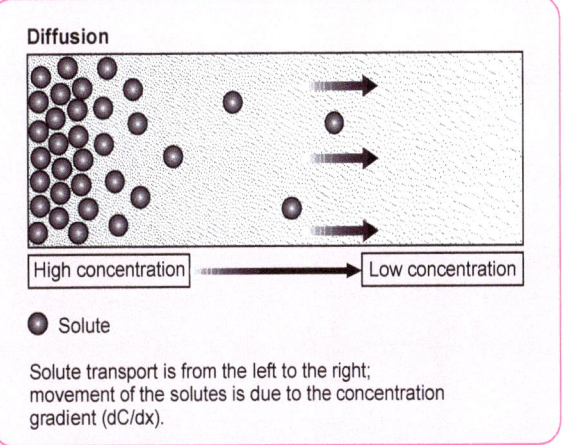

Fig. 4.2 : Movement of solute from high concentration to low concentration

(c) Osmosis : Osmosis is also a form of diffusion. In this process, water molecules diffuse from a more dilute solution to a less dilute solution across a semi-permeable membrane (Fig. 4.3). If the water molecules are in a higher concentration (in a dilute solution or in the pure water form) they move to that in a lower concentration (in stronger solution or just a solution in relation to pure water). There are two forms of osmosis : Endosmosis and Exosmosis.

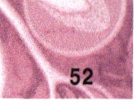

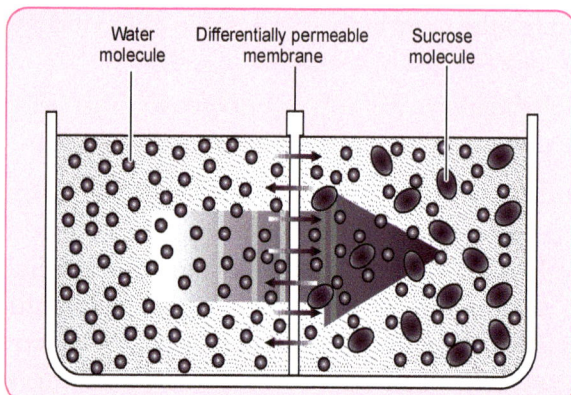

Fig. 4.3 : Absorption by osmosis

(i) **Endosmosis** (endo: inward, osmo: push/thrust) is inward movement of water into a cell through a semi-permeable membrane. It takes place when the solution around it is less concentrated. It causes the cell to swell up.

(ii) **Exosmosis** is (exo: outward), outward flow of water through a semi-permeable membrane. It takes place when the solution around it is more concentrated. Cells shrink because of exosmosis.

4.5. EXPERIMENTS ON OSMOSIS

Experiment–1

Aim : To understand the process of Osmosis (Fig. 4.4).

Apparatus : Two retort stands, two thistle funnels with wide bulbs and narrow stems, two beakers, water, sucrose, parchment paper, liquid wax.

Procedure : Prepare two solutions, A and B which have the following percentage compositions :

Solution A : 20% solute; 80% solvent

Solution B : 5% solute; 95% solvent

Close each of the thistle funnels ends with parchment paper and seal them with liquid wax. Suspend each inverted funnel in a beaker.

Set-up A : *Beaker* : Plain water (as control)

Thistle funnel: 20% sucrose solution

Set-up B : *Beaker* : 5% sucrose solution

Thistle funnel : 95% sucrose solution

Mark the initial levels of sucrose solution in each funnel.

Allow the apparatus to remain in this state for a few hours.

Observation

Set-up A : Level of solution in the stem of the thistle funnel rises.

Set-up B : Level of solution in the stem of the thistle funnel falls.

Inference : Water molecules move from the beaker to the thistle funnel in set-up A, i.e., from their region of higher concentration to their region of lower concentration across the parchment paper. Water molecules move from the thistle funnel to the beaker in set-up B i.e., from the region of lower concentration to their region of higher concentration across the parchment paper.

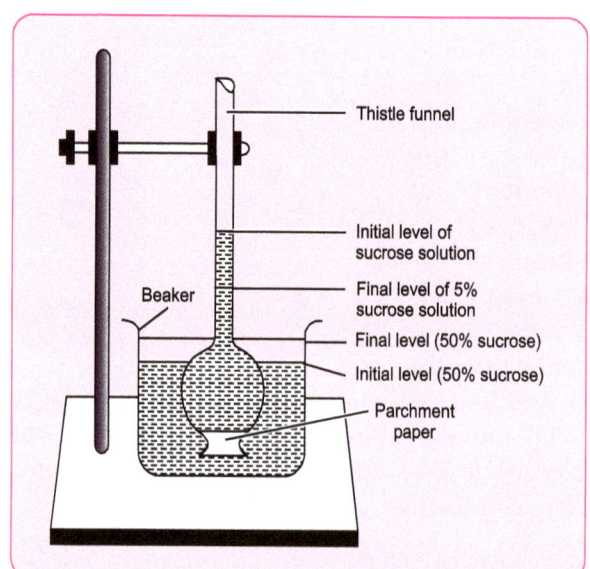

Fig. 4.4 : Set up–'A' Fig. 4.4 : Set up–'B' Experimental setup to demonstrate osmosis

Experiment–2

Aim : To demonstrate how osmosis works using a potato osmoscope (Fig. 4.5).

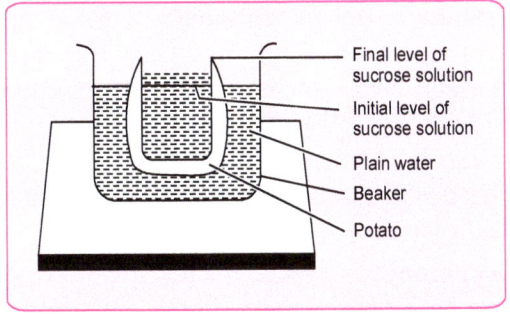

Fig. 4.5 : Demonstration of osmosis using potato osmoscope

Apparatus : A peeled potato, a petri-dish, sucrose, water, pins.

Procedure : Make a cavity in the peeled potato. Slice the bottom to make it flat and even. Place it in the beaker containing water in a manner that the potato is immersed. Fill the cavity with 25% sucrose solution. Mark the level of the solution with a pin. Allow the apparatus to remain in this state for sometime.

Observation : The level of liquid in the potato cavity rises.

Inference : Osmosis takes place. The water passes into the cells of the potato and accumulates inside the cavity in which the concentration of water molecules was lower.

PROGRESS CHECK

FILL IN THE BLANKS

1. Substances made up of .... and .... have a strong attraction for water.
2. Osmosis is a form of, ... and ....
3. Some minerals such as .... and .... are absorbed in the form of ions.
4. The roots .... the plants to the ....
5. Turgidity takes place when a cell cannot .... any more.

Osmotic pressure : It is the minimum pressure required to prevent the passage of pure solvent into the solution across a semipermeable membrane.

Osmotic pressure can also be defined as the maximum that can develop in an osmotically active solution across a semipermeable membrane to stop further endosmosis from a region of lower concentration to a region of higher concentration.

Experiment–3

Aim : To understand osmotic pressure (Fig. 4.6).

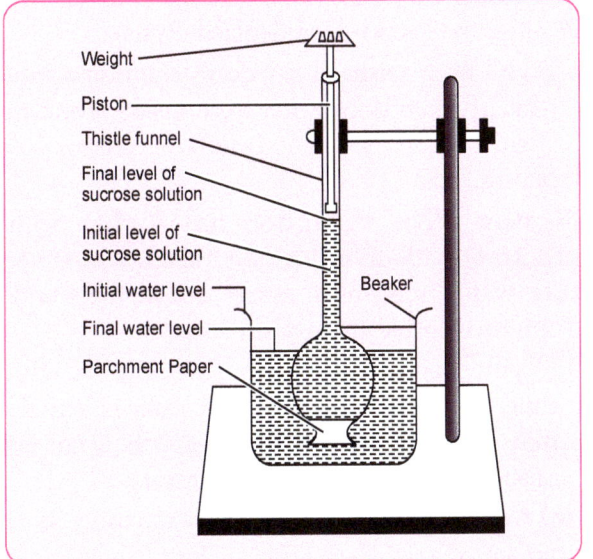

Fig. 4.6 : Demonstration of osmotic pressure

Apparatus : A retort stand, thistle funnel, parchment paper, beaker, water, 20% sucrose solution, a piston of narrow diameter that comfortably fits into the stem of the thistle funnel.

Procedure : Set up the apparatus as in Experiment 1. Place the piston in the thistle funnel so that it touches the surface of the liquid. As the piston moves upwards, weights are placed on the piston until the movement of the piston stops.

Explanation : The piston gradually moves upwards due to osmosis of water from beaker into the thistle funnel. The movement of the piston is stopped by applying extra external pressure on the piston. This is because the solute molecules move and possess kinetic energy. They spread evenly in the entire space because of diffusion. Thereafter, they exert a pressure on the solution and this pressure is known as osmotic pressure.

Experiment–4

Aim : To understand endosmosis and exosmosis.

Apparatus : A bag made up of a semi-permeable membrane, 2% sucrose solution, 10% sucrose solution, two beakers and water.

Procedure : Fill up the bag partially with 2% sucrose solution and suspend it in a beaker of water. After some time, suspend the same bag in a beaker containing 10% sucrose solution. Leave the apparatus like this for some time.

Observation : When the bag is suspended in the beaker of water, the bag distends fully. When it is placed in the 10% sucrose solution, the bag shrinks.

Inference : Endosmosis takes place when the bag is placed in a hypotonic solution (pure water). Exosmosis takes place when the bag is placed in a hypertonic solution (10% sucrose solution).

Osmosis and its Importance

In plants

(a) Water absorption from the soil : Osmosis enables water from the soil to move from the root hair and the cortical cells. It reaches the xylem cells by passing through the passage cells and the thin sections of the endodermis. Thus, water is absorbed from the soil due to the formation of a channel from the root hairs to the xylem tissue, enabling water to move upwards.

(b) Opening and closing of stomata : Osmosis also regulates the opening and closing of stomata. Solutes (mainly potassium) are absorbed by the guard cells of the stomata from the epidermal and mesophyll cells. We are now aware of the role of potassium ions in the stomatal opening. The size of thestomatal opening is governed by the amount of potassium ions that accumulate in the guard cells. Higher the potassium ion level, greater is the stomatal opening.

In animals : The membranes of animal cells, unlike that in plant cells, allow the movement of water and some solutes. In animals, osmoregulation is carried out to maintain osmotic balance.

(a) Amoeba : In amoeba, water enters the body (a single cell), through osmosis and collects in an open space in the endoplasm called the contractile vacuole. This space gradually becomes larger and distends. This process leads to the release of metabolic wastes and water.

(b) Frog and fish : In fishes and frogs, the metabolic wastes collect in the blood and raise the osmotic pressure inside the body. They draw in water from the environment and distend. As a result, their blood dilutes and their vital processes are hampered. This is the reason why these animals have organs like the kidney.

(c) Land creatures : Land creatures also take in water and fluids which are lost by evaporation or respiration. The balance is maintained by organs like the kidneys.

Tonicity

Tonicity is the relative concentration of two solutions that determines the extent of diffusion and its direction. It is usually determined when two solutions are compared for their osmotic pressure. Tonicity is of three types:

(a) Isotonic : 'Iso' means same and tonus means concentration. In a solution where the relative concentration of the solute and water molecules on either side of the cell membrane is the same, there is no osmosis or there is no movement of water molecules across the cell membrane. Such solutions are called isotonic.

(b) Hypotonic : 'Hypo' means lower. In this, condition lesser amount of dissolved solutes are present outside the cell than inside which (as compared to the fluids inside the cell), cause the water molecules to move from outside to inside. This is also known as endosmosis.

(c) Hypertonic : 'Hyper' means higher. In this, greater amount of dissolved solute are present outside of the cell than inside, causing the water molecules to move from inside the cell to outside. This is also known as exosmosis.

If a living cell is put in isotonic solution then neither the cell will gain nor lose water, but living cell kept in hypertonic solution will lose water and a living cell when kept in hypotonic solution will gain water.

Osmosis affect raisin in different ways pertaining to the solution in which it is kept. It can behave in three ways :

(i) If you keep raisin in pure water raisins absorbs water and swells up.

Reason : Pure water has very low solute concentration than the raisin, so osmosis occurs, water enters the raisin, and raisin swells up (it is also called endosmosis or deplasmolysis).

(ii) If you keep raisin in a sodium chloride solution (NaCl), raisin loses water from inside it and gets shrunk. (It is also called exosmosis or plasmolysis).

Reason : NaCl solution has higher solute concentration than inside the raisin, so osmosis occurs, water from raisin moves out in the solution of sodium chloride thus raisin shrinks.

(iii) If you keep raisin in a solution in which concentration (or amount) of salts is equal to that inside raisin no osmosis will occur and raisin will neither swell nor shrink.

(d) Active transport : Active Transport is the movement of a substance (salt or ion) from its lower to higher concentration through a living cell membrane. It takes place against the concentration gradient. This process is the opposite of diffusion. Energy from the cell is used in this process. Ions of nitrates, sulphates, potassium, zinc, manganese are unable to move through the cell membrane of the root cells easily. They are at a higher concentration inside the root cells so as to develop osmotic pressure for absorbing water. There are carrier molecules, mainly proteins, present in cell membrane to pick up these ions and transport them into the cell cytoplasm. Active transport requires energy provided by the cell (i.e. by using ATP present as the chemical form of energy in biological systems).

(e) Turgidity and flaccidity (Plasmolysis) : When a cell is kept in water or in a solution less saturated than the cell sap, water enters the cell. This increases the volume of the cell and the protoplasm exerts pressure against the cell wall. As a result of this, the cell wall becomes stretched. This state of the cell is termed turgid condition (Fig. 4.7).

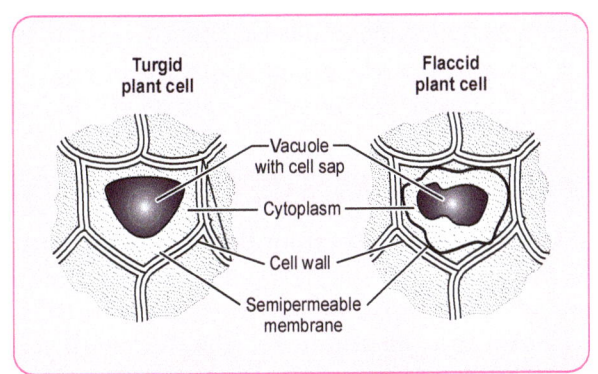

Fig. 4.7 : Turgid plant cell and flaccid plant cell

Turgor Pressure and wall pressure : Turgidity is the fully expanded condition of a cell with its wall stretched due to excessive accumulation of water. The outward pressure exerted by the cell fluid on the cell wall is called turgor pressure. The inward pressure exerted on the cell contents by the stretched cell wall is called wall pressure.

Normally these two pressures counterbalance each other and a state of equilibrium is maintained between them. Three factors influence the turgidity of a living cell. These are : (a) formation of osmotically active substances inside the cell, (b) an adequate supply of water, and (c) presence of a semi-permeable membrane.

Plasmolysis and flaccidity : In the turgid state, the cell is balanced i.e. no water enters or leaves it. The turgor pressure and the wall pressure balance each other and no absorption of water occurs. If a living cell is placed in fresh water, its condition remains fully distended. The plasma membrane and the cell wall remain in close contact. When the plant cell is placed in a 5% salt solution for a couple of minutes the cytoplasm shrinks. Cell membrane separates from the cell wall and gets localized. This phenomenon is called *plasmolysis* and state is called *flaccidity*.

Deplasmolysis : If the flaccid cell is once again placed in hypotonic solution before it perishes, its protoplasm distends and it presses tight against the cell wall as water from outside enters the protoplasm due to endosmosis. This phenomenon is called *deplasmolysis*.

Uses of turgidity

(i) Water transportation : Water is transported through cells (especially the root cortex) due to turgidity; water moves from a more turgid cell to less turgid cell.

(ii) Growth of the cell : Turgidity also contributes to the growth of the cell because the cell wall swells.

(iii) Rigidity to plant tissue : Turgidity also provides support to the thin-walled parenchyma tissues in the green leaves and the growing parts of the plant.

(iv) Locomotion of cells : The locomotion of cells is also regulated by turgidity, like drooping of leaves of sensitive plant, the sleep movements of certain plants.

(v) Movement of stomata : The turgidity of the guard cells is responsible for movement of the stomata. When the guard cells are turgid the walls distend and the stomata open while flaccidity leads to the closure of the stomatal opening. This regulates *transpiration*.

(vi) Turgidity in root cells builds up root pressure : As a result of turgidity, water passes from living cells into xylem and rises up through the stem.

Example : Leaf movement of many plants like sensitive plant (*Mimosa pudica*) are controlled by loss and gain of cell turgidity.

Imbibition and turgor : Passive absorption of water by substances such as cellulose and starch is called imbibition. The hydrostatic pressure inside the plants cells due to endosmosis is called turgor.

Imbibition and endosmosis cause the seeds and grains to swell up when soaked in water. The force generated by this absorbed water is usually strong enough to cause the seed coats to burst. A similar case is when soaked seeds are kept in fully filled containers, they generally tend to cause the container to burst open with pressure.

Suction pressure : The vigour with which substances absorb water varies from substance to substance. Suction pressure is the force responsible for exerting pressure on the water to drive it into the absorbing material. Suction pressure is also a way to measure a cell's ability to absorb water. The difference between osmotic pressure (OP) and turgor pressure (TP) gives us the magnitude of the suction pressure (SP).

$$OP - TP = SP$$

When TP = OP, it implies no further movement of water. In such a case SP = 0. A reduction in turgor pressure causes the suction pressure to increase.

Experiment–5

Aim : To understand what happens to a cell when it is placed in (a) hypertonic and (b) hypotonic solution.

Apparatus : Leaf of hydrilla, 10% sucrose solution, distilled water, two petri-dishes, a microscope, a glass slide.

Procedure : A section of the hydrilla leaf is placed under the microscope for observation. It is then placed in the petri-dish containing 10% sucrose solution and removed after 5 to 10 minutes. It is then mounted on a slide in the same solution and observed under the low and high powers of the microscope. The leaf then placed in distilled water taken out and mounted in water and placed under the microscope. Thereafter, take a fresh section of the leaf, place it in boiling water or alcohol for a few minutes and replicate the above procedure.

Observation : Before the leaf is placed in the water we can see that its plasma membrane is so closely pressed against the cell wall that they appear as one. We can see a large colourless central vacuole which presses the cytoplasm against the cell wall. When the section is totally immersed in the 10% sucrose solution, the entire cell contracts. The plasma membrane and the cytoplasm moves away from the cell wall and appear as a rounded mass in the centre. The vacuole also contracts completely. When we immerse the section in distilled water, the protoplasm reverts to the normal condition and the vacuole is visible once again.

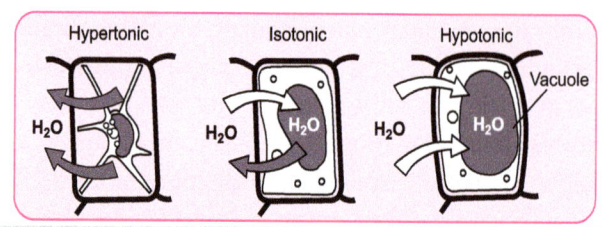

Fig. 4.8 : Plant cell placed in a different solution

Inference : In a hypertonic solution, the cell undergoes exosmosis while in a hypotonic solution the cell undergoes endosmosis.

As the cell wall and the cell membrane are separate we may conclude that the cell wall is permeable and the cell membrane is semi-permeable.

Osmotically active substances of the sap can be retained by the protoplasm.

We can determine through the process of plasmolysis whether cells are living or dead.

Significance of Plasmolysis :

(a) Helps to understand the living nature of a cell.

(b) Helps to preserve meat, jellies and used in pickling as their salting kills bacteria by plasmolysis.

(c) Used to prove the permeability of cell wall and selectively permeable nature of plasma membrans.

4.6. TRANSPORTATION IN PLANTS

Movement of water from the soil to the plant : The process of transpiration leads to an unending process of water loss by the plant into the surrounding environment. As a result, the concentration of water in the cell sap is reduced. We know that the root hair has a semi-permeable membrane and the cell sap is hypertonic. These materials establish an osmotic system with the water that surrounds the root hair. The water enters through the root hair. Inside the root hair an osmotic system develops between the cell of the root hair and the cell of the root cortex which has a relatively lower concentration of water molecules. Water from the root hair diffuses into the cells of the cortex. The root hair becomes flaccid. The absorption of water continues. The cells of the cortex establish an osmotic system with the cell around it and water passes inward into the inner cortical cell. Thus, a cell to cell osmosis is established. The water passing on in this manner reaches the xylem vessels through the passage cells and the thinner areas of the endodermis.

Ascent of sap : The upward movement of water from the root to aerial parts of the plant body is called ascent of sap or often called translocation of water.

The water that is absorbed collects in the tissue of the cortex. The upward movement of water and dissolved minerals from the xylem of root to the leaves is termed ascent of sap. The upward movement takes place through the lumen of xylem vessels and tracheids. The ascent of sap takes place due to the following :

(a) Root pressure : During osmosis from cell to cell, each cortical cell turns turgid and flaccid alternately. A considerable amount of pressure develops. This pressure is called root pressure. The water is pushed into the xylem cells through the passage cells and the thin areas and pits in the endodermis. The lignified walls of the xylem vessels also absorb water. Magnitude of root pressure never exceeds 2-3 atmospheres. As such it can move the water only up to a short distance, but not in very tall trees.

(b) Transpiration pull and force of cohesion : Inside the xylem vessels, the water collects in columns from the root to the mesophyll cells in the leaves. The loss of water leads to the water column becoming highly stretched. But, cohesion among the water molecules and adhesion between the water and the wall of the xylem vessels does not allow the water column to break. The transpirational pull is so strong that even the tallest of trees receives the water from the ground.

(c) Capillarity : The xylem vessels in plants are like capillary tubes. The water moves in them by capillary action. The sap does not rise beyond one or two metres due to capillarity.

(d) Imbibition force : Imbibition is not enough for the rapid rise of water; hence water lost through transpiration cannot be compensated in this way.

Root pressure and transpirational pull accounts for the ascent of sap. Root pressure *'pushes'* the sap in the xylem tubes and transpiration *'pulls'* the water up the xylem vessels.

PROGRESS CHECK

NAME THE FOLLOWING

1. Assimilation of water by living or dead plant cells through surface attraction.
2. The method by which water moves in the xylem vessels.
3. The movement of a substance from lower to higher concentration.
4. A process in which green leaves employ water to synthesize food for the plant.
5. The drooping of leaves.

Animations for Transport of Water and Salts in Plants

http://www.youtube.com/watch?v=rK2DIF_tgCg
http://www.youtube.com/watch?v=L0Z5l__RiyE

Importance of root hair :

Absorption of water by the root : Root hairs are unicellular, thin-walled outgrowths of the epidermis. They are in close contact with the thin film of water surrounding the soil particles. Soil solution is a weaker solution as compared to the cell sap of root hair. Hence osmosis (*endosmosis*) occurs and the water is absorbed by the root hairs through cell membranes from the soil. Due to this, the root hair cells become more turgid and their osmotic pressure falls. Adjacent cells of cortex have higher osmotic pressure. This results in the diffusion of water from the root hair to cortical cells which push the water in the xylem tubes.

Absorption of minerals : Mineral salts are absorbed by the root through the process of diffusion. Inorganic salts are absorbed in the form of ions. Each type of ion is taken up according to its requirement.

The dilute solution of water and mineral salts absorbed by plant roots can be used for the manufacture of food in the leaves only if it can travel up to the highest points of the plant through the xylem.

4.7. EXPERIMENT 6 : RINGING OR GIRDLING EXPERIMENT

Aim : To understand the role of xylem and phloem in the ascent of water and the translocation of food in the plant (Fig. 4.8).

Procedure

(a) The phloem and other peripheral tissues upto the cambium of a leafy shoot are removed, leaving the xylem intact. A retort stand is used to suspend the twig in a beaker of water.

(b) The xylem is cautiously removed with a scalpel from a portion of another twig. Then a retort stand is used to suspend the twig in a beaker of water.

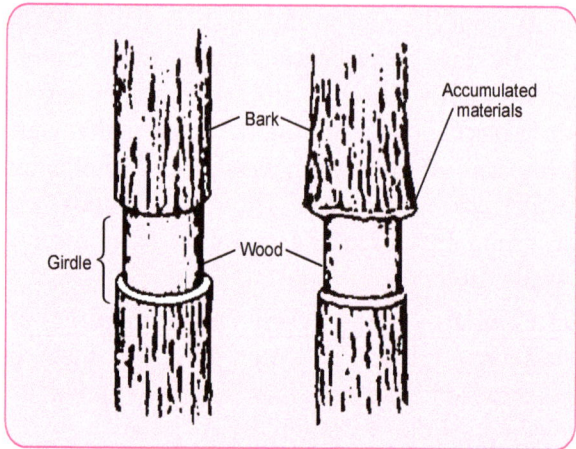

Fig. 4.8 : Tree trunk immediately after girdling (left) and later (right). Girdling is the removal of the bark of a tree in a ring around the trunk. At right, materials translocated from the leaves have accumulated in the region above the girdle and caused it to swell

Observation

(a) The leaves remain turgid. At the base of the upper end of the cut portion adventitious roots appear. The portion below the leaf shrivels up.

(b) Leaves become flaccid and the shoot perishes.

Inference

(a) The upward movement of water and solutes remains constant. This demonstrates that the shoot remains turgid, healthy and growing. But, the food does not reach below the ring demonstrating that water is transported upwards by the xylem and food translocated downwards by the phloem.

(b) Water does not reach above the ring. Water is transported upwards by the xylem. The leaves cannot prepare food as the water does not reach them. As a result, the shoot ultimately perishes.

Table 1 : Differences between Osmosis and Diffusion

Osmosis	Diffusion
1. It is the movement of water particles.	1. It is the movement of solute particles.
2. Occurs through a semi permeable membrane.	2. Membrane is not required.
3. Movement from low concentration to high concentration of solute.	3. Movement from high concentration to low concentration of solute.
4. It is associated with liquids.	4. It is associated with solids, liquid and gases.
5. It occurs over short distances.	5. It can occur over long distances too.

EXERCISE

A. VERY SHORT ANSWER TYPE

(I) Define the Following
1. Plasmolysis
2. Osmosis
3. Imbibition
4. Turgidity and Flaccidity
5. Root Pressure
6. Ascent of sap
7. Osmotic Pressure
8. Solvent
9. Turgor pressure
10. Transpiration pull

(II) Classify the following into Osmosis/Diffusion
1. Swelling up of a raisin on keeping in water.
2. Spreading of virus on sneezing.
3. Earthworm dying on coming in contact with common salt.
4. Shrinking of grapes kept in thick sugar syrup.
5. Preserving pickles in salt.
6. Spreading of smell of cake being baked throughout the house.
7. Aquatic animals using oxygen dissolved in water during respiration.

B. SHORT ANSWER TYPE

1. How does a living cell behave in
   (a) hypotonic and   (b) isotonic solution.
2. What types of minerals are absorbed by the roots?
3. What is endosmosis and exosmosis?
4. Give one example of osmosis occurring in the human body and in a green leaf.
5. Give two examples of plasmolysis from our daily lives.
6. What is cell sap?
7. What is the utility of plasmolysis?
8. Seeds when kept in water swell up and burst. Why?
9. Why do grapes shrink when kept in honey?
10. How can you demonstrate root pressure experimentally?

C. LONG ANSWER TYPE

1. Explain the phenomenon of ascent of sap.
2. What is the importance of osmosis in animals?
3. Demonstrate with the help of an experiment the working of osmotic pressure.
4. What are the factors based on which roots absorb water from the soil?
5. What is the difference between hypertonic and hypotonic solution?
6. Osmosis is a special kind of diffusion. Comment.

(I) Differentiate between

1. Turgor pressure and wall pressure.
2. Tonoplast and plasma membrane.
3. Hypertonic and hypotonic solution.

(II) Explain Why

1. Raisins swell up when kept in water.
2. Fresh water fish cannot survive in sea water.
3. Leaves of Mimosa pudica droop down when touched.
4. Transpiration pull can transport water in tall trees.

D. STRUCTURED/APPLICATION BASED QUESTIONS

1. The following diagram represents an experimental set up. Study the same and answer the questions :

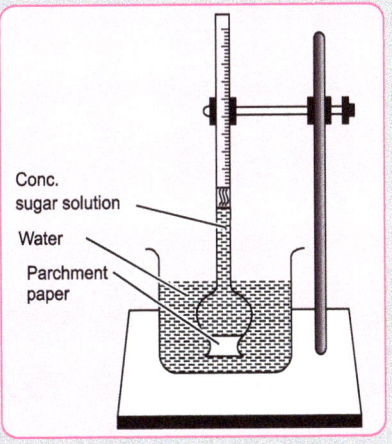

(a) Name the process.
(b) Define the process.
(c) What would you observe after an hour?
(d) What can be used instead of parchment paper?
(e) Give two advantages of this process to the plant.

2. The figure given below is a diagrammatic representation of a part of the cross section of the root in the root hair zone. Study the same and then answer the questions that follow:

(a) Name the parts indicated by guidelines '1' to '5'.
(b) Is the root hair cell unicellular or multi-cellular?
(c) Name the process responsible for the entry of water molecules from the soil into A_1 and then A_2.
(d) What pressure is responsible for the movement of water in the direction indicated by arrows?
(e) How is this pressure set up?

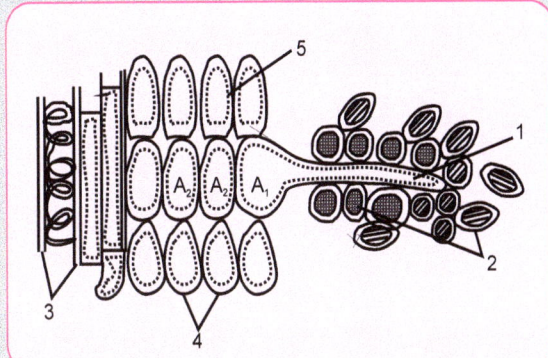

DO YOU KNOW ?

> Plants seem to grow well without ultraviolet light.
> Plants will absorb nutrients in proportion to the amount that is present in the nutrient solution within certain limits determined by the needs of the plant. To a certain degree plants can react by concentrating an element or limiting an element in themselves. But, generally they always contain at least some of everything found in their growing medium.
> A mineral is an inorganic substance occurring naturally in the earth and having a consistent and distinctive set of physical properties e.g. colour, hardness and crystalline structure, and a composition that can be expressed by a chemical formula expressing the elements involved and the form of their occurrence.
> Plants have a minimum and maximum temperature beyond which activity ceases. Some plants grow well at low temperatures and become inactive at room temperature.
> Plants absorb their nutrient salts in the form of ions.

5

TRANSPIRATION

CHAPTER HIGHLIGHTS

5.1. Transpiration
5.2. Plants Transpire in the Form of Water Vapour
5.3. Measurement of Transpiration
5.4. Kinds of Transpiration
5.5. Factors that Affect Transpiration
5.6. Adaptations in Plants to Reduce Transpiration
5.7. Importance of Transpiration
5.8. Disadvantages of Transpiration
5.9. Guttation and Bleeding

5.1. TRANSPIRATION

Transpiration is a process during which water in the form of water vapour is lost from the internal tissues of plants, through aerial parts of the plant.

The roots of plants absorb water from the soil. This water is transported to the aerial parts of the plant including the leaves. The total water absorbed by the roots, only a small amount (2%) is consumed during photosynthesis and other activities. The remaining water is lost to the atmosphere by the plant during transpiration. A large tree may lose as much as a 1,000 litres of water per day by way of evaporation due to transpiration.

This excess water evaporate from the plant or tree is important for its survival, as without it the metabolic activity of the plant would be adversely affected. Without transpiration, the water would accumulate in the plant tissue, causing hydrostatic pressure to build up in the cells, eventually resulting in its rupture.

The moisture thus, added to the environment, cools the climate, there by influencing the weather. This moisture, eventually falls to the ground as rain, is absorbed by the roots of plants and hence, again becomes a part of the water cycle.

5.2. PLANTS TRANSPIRE IN THE FORM OF WATER VAPOUR

Experiment–1

Requirement : A well-watered potted plant and a transparent polythene bag (Fig. 5.1).

Fig. 5.1 : Experiment to prove that plants transpire in the form of water vapour

Procedure : Cover the plant with the polythene bag. Tie its mouth to the base of the stem. Leave this setting undisturbed in the sunlight for around 2 hours.

Take another polythene bag and tie its mouth. Leave this bag also undisturbed in the sunlight for around 2 hours.

Observation
(a) Water droplets are observed on the inner side of the polythene bag that was tied to the plant.

(b) The polythene bag without the potted plant is devoid of any moisture.

Conclusion : Formation of water droplets inside the polythene bag tied to the plant is due to the condensation of water vapour. This water vapour could have come only from the potted plant. This shows that plants transpire in the form of water vapour.

Experiment–2

Requirement : Three bell jars labelled A, B and C, two well watered potted similar plants (broad leaves preferred), two polythene bags, two strips of cobalt chloride paper.

Procedure : Take bell jar labelled 'A' and use it to cover one of the plants whose pot has been enclosed within a polythene bag (Fig. 5.2).

Take bell jar labelled 'B' and enclose within it the other plant whose pot is also well covered with a polythene bag. Also attach a strip of cobalt chloride paper to the interior of the bell jar.

Take a third bell jar labelled 'C' and attach a strip of cobalt chloride paper to the interior of this bell jar too. Note that there is no plant in this bell jar.

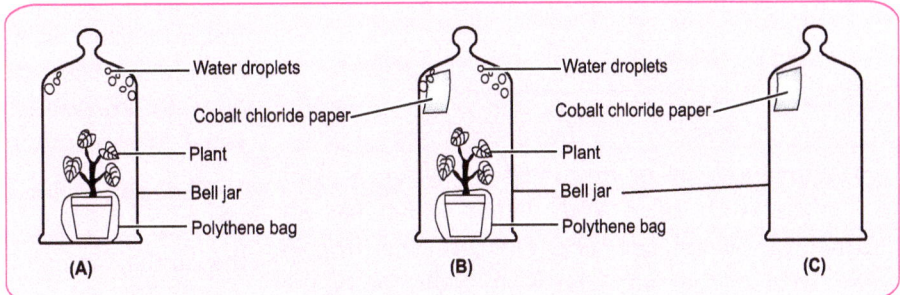

Fig. 5.2 : Bell jar experiment to prove that plants transpire in the form of water vapour

Now place all the three bell jars A, B and C in the sunlight for about an hour.

Observation
(a) Water droplets are formed in the interior of the bell jar A.

(b) Water droplets are formed within the bell jar B too, and the colour of the cobalt chloride stripchanges from blue to pink.

(c) No water droplets are formed in the interior of the bell jar C. The colour of the cobalt chloride paper remains unchanged.

Conclusion : Formation of water droplets in the interior of the bell jars A and B and not in C is proof that plants give off water vapour during transpiration. Colour change of the cobalt chloride paper from blue to pink also supports the same.

The bell jar 'C' in the above experiment was a control that serves to show that there was no moisture in the air to begin with.

5.3. MEASUREMENT OF TRANSPIRATION

Transpiration can be measured by the following methods :

(a) Weighing method (Fig. 5.3) : The weight of a small well watered potted plant, preferably with broad leaves, can be measured before and after a specific time period to know the amount of water lost during transpiration. The pot and the soil surface are covered with a polythene bag to prevent any additional loss of water apart from transpiration. The difference in weight gives the weight loss by potted plant due to transpiration. However, this is an inaccurate method of measuring transpiration.

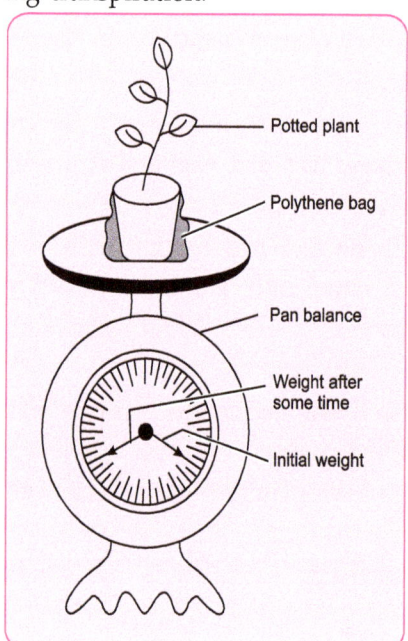

Fig. 5.3 : Weighing method

This method can be improved by taking a plant in a glass bottle filled with water, which has an attached graduated side tube (Fig. 5.4). The drop in water level in the side tube is an indicator of the loss of water due to transpiration.

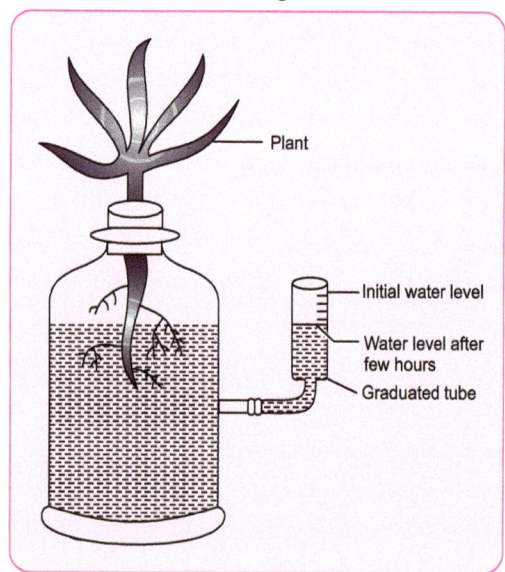

Fig. 5.4 : Measurement of water loss volume due to transpiration

This volume loss can be compared with its weight loss by using volume to weight conversions. (1 cc water = 1 gram)

The water loss due to transpiration can also be measured by keeping a small plant in a test tube filled with water (Fig. 5.5). Pour a little oil on the water surface to make a thin film. Weigh this test tube. Leave the test tube undisturbed in a stand for a few hours. The water in the test tube is sealed with the oil film. This prevents any direct loss of water.

Now check the weight of the test tube. The loss in weight of the test tube is due to loss of water through transpiration from the plant.

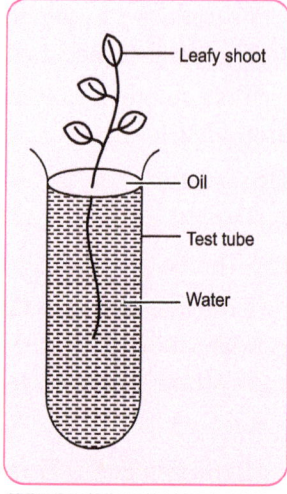

Fig. 5.5 : Measurement of water loss due to transpiration

(b) Potometer method : *Potometer*, also known as *transpirometer* is a device that can measure the amount of water intake by the plants. The amount of water consumed by the plant is approximately equal to the amount lost during transpiration.

The potometer consists of bent capillary tube attached to a reservoir (Fig. 5.6). The bent end of the capillary tube is immersed in a beaker filled with water. The other end of the capillary tube has a small twig of some suitable plant. Water is filled in the entire apparatus in such a way that there are no air spaces.

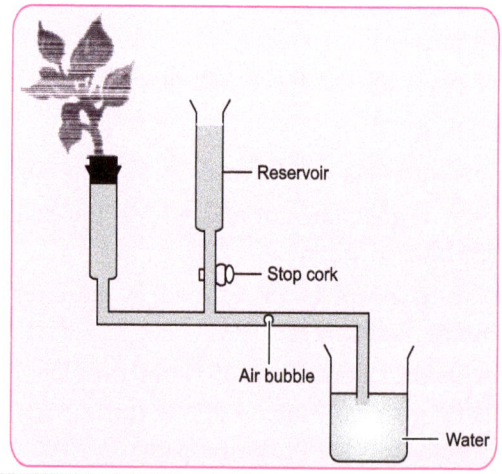

Fig. 5.6 : Ganong's potometer

An air bubble is introduced into the horizontal graduated capillary tube by lifting it above the water level in the beaker and then immersing it again. Air bubble is formed due to suction pull. We have to take a fresh leafy shoot of some suitable plant, cut it under water to prevent entry of air from the cut end and fix it into the upper wide tube of the potometer.

As the water from the plant is lost through transpiration, a suction force is developed. This pulls the water from the beaker and the air bubble moves along in the capillary tube. The volume of water lost can be measured with the help of readings on the capillary tube. By adding water from the attached reservoir, the air bubble can be brought back to its original position.

NOTE

Potometer does not measure the water lost during transpiration. It measures the total water intake of the twig. The water taken in is consumed during photosynthesis (2%) and lost during transpiration (98%). For better accuracy, the following steps need to be taken :

(i) The potometer should be kept air tight.

(ii) The twig should be cut obliquely for allowing larger surface area for water intake.

(iii) The twig should be well immersed in the water to avoid any absorption of air into the xylem.

Limitations of the use of potometer

(i) Air bubble introduction is difficult.

(ii) The twig does not remain alive for a long time.

(iii) Fluctuations in the room temperature, humidity, air velocity etc. affect the position of the air bubble in the capillary tube.

PROGRESS CHECK

TRUE OR FALSE

(1) Only 2% of water absorbed by the roots is lost during transpiration. (T/F)

(2) Water does not affect cobalt chloride paper. (T/F)

(3) The evaporative loss of water from the aerial parts (leaves, stem) of the plants is called photosynthesis. (T/F)

(4) Fluctuation in the room temperature does not affect the position of the air bubble in the capillary tube of photometer. (T/F)

5.4. KINDS OF TRANSPIRATION

All the aerial parts of the plant transpire but with varying degrees of efficiency. Based on these variations, transpiration can be of three kinds :

(a) Stomatal transpiration : Through the stomata of leaves.

(b) Cuticular transpiration : Directly from the surface of leaves and stems.

(c) Lenticular transpiration : From the minute openings (lenticles) on the surface of old stems.

Of the three types, maximum transpiration occurs through the stomata of the leaves.

(a) Stomatal transpiration

The minute openings in the lower epidermal layer of the leaves are called stomata (singular: stoma) (Fig. 5.7). The number of stomata in a square cm area of leaf could range anything from 1000 to 10,000. Each stoma has two bean shaped guard cells around it. When the guard cells are turgid, stomata are open and when they are flaccid, stomata are closed. During day, the stomata are wide open to facilitate intake of carbon dioxide for photosynthesis.

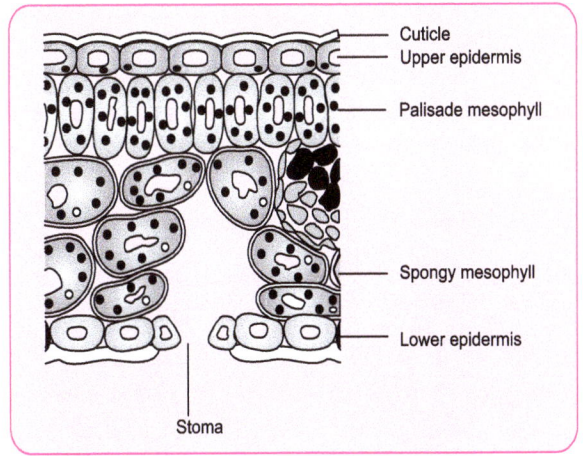

Fig. 5.7 : Stomatal transpiration

The roots of plants absorb water from the soil. This water is transported to the rest of the plant through the xylem vessels. Water reaches the tissues of the leaves through veins. A large number of spongy mesophyll cells in the leaves have their surfaces exposed to the intercellular spaces. The surfaces of the mesophyll cells give out a small quantity of water in the form of a thin film. The thin film of water evaporates to give water vapour that gets accumulated in and saturates the air in the intercellular spaces. This water vapour reaches the inter-stomatal spaces, from where it escapes the stomata (higher concentration region) to the outside atmosphere (lower concentration region).

Thus, diffusion is responsible for stomatal transpiration since water vapour, like other gases, has a tendency of moving from a region of higher concentration to a region of lower concentration region.

The water thus lost is replaced by drawing more from the nearing veins. Most of this water travels by imbibition (along cell walls) and only a small quantity enters the cell by osmosis.

As mentioned earlier, during photosynthesis the stomata of the leaves are wide open essentially for intake of CO_2. Sugar produced during photosynthesis in the daytime increases the osmotic pressure. As a result, water enters the guard cells by endosmosis, making them turgid and causing the stomatal pores to open. But at night osmotic pressure of guard cells decreases because there is no photosynthesis, the stomatal guard cells become flaccid and the stomata remain closed.

Transpiration occurs only when the stomata are open and stops when the stomata close (Fig. 5.8). The fluids (water and solutes) in the guard cells govern the opening and the closing of the stoma. Diffusion of gases in and out is possible only when the stoma is open. If the water level of the plants starts falling, the stoma closes because the guard cells turn flaccid (relax). This is common during mid-day when the rate of transpiration exceeds the rate of absorption of water by roots.

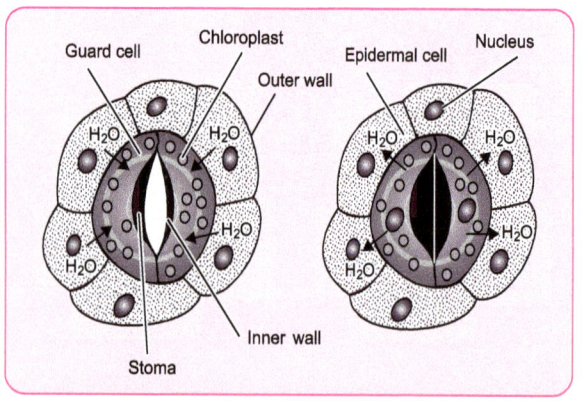

Fig. 5.8 : Opening and closing of stoma

Thousands of leaf cells lose water by transpiration in this way and cause more and more water to be pulled from below via the xylem tissue. The transpiration pull thus created can draw up water to heights as much as 50 metres or more in the tallest trees.

The guard cells become turgid (contract) during the nights when the rate of transpiration is low.

The under surface of the leaf is the place from where the maximum transpiration takes place. This is mainly due to the fact that there are more stomata on leaf's under surface as compared to its top surface.

It can be concluded that stomatal transpiration is controlled by adjusting the size of stoma by the guard cells. Under normal conditions of temperature, humidity and light, nearly 80–90% of all transpiration is stomatal.

(b) Cuticular transpiration : The epidermis of the leaves secretes a waxy substance that forms a layer, called the cuticle, on the leaf surfaces. The main function of the cuticle is to block evaporation of water from the leaf surfaces. The greater the thickness of cuticle, lesser is the evaporation (transpiration). The cuticle thickness varies from plant to plant and it is the thickest in the plants from dry arid regions like desert, resulting in minimal loss of water through transpiration.

Even though the cuticle blocks transpiration, a small amount of water is still lost. This type of transpiration is only 3-10% of total transpiration. While stomatal transpiration takes place during day time, cuticular transpiration can occur both during the day as well as at night.

(c) Lenticular transpiration : The old stems and branches of trees of plants have minute openings called lenticels in place of the stomata. Unlike the stomata, lenticels remain open perpetually. The lenticels serve dual purpose of diffusing gases (for respiration and photosynthesis) and water evaporation (transpiration).

The amount of water lost due to lenticular transpiration is more than cuticular transpiration but much less as compared to stomatal transpiration.

Links for Transpiration

http://www.youtube.com/watch?v=U4rzLhz4HHk
http://www.youtube.comwatch?v=IImgFYmbAUg

PROGRESS CHECK

DEFINE THE FOLLOWING TERMS

(1) Lenticel　　(2) Cuticle　　(3) Stoma　　(4) Guard cells

5.5. FACTORS THAT AFFECT TRANSPIRATION

The factors that affect transpiration are both external and internal.

The external factors that affect transpiration are :

(a) Temperature : The ambient temperature is directly related to transpiration rate; higher the temperature, greater is the rate of transpiration. Because of high ambient temperature the humidity decreases and more evaporation takes place. The amount of air retained by cold air is less as compared to warm air.

(b) Sunlight : Sunlight is one of the essential factors to carry on photosynthesis. During photosynthesis, the stomata open to enable diffusion of gases. This is responsible for increased transpiration. The rate of transpiration reduces during the night and also on cloudy days. Intense sunlight also increases the temperature which will decrease humidity in the air and result in a higher transpiration rate.

(c) Velocity of wind : Wind velocity is directly responsible for rate of transpiration; higher the wind velocity, greater is the rate of transpiration. Moving air constantly replaces the air in the area immediately surrounding the transpiring leaf. This allows the air to be free of water vapour thus allowing the leaf to transpire freely. When air is still, the air surrounding the plant or tree gets saturated with water vapour, thus limiting the amount of transpiration from the leaf.

(d) Humidity : This factor is inversely related to transpiration rate; higher the humidity, lower is the rate of transpiration. High levels of humidity in the air reduce the rate of outward diffusion of the water in the leaf through the stomata. This reduces the rate of transpiration. When humidity is low, air becomes drier and can receive more moisture readily. Hence the rate of transpiration is greater when humidity levels are low.

(e) Carbon dioxide : This factor is also inversely related to transpiration as higher the level of CO_2 (more than 0.03% in air), lower is the rate of transpiration. The stomata close due to higher levels of CO_2 resulting in decrease in transpiration rates.

(f) Atmospheric pressure : The rate of transpiration increases with a fall in atmospheric pressure. That is why plants in the hills show higher rates of transpiration.

(g) Soil water : Only if the roots of the plant are able to absorb water from the soil and makeup for the moisture content lost due to transpiration, can the process of transpiration be maintained. In the absence of soil water or where soil water is depleted, rate of transpiration decreases.

The internal factor affecting transpiration is the water content of leaves. This is directly related to transpiration as higher the level of water content in the leaves, higher is the rate of transpiration. Beside this, leaf surface area, leaf structure and age of the plant also affect the rate of transpiration.

5.6. ADAPTATIONS IN PLANTS TO REDUCE TRANSPIRATION

In order to avoid excessive transpiration, some plants, especially those found in dry and arid areas, have modified themselves to adapt to their surroundings.

Some adaptations commonly observed in plants to control excessive transpiration are:

(a) Morphological adaptations : The amount of transpiration a leaf experiences is a direct function of the surface area of the leaf. A reduction in the surface area of the leaf is bound to impact and control the transpiration rates from the leaf. This is achieved in the following ways :

(i) Modification of leaves of desert plants like cactus into spines to limit the surface area for transpiration.
(ii) Modification of the pine tree leaves into needles.
(iii) The folding or rolling up of leaves to reduce the surface area.
(iv) The shedding of leaves, like in deciduous trees.
(v) Leaves of some plants may be covered by a thick cuticle (e.g. Banyan tree) and most evergreen trees.

However, one should bear in mind that due to a reduced surface area, the process of photosynthesis would also be adversely impacted. In such plants, the stem adapts to perform photosynthesis effectively, given the circumstances.

(b) Anatomical adaptations : These may occur in the following ways :

(i) The development of a thick waxy cuticle on the epidermis, like in the case of evergreen trees.
(ii) A waterproof covering of cork or bark on shrubs and trees.
(iii) The creation of multiple epidermises on some leaves.

(iv) The emergence of dense cutinized bark, and scales on the leaf surface.

(v) Reduction in the number of stomata that remain sunken in pits as in *Oleander* or covered with hair as in *Neriun*.

There are also man-made measures to reduce transpiration in plants called *anti-transpirants*. They are sprayed on the stem and leaves of plants to reduce the rate of water loss. Often used by farmers in drought situations, *anti-transpirations* protect evergreens from dry winds and climate. These are of two types :

(1) Metabolic inhibitors : They increase the leaf's resistance to transpiration by reducing the stomatal opening. This, however, does not impact CO_2 intake by the plant e.g., Aspirin, phenyl mercuric acetate.

(2) Film forming anti transpirants : A colourless substance, this forms a coating on the leaf surface which allows diffusion of gases, but not of water vapour e.g., Silicon oils, waxes.

5.7. IMPORTANCE OF TRANSPIRATION

(a) Temperature balance : Transpiration helps in cooling the plants during hot days. It reduces the temperature of leaves and of the entire plant.

(b) Ascent of sap : Transpiration creates a suction force at the top of the plant. This is helpful in the rise of sap and its concentration in the leaves. The osmotic pressure in the leaves increases causing the water to be pulled up. This finally leads to absorption of water from the soil by roots.

(c) Mineral salts and water distribution : Transpiration is responsible for absorption of water from the soils. Along with the water, essential mineral salts are also absorbed. The water and absorbed mineral salts get distributed throughout the plant by suction force.

(d) Climate control : Transpiration releases water to the atmosphere. A single apple tree looses approximately 30 liters of water per day due to transpiration. This cools down the environment.

(e) Removal of excess water : Roots of a plant often tend to absorb more water than they require. This excess water is removed from the plant by way of transpiration. Trees in the forest add moisture and humidity to the air as a result of huge quantity of water that is lost through transpiration. This increase in moisture in the atmosphere brings more rains and maintains the climatic cycle.

(f) Prevents drying up : Water evaporation from the leaf surface leaves behind hygroscopic salts which have the ability to absorb moisture from the environment and do not allow the plant to dry up.

(g) It increases sugar content in fruits.

5.8. DISADVANTAGES OF TRANSPIRATION

(a) Wilting : Excess transpiration often leads to more moisture loss than has been absorbed by the roots of the plants. This leads to the plant wilting and dying. The shrinkage in the volume of water in plant cells resulting in the loss of turgidity due to excessive transpiration is called wilting.

(b) Stunted growth : Ample water content is essential for the full and complete growth of the plant. Water provides turgidity to plants allows photosynthesis and facilitates the movement of minerals & food in the plant. Less than adequate water can cause slow or stunted growth in the plant.

(c) Energy expenditure : If the amount of transpiration is high, a large amount of energy has to be spent by the plant in regaining the moisture and compensating for the loss.

5.9. GUTTATION AND BLEEDING

Plants can release water in its true liquid form in two ways :

Guttation : Secretion of droplets of water by leaves is called *guttation*. Guttation occurs at night when there is no transpiration. It can take place during day time also when plants grow in humid condition.

This is very common in plants from warm humid regions. Excessive humidity adversely affects the rate of transpiration. The roots continue to absorb water from the soil which is responsible for development of hydrostatic pressure. This continues till the leaves are saturated and finally expel copious amounts of water in the form of droplets. This water is expelled directly from the tip of veins where special pore bearing structures called *hydathodes* are present. Guttation is very common in banana and strawberry plants. The difference between transpiration and guttation is given in table 5.2.

Bleeding: Exudation of cell sap or watery solution from the injured parts of a plant is called bleeding. The root pressure generated is responsible for bleeding. When rubber plant stem is injured, latex will come out.

Table 1 : Difference between Transpiration and Evaporation.

Transpiration	Evaporation
1. It is a physiological process.	1. It is a physical process.
2. Transpiration is the loss of water from the aerial parts of the plants.	2. Evaporation is the loss of water from the sur of water bodies in the form of water vapour.
3. External factors (Temperature, Sunlight, wind velocity etc.) and water content of the plants control transpiration.	3. Temperature and Humidity of the atmosphere control evaporation.
4. It is a slow process.	4. It is a fast process.
5. Stomata open in light and thus more transpiration occurs in day time.	5. No direct effect of light on evaporation.

Table 2 : Difference between Transpiration and Guttation.

Transpiration	Guttation
1. Water is lost in the form of vapour.	1. Water is lost in the form of droplets.
2. Vapour contains pure water only.	2. The water droplets lost contain organic and inorganic salts.
3. Transpiration occurs through stomata, lenticels and cuticle.	3. Guttation occurs through tip of veins of leaves where special pore bearing structures called hydathodes are present.
4. It may affect the turgidity of leaves and cause wilting.	4. It does not affect the turgidity of leaves.
5. Stomatal transpiration is controlled by guard cells.	5. The hydathodes do not have any controlling cells.
6. Transpiration occurs in the presence of sunlight.	6. Guttation occurs in the night or early morning
7. Transpiration has a cooling effect on plant.	7. It has no such effect on the plant.
8. Transpiration occurs in dry conditions.	8. Guttation occurs in humid conditions.
9. Transpiration causes negative root pressure.	9. It occurs when there is positive root pressure.
10. Excessive transpiration causes wilting.	10. Excessive guttation does not cause wilting.

EXERCISE

A. VERY SHORT ANSWER TYPE

(I) Fill in the Blanks
1. During photosynthesis, the stomata of the leaves are wide open essentially for intake of_____.
2. The guard cells become _____ during the night when the rate of transpiration is low.
3. Potometer also known as_____ is a device that can measure the amount of water intake by the plants.
4. The internal factor that affects transpiration is the _____ of leaves.

(II) State whether True or False
1. Humidity is directly related to transpiration.
2. Plant sap is secreted from cut surfaces or ruptures that are formed due to injury.
3. As the water from the plant is lost through transpiration, a suction force is developed.
4. Transpiration increases the temperature of leaves.

B. SHORT ANSWER TYPE

1. What is guttation?
2. In what ways do plants adapt themselves to reduce transpiration?
3. Explain cuticular and lenticular transpiration.
4. Enlist the limitations of use of the potometer.
5. How can transpiration be measured by weighing?

C. LONG ANSWER TYPE

1. State the importance of transpiration.
2. State the factors that affect transpiration.

3. Explain stomatal transpiration.
4. With the help of a labelled diagram, explain the working of a potometer.
5. Prove that plants transpire in the form of water vapour with the help of bell jar experiment.

(I) Write one Main Function of the Follownig
1. Hydathode.
2. Sunken stomata.
3. Needle like leaves.
4. Lenticels.

(II) Differentiate between
1. Stomata and hydathodes.
2. Transpiration and guttation.
3. Guttation and bleeding.

(III) Give Reasons for the Following
1. Leaves are reduced to spines in cactus.
2. Presence of sunken stomata.
3. In hot summer months, most herbaceous plants wilt at noon and recover in the evening.
4. To keep cut flowers fresh we use antitranspirants.
5. Leaves of certain plants roll up on a bright sunny day.

D. STRUCTURED/APPLICATION BASED
1. Given below is a diagram of an experimental set up to study the process of transpiration in plants. Study the same and then answer the questions that follow :
   (a) What is the colour of dry cobalt chloride paper?
   (b) Is the experimental leaf a monocot or A dicot? Give reasons to support your answer.

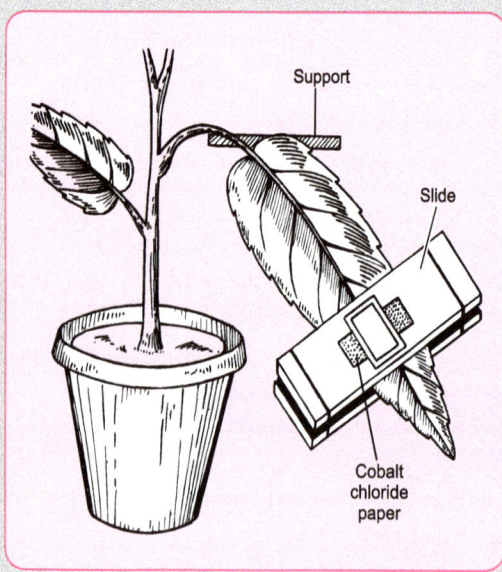

   (c) Why is the glass slides placed over the dry cobalt chloride paper?
   (d) After about half an hour what change, if any, would you expect to find in the cobalt chloride paper? Give a reason to support your answer.
   (e) Define the term 'transpiration'.

2. Given below is an apparatus used to study a particular process in plants. Study the same and answer the questions that follow :
   (a) Name the apparatus.
   (b) Mention one limitation of this apparatus.
   (c) Which phenomenon is studied with the help of this apparatus?
   (d) What is the function of the part marked 'reservoir'?
   (e) What is the role of the air bubble in the experiment?

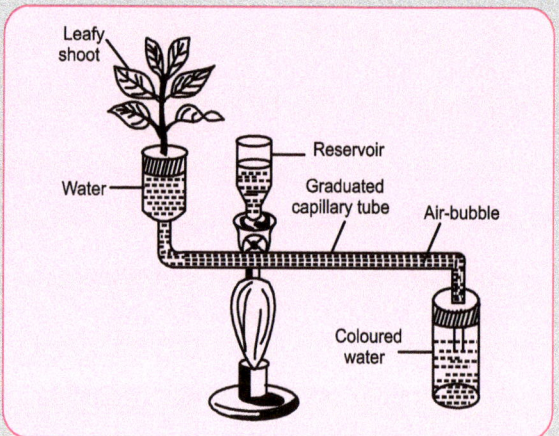

3. The apparatus shown here is Ganong's potometer designed to demonstrate unequal transpiration from the two surfaces of a dorsi-ventral leaf. Before keeping the leaf in between the tubes anhydrous calcium chloride ($CaCl_2$) contained in two small vials were weighed and placed in both the tubes. The ends of the tubes were closed with connected. After a few hours, $CaCl_2$ vials were taken out and weighed again.
   (a) What is the purpose of keeping $CaCl_2$ vials inside the tubes?
   (b) After a few hours $CaCl_2$ vials were taken out and weighed again. Will you expect any difference in weight? If so give reasons.
   (c) What was the purpose of using a mano-meter ?
   (d) What do you mean by transpiration?

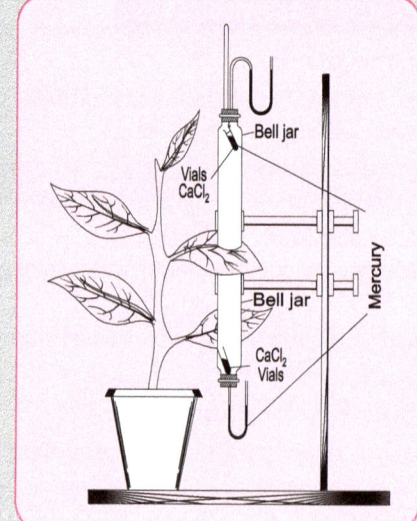

TRANSPIRATION

DO YOU KNOW?

- In one growing season, a corn plant transpires over 200 litres of water.
- Transpiration, along with evaporation of moisture on land, provides almost two-thirds of the atmospheric moisture that falls as precipitation on land surfaces.
- As with human respiration, trees tend to transpire more with increased temperatures, sunlight intensity, water supply, and size. When it gets too hot, though, transpiration will shut down.
- Cacti, since they don't have leaves, only have a few stomata in their green stems and so transpire very little.
- Many Eric plants have small leaves, silvery reflective leaves and hairy leaves and/or produce essential oils which are all strategies to reduce transpiration by reducing evaporation.
- In the summer, a large maple tree can transpire 50-60 gallons of water per hour into the atmosphere. This adds to the humidity which makes us to feel more comfortable, is less drying for our skin and reduces bronchial problems.
- The Snows of Mount Kilimanjaro have disappeared primarily because deforestation has reduced local transpiration, resulting in less (or no) snowfall.

6

PHOTOSYNTHESIS

CHAPTER HIGHLIGHTS
6.1. Photosynthesis
6.2. Role of Chlorophyll
6.3. Regulation of Stomatal Opening
6.4. Process of Photosynthesis
6.5. Phases of Photosynthesis
6.6. Leaf Adaptations for Photosynthesis
6.7. End Products of Photosynthesis
6.8. Factors Affecting Photosynthesis
6.9. Experiments on Photosynthesis
6.10. Significance of Photosynthesis
6.11. Carbon Cycle

6.1. PHOTOSYNTHESIS

Green plants are the only living organisms which prepare their own food in the presence of carbon dioxide, water and sunlight through a process called photosynthesis. They are not dependent on other plants or animals for their nutrition needs. In plants, food in the form of carbohydrates and proteins is utilized for energy and growth of the plant.

Photosynthesis can be defined as the biochemical process by which green plants containing chlorophyll prepare their own food (glucose and starch) from carbon dioxide and water in the presence of sunlight, liberating oxygen as a by-product. Photosynthesis is a vital biochemical process, since almost all organisms depend upon the products of photosynthesis directly or indirectly.

Since they manufacture their own food, green plants are called *producers* or *autotrophs* and their mode of nutrition is called *Autotrophic*.

Significance of Photosynthesis
(a) Photosynthesis is the ultimate energy producing process necessary for survival for all living organisms. The energy produced is directly consumed by plants and indirectly consumed by other living organisms that depend upon plants for nutrition.
(b) Photosynthesis is the only process which releases oxygen into the environment which is essential for sustaining life on earth.
(c) It also helps in making ozone in the outer layer of the atmosphere. This ozone helps in stopping harmful UV rays from reaching earth.
(d) Wood, rubber, fodder, fibres, resins, oils, coals, petroleum are all products of photosynthesis, directly or indirectly.
(e) It acts as purifier of the atmosphere by absorbing carbon dioxide during photosynthesis and liberating oxygen.

6.2. ROLE OF CHLOROPHYLL

Chlorophyll is the green coloured pigment of plants that is present in the microscopic cell organelles called *chloroplasts*.

In leaves they mainly occur in mesophyll cells, located between the upper and lower epidermis.

Chloroplasts are elongated oval shaped bodies enclosed in a double layered membrane. Each membrane is selectively permeable. The chloroplast contains flattened sacs called thylakoids that are arranged in stacks called *grana* and lie in a colourless ground substance called stroma (Fig. 6.1). The grana are connected with each other by *stroma lamellae* or

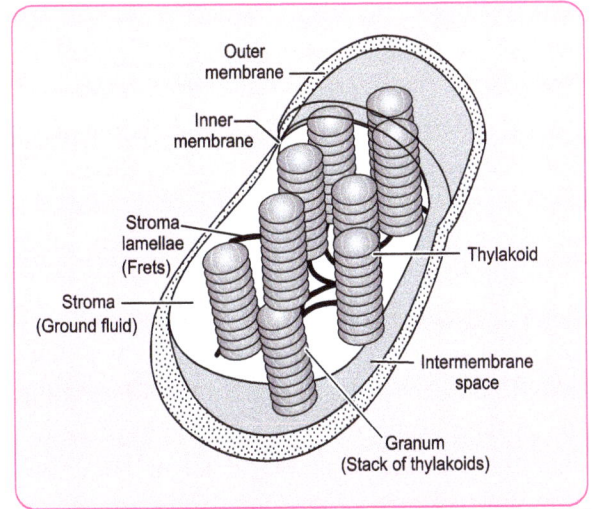

Fig. 6.1 : Internal structure of chloroplast

frets. Chlorophyll is present in the walls of thylakoids and is a highly complex substance made of carbon, hydrogen, oxygen, nitrogen and magnesium.

There are around 40-50 chloroplasts in a cell and around 500,000 per square mm of leaf surface.

Chloroplasts are Present in

(a) *Mesophyll cells* that are found in between the lower and the upper epidermis of leaves.

(b) *Guard cells* of stomata.

(c) Outer layers of younger green cells.

Why is chlorophyll green?

There are 9 types of chlorophyll of which chlorophyll-a and chlorophyll-b are best known and most abundant. Chlorophyll absorbs light from both ends of the visible spectrum and reflects green light that is why the colour of chlorophyll is green.

Formation of chlorophyll is a light dependant process : Leaves that do not have a sufficient supply of light will turn yellow. This is due to discontinuation of new chlorophyll formation and disintegration of the older chlorophyll. Excess of light is also harmful to chlorophyll and can destroy it. Hence chlorophyll is extremely light sensitive.

Colours in plants : In autumn, leaves often develop colours other than green. These different coloured leaves may appear due to the following reasons :

(i) Yellow : *Carotenoids* cause orange red colour in leaves in autumn. Xanthophylls are yellow in colour. When the plant receives less light, the pigment etiolin is formed giving the plant a yellowish colour.

(ii) Red : *Anthocyanins* cause red colour in leaves.

(iii) Brown : *Tannin* deposits in leaves cause them to turn brown.

6.3. REGULATION OF STOMATAL OPENING

The minute openings in the lower epidermal layer of the leaves are called stomata (singular: stoma). Their number per square cm. of leaf area can range between 1000 and 10,000. Each stoma has two bean shaped guard cells around it.

The main role of stomata is to let in CO_2 from the atmosphere for photosynthesis. Transpiration occurs simultaneously with photosynthesis during day time, and the open stomata allow CO_2 to enter the leaf. Simultaneously water vapour escapes into the atmosphere. During the night, the stomata remains closed and the loss of water is minimized. Hence, to accomplish photosynthesis, a plant has to undergo the process of transpiration.

The two bean shaped guard cells surrounding each stoma control their opening and closing by the movement of water in and out of the guard cells. The inner wall of the guard cell that faces the stoma is thicker than the outer wall. The cytoplasm of the guard cell contains chloroplasts.

Opening and closing of stomata : Opening and closing of the stomata (Fig. 6.2) can be explained by the following two hypotheses :

(a) K^+ ion concentration : This theory, given by **Levitt in 1974** is the more recent explanation for stomatal opening and closing.

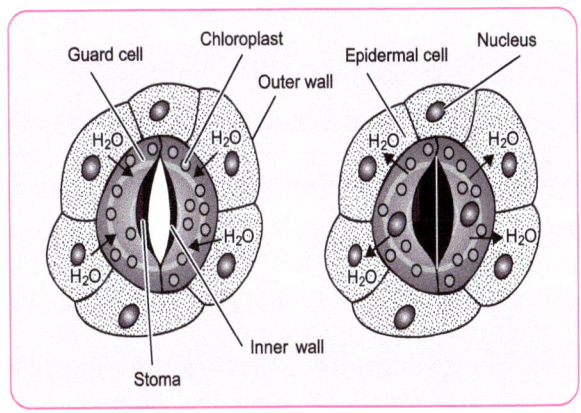

Fig. 6.2 : Opening and closing of stoma

In sunlight, starch is converted to malic acid which breaks down to malate and H^+ in guard cells. H^+ ions migrate to epidermal cells of leaf and K^+ ions are balanced by organic anions.

According to this theory the generation of K^+ ion (potassium ion) gradient controls the opening and closing of stomata. The chloroplasts present in the guard cells photosynthesize during the day and produce ATP (Adenosine triphoshate). This ATP is actively consumed to draw the K⁺ ions from the adjacent cells into the guard cells. Increased K⁺ ion concentration increases osmotic pressure in the guard cells making them draw water from the adjacent cells. As a result of this, guard cells become turgid (contract) and open the stomatal pore. This process is reversed during the night. Decrease in the K+ ion concentration relaxes the guard cells making them flaccid and the stomatal pore closes.

(b) Sugar concentration

$$\text{Starch} \rightleftharpoons \text{Sugar hypothesis}$$

Lloyd (1908) observed that the amount of starch in guard cells is high during night time and less during day.

According to this theory the concentration of sugar in the guard cells controls the opening and closing of stomata. The chloroplasts present in the guard cells photosynthesize during the day and produce sugar. Increased sugar concentration increases the osmotic pressure of the guard cells making them draw water from the adjacent cells. As a result of this, guard cells become turgid (contract) and bulge outwards causing the stomatal pores to open. The open stomatal pore facilitates the diffusion of gases for photosynthesis. This process is reversed during the night when the water content of the leaf decreases. The water is drawn out of the guard cells due to exosmosis making them flaccid (relaxed). This closes the stomatal pore. During night there is no photosynthesis in the guard cells so neither there is accumulation of sugar or a rise in K⁺ ion concentration. Therefore, water moves out of the guard cells by exosmosis making them flaccid and stomatal opening close.

PROGRESS CHECK

FILL IN THE BLANKS

1. Chlorophyll is present in the walls of _____.
2. The minute openings in the lower epidermal layer of the leaves are called _____.
3. Chlorophyll is the green coloured pigment of plants that is present in the microscopic cell organelles called _____.
4. The colourless ground matter is called _____.

6.4. PROCESS OF PHOTOSYNTHESIS

Mesophyll cells (*palisade* and *spongy* both) of the leaf are responsible for photosynthesis. The chlorophyll present in the mesophyll cells, especially the palisade cells, traps the light energy available during day light. This energy is then used for the manufacture of food in the presence of carbon dioxide and water.

(a) Water is absorbed by the roots from the soil and passed on through the stem to the leaves where it finally enters the mesophyll tissue by osmosis.
(b) CO_2 is made available to the plants from the atmosphere. CO_2 enters the leaves through the stomatal openings by diffusion. During daytime when the intensity of sunlight is high, the rate of photosynthesis is fast and the rate of consumption of CO_2 by the plants is also correspondingly high.

The chemical reaction involved in photosynthesis is :

$$6CO_2 + 12H_2O \xrightarrow[\text{Chlorophyll}]{\text{Sunlight}} C_6H_{12}O_6 + 6H_2O + 6O_2$$

The end product of photosynthesis, glucose, is a simple sugar that is easily soluble in water. The 6 molecules of water formed as end products are newly formed and do not include the already existing ones. The glucose molecule thus formed is represented as $C_6H_{12}O_6$.

6.5. PHASES OF PHOTOSYNTHESIS

The two main phases of photosynthesis are :

(a) Photochemical phase : This phase is also called light dependent phase or light reaction since light plays a vital role in this reaction. This phase is constituted of a series of steps that are triggered by light. This reaction is carried out in the *thylakoids* (containing chlorophyll) of chloroplasts. The steps involved are as follows :

STEP 1

Activation of chlorophyll by absorption of photons of light in the smallest units of light energy.

STEP 2

Breaking down of water molecule into its two components (Oxygen and Hydrogen) by the energy absorbed through a reaction called photolysis (photo means light and lysis means breaking)

$$2H_2O \xrightarrow{\text{Energy of 4 photons}} 4H^+ + O_2 + 4e^-$$

Please note that O_2 released during photolysis comes from water.

The products of photolysis are

(i) The 4H⁺ (hydrogen ions) are used by a compound Nicotinamide adenine dinucleotide phosphate with positive charge (NADP⁺) to give NADPH.

$$NADP + e^- + H^+ \xrightarrow{Enxyme} NADPH$$

(ii) Elemental oxygen combines to form oxygen molecule. Hydrogen peroxide (formed as a result of the oxidation of hydroxide) decomposes due to the action of enzyme catalase, thus leading to release of molecular oxygen.

$$2O \longrightarrow O_2 \text{ (Molecular Oxygen)}$$

Addition of phosphate group is called *phosphorylation*. Since the addition is done in the presence of light with the help of energy of e^-, it can be termed as *photophosphorylation*.

(iii) The electrons are consumed for conversion of adenosine diphosphate (ADP) to adenosine triposphate (ATP) by addition of one inorganic phosphate group (Pi group).

$$ADP + Pi \longrightarrow ATP$$
$$\text{(inorganic phosphate)}$$

Thus the net result of light reaction is the formation of ATP and NADPH molecule and release of O_2. Light energy absorbed by chlorophyll is converted to chemical energy in ATP and NADPH.

PROGRESS CHECK

COMPLETE THE FOLLOWING REACTIONS

(i) $6CO_2 +$ _____ $\xrightarrow[\text{Chlorophyll}]{\text{Light energy}}$ _____ $+ 6H_2O + 6O_2$

(ii) $2H_2O \longrightarrow 4H^+ + O_2 + 4e^-$

(iii) $NADP + e^- + H^+ \longrightarrow NADPH$

(iv) _____ $+ Pi \longrightarrow ATP$
(inorganic phosphate)

(b) Biosynthetic phase or dark phase : This phase is also called light independent phase or dark reaction as it does not require light and occurs simultaneously with the light reaction.

This reaction results in the production of glucose.

Glucose is produced by utilizing energy stored in ATP to combine the hydrogen (from NADPH) with CO_2.

This fixation of CO_2 occurs in a number of steps triggered by enzyme Rubisco using a special CO_2 acceptor compound RuBP (ribulosebiphosphate).

Glucose is converted to starch as soon as it is formed during photosynthesis. This is done by polymerization in which several glucose molecules combine to give a single starch molecule. Glucose can also be converted to sugars or into some oils by plants.

$$RuDP + CO_2 + NADPH + ATP \longrightarrow$$
$$RuDP + Glucose + NADP + ADP + Phosphate$$

In the above equation we have noted that RuDP is regenerated at the end of the reaction. This process of formation of glucose is called **Calvin Benson** or only *Calvin cycle*.

6.6. LEAF ADAPTATIONS FOR PHOTOSYNTHESIS

(a) Presence of broad leaves for maximum exposure to light.

(b) Leaf arrangement perpendicular to the light source for maximum exposure to light.

(c) Transparent cuticle and upper epidermis for easy entry of light.

(d) Water proof cuticle & upper dermis to allow for light to enter easily

(e) Numerous stomata for allowing rapid gas exchange (oxygen with CO_2).

(f) Reduction in thickness of leaves to decrease distance between cells for better transport.

(g) Concentration of chloroplasts in the upper layers of leaf for receiving light quickly.

(h) Extensive vein system to allow for quick transport to and from the mesophyll cells.

6.7. END PRODUCTS OF PHOTOSYNTHESIS

The three end products of photosynthesis are :

(a) Glucose : (i) immediately used by plant cells for release of energy for metabolic activities of cell. (ii) Stored in the form of insoluble starch. (iii) Converted to sucrose. (iv) Used in synthesizing fats, proteins etc.

(b) Water : It is re-used for the continuation of photosynthesis.

(c) Oxygen : Oxygen produced is partially used in respiration of leaf cells. The remaining oxygen is released into the atmosphere and used up by other organisms for their life processes.

Translocation of food : The food produced during photosynthesis is needed by all the parts of the plant. Photosynthates are very much energy rich compounds. Sucrose is the principal form of carbohydrate that is translocated from leaf to the non-photosynthetic organs. Glucose cannot be transported to other parts of plants as quickly it is produced. For this purpose, glucose is converted to insoluble starch for temporary storage. This starch is reconverted into soluble sugar at night. This sugar in the solution form is passed through the veins of the leaf down through the phloem of the stem. After reaching the different parts of the plants, the sugar can be reconverted to starch for storage. This can later be used as an energy source for various functions of the plants.

6.8. FACTORS AFFECTING PHOTOSYNTHESIS

The factors that affect photosynthesis are both external and internal in nature :

External Factors Affecting Photosynthesis

(a) Light intensity : The rate of photosynthesis increases with the increase in the intensity of light. This is true only to a certain limit beyond which it gets stabilized (0.02 % CO_2). Higher light intensity can cause solarisation due to which photosynthetic activity is reduced. Solarisation causes disintegration of chlorophyll molecules. At low intensity of light too, stomata are close and intake of CO_2 is reduced resulting in lower photosynthetic activity.

(b) Carbon dioxide concentration : When light energy is sufficient and the concentration of CO_2 increases, the rate of photosynthesis increases again to a limit (0.05% CO_2) and stabilizes again for both factors. Very high CO_2 concentration is toxic to plants.

(c) Temperature : Temperature is directly related to rate of photosynthesis i.e. increase in the temperature upto 35 degrees centigrade, the rate of photosynthesis also increases. Beyond this temperature the rate falls and stops completely above 40°C. This is because enzymes cannot survive at such high temperatures. The rate of photosynthesis doubles of every 10°C rise up to the optimum temperature of 35°C. There are, of course, exceptions like the desert cactus that can continue to photosynthesis even at 50°C. Optimum temperature for photosynthesis is 25°–35°C. Thermal algae can perform photosynthesis even at 70°C.

(d) Decreased water content either due to reduced water absorption from soil or due to excessive transpiration, the rate of photosynthesis decreases. This is due to closure of stomata during reduced water levels in plants. Of the total volume of water absorbed by the roots, only 1–2% is used for photosynthesis. Water helps in developing turgor pressure in the guard cells due to which stomata are open. So if amount of water is decreased then the stomata close and photosynthesis may also stop.

Internal Factors Affecting Photosynthesis

(i) Loss of chlorophyll due to deficiency of essential minerals reduces the capacity to absorb light. This decreases the rate of photosynthesis.

(ii) Dehydration of protoplasm and accumulation of carbohydrates (sugar and starch) reduces the rate of photosynthesis as photosynthetic enzymes are cytoplasmic in origin and remain active in the hydrated state only.

(iii) Structure of leaf which includes the thickness of cuticle, the stomatal distribution and leaf size affects the amount of light and amount of CO_2 entering the leaf and hence effect the rate of photosynthesis.

PROGRESS CHECK

STATE TRUE OR FALSE

1. The three end products of photosynthesis are protein, water and oxygen.
2. Dehydration of protoplasm and accumulation of carbohydrates reduces the rate of photosynthesis.
3. Enlargement of surface area of leaves enables maximum exposure to light.
4. Decreased water content increases the rate of photosynthesis.

Animations for Photosynthesis

1. http://www.sumanasinc.com/webcontent/animations/content/harvestinglight.html
2. http://highered.mcgraw-hill.com/olcweb/cgi/pluginpop.cgi?it=swf::535::535::/sites/dl/free/0072437316/120072 bio13.swf::Photosynthetic%20Electron%20Transport%20and%20ATP%20Synthesis

6.9. EXPERIMENTS ON PHOTOSYNTHESIS

Experiment–1

Objective : *To show that starch is present in leaves (Fig. 6.3).*

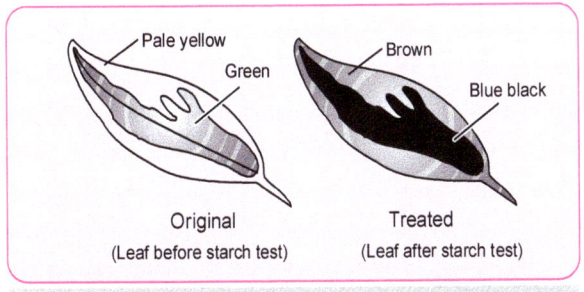

Fig. 6.3 : Treatment of a variegated colour leaf with Iodine solution

Requirement : Methylated spirit, destarched leaf, water bath, iodine solution.

Procedure : Detach a leaf from the destarched plant and place it in boiling water for few minutes so that no further reaction takes place in its cells. This leaf is then boiled in methylated spirit over a water bath till the chlorophyll is completely removed (leaf turns pale white) and the leaf turns hard and brittle. Soften the leaf by dipping in hot water and then place it in a dish containing iodine solution (Iodine solution contains 0.3g Iodine and 1.5g Potassium Iodide in 100 ml water).

Observations : Some parts of the leaf turn bluish black.

Conclusion : The colour change of parts of the leaf to bluish black indicates of presence of starch. Parts of the leaf that merely stain brown by iodine indicate the absence of starch.

How to destarch leaf?

A leaf can be destarched by keeping it in the dark for 2–3 days. This is essential for most experiments discussed here as this will ensure that any starch present in the leaf has been formed during the experiment itself.

Experiment–2

Objective : *To show that light is necessary for photosynthesis (Fig. 6.4).*

Requirement : Plant with destarched leaves (Destarch the leaves according to procedure given after experiment 1), black paper.

Procedure : Take the plant with destarched leaves and cover one of its leaves with black paper on which a design has been cut. Place this plant in sunlight for few hours. Now test this leaf for starch with Iodine solution.

Observations : Only the parts that were exposed to sunlight i.e. the parts that were not covered with sunlight turn bluish black.

Conclusion : Only the parts that were exposed to sunlight tested positive for starch which indicates that photosynthesis requires sunlight.

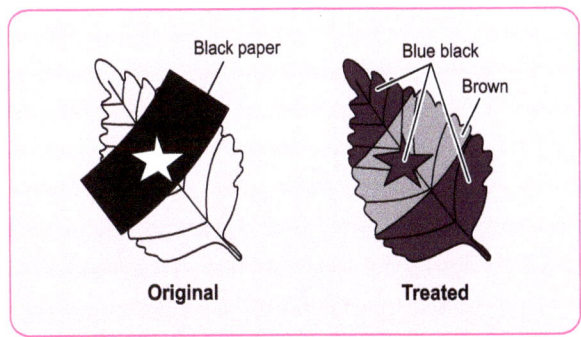

Fig. 6.4 : Parts exposed to sunlight give positive result for starch when tested with Iodine solution

Experiment–3

Objective : *To prove that carbon dioxide is necessary for photosynthesis (Fig. 6.5).*

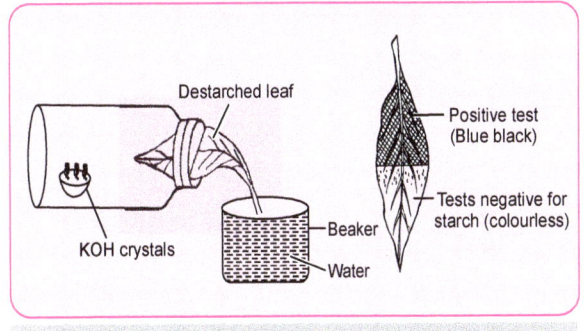

Fig. 6.5 : Experiment to show that CO_2 is necessary or photosynthesis

Requirement : Plant with destarched leaves, conical flask, potassium hydroxide crystals.

Procedure : Take the plant with destarched leaves and, with the help of a split cork; insert one of its leaves into the conical flask containing potassium crystals. Put this plant in sunlight for a few hours. Test the leaf that is in the conical flask and any other leaf of the plant for starch using Iodine solution.

Observations : The leaf that was outside the conical flask changes colour and turns bluish black but the one in the conical flask does not change colour.

Conclusion : Potassium hydroxide present in the flask absorbed the carbon dioxide. That is why the leaf inside did not show positive results for starch test as it was not able to perform the process of photosynthesis.

This proves that photosynthesis requires carbon dioxide.

Experiment–4

Objective : *To show that O_2 is produced during photosynthesis (Fig. 6.6).*

Requirement : Water plants (*Elodea* or *Hydrilla*), beaker containing pond water, short stemmed funnel, test tube.

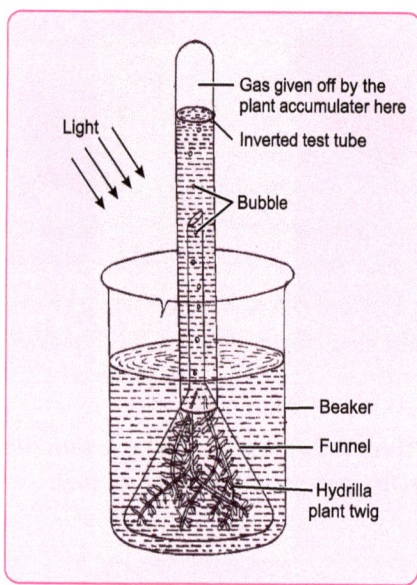

Fig. 6.6 : Experiment to show that O_2 is evolved during photosynthesis

Procedure : Take the beaker containing pond water and put one to two twigs of Hydrilla, tie it and keep its root upside and cover the plant with funnel. Invert a test tube full of water on the stem of the funnel in such a way that the water level in the test tube is more than that in the beaker. Allow this set up to stand in sunlight for few hours. Bubbles of gas start to collect. Test this with a glowing splinter.

Observations : The glowing splinter bursts into flames when it comes in contact with the gas.

Conclusion : The flames produced indicate the presence of oxygen which has been produced during photosynthesis.

6.10. SIGNIFICANCE OF PHOTOSYNTHESIS

(a) Manufacture of food : Photosynthesis is the ultimate energy producing process which is required for survival for all living organisms. The energy produced is directly consumed by plants. In turn, herbivores consume plants for food and get this energy indirectly. Similarly carnivores that eat other animals for survival also get this energy. This chain of food dependence is called the food chain (Fig. 6.7). No matter how long or complex the food chain becomes, its starting point is always a plant.

Several non-green plants such as fungi and bacteria derive their nourishment from decaying organic matter, which primarily comprises of dead animals and plants.

(b) Oxygen generation : Photosynthesis is the only process which releases oxygen, vital for the survival of living organisms. The life supporting oxygen was absent in the early atmosphere (around 2 billion years ago). Proliferation of plants built up the oxygen content of atmosphere making it conducive for survival of animals. It also helps in the formation of ozone layer. In this process O_2 is released and CO_2 is absorbed.

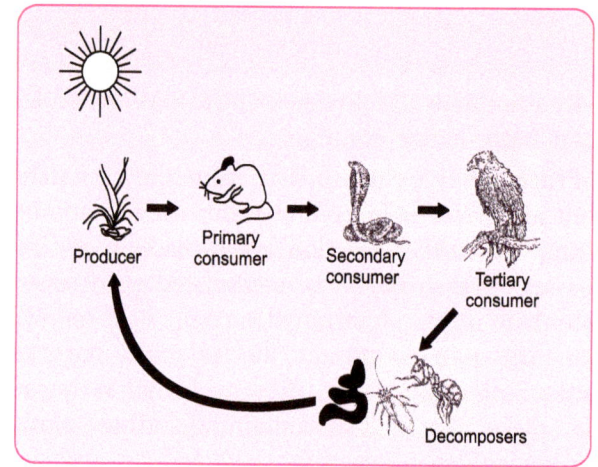

Fig. 6.7 : Food chain

6.11. CARBON CYCLE

Carbon cycle (Fig. 6.8) is a biogeochemical cycle by which carbon in the carbon dioxide is removed from the air, utilized by living organisms in their body processes and is then returned to the air.

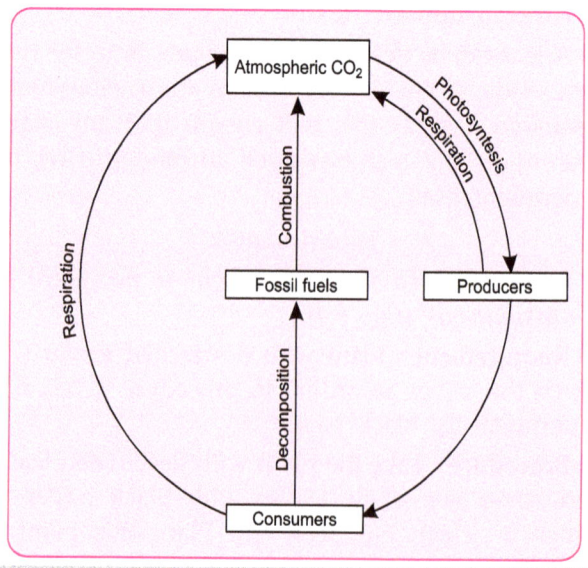

Fig. 6.8 : Carbon cycle

The 5 steps in carbon cycle are :

(a) Photosynthesis : Plants consume carbon dioxide from the atmosphere for photosynthesis to produce carbohydrates (sugar, starch, etc.)

(b) Consumption : Food (carbohydrates) is passed on from plants to animals. Carbon is an important part of tissues of animals and plants.

(c) Respiration : All plants and animals respire to give carbon dioxide which is produced from the oxidation of carbohydrates in their cells for energy production.

(d) Decomposition : Breaking down of dead organic matter (dead animals and plants) by bacteria is called decomposition which releases carbon in the form of carbon dioxide back into the atmosphere.

(e) Combustion : Burning of fossil fuels like coal, petroleum etc. produces carbon dioxide and carbon monoxide gases which are released back into atmosphere. A small amount of carbon dioxide is also released due to burning of limestone in lime furnace. External and manmade combustion of fuels, such as the burning of lime scale in lime kilns adds to the combustion process in the carbon cycle.

Burning of fossil fuels these days increase the amount of CO_2 which leads to global warming, responsible for trapping more heat and does not allow the heat to escape, as a result increasing the temperature of earth.

PROGRESS CHECK

STATE WHETHER TRUE OR FALSE

1. Photosynthesis requires Carbon dioxide.
2. Breaking down of dead organic matter (dead animals and plants) by bacteria is called combustion.
3. Photosynthesis is the only process which releases oxygen which is essential for survival of living organisms.
4. Bluish black colour change due to Iodine solution is an indicator of the presence of starch.

EXERCISE

A. VERY SHORT ANSWER TYPE

(I) Fill in the Blanks

1. A small amount of carbon dioxide is also released due to burning of _____ in lime furnace.
2. Dehydration of _____ and accumulation of _____ reduces the rate of photosynthesis.
3. Decreased water content either due to reduced water from soil or due to excessive _____ decreases the rate of photosynthesis.
4. _____ phase is also called as light dependent phase as light plays a major role in this reaction.
5. There are 9 types of chlorophyll of which _____ and _____ are best known and most abundant.
6. Light reaction takes place in _____.
7. During photosynthesis O_2 comes from _____.
8. Splitting of water results in the release of _____.
9. CO_2 is absorbed by _____.
10. The process of conversion of ADP into ATP during photosynthesis _____.

(II) Match the Column

1. Dehydration of protoplasm
2. Numerous stomata
3. Enlargement of surface area of leaves
4. Oxidation of carbohydrates

(i) Allows rapid gas protoplasm exchange.
(ii) Increases exposure to sunlight.
(iii) Reduces the rate to photosynthesis.
(iv) Produces CO_2.

B. SHORT ANSWER TYPE

1. What is photolysis of water?
2. State two main events of dark reaction?
3. State any three ways in which a leaf adapts for increasing the rate of photosynthesis.
4. What is thylakoid?
5. What does a granum consist of?
6. What happens to chlorophyll when plants are kept in dark?
7. State four limiting factors of photosynthesis.

C. LONG ANSWER TYPE

1. What is the significance of photosynthesis?
2. With the help of appropriate experiments demonstrate that photosynthesis requires carbon dioxide and releases oxygen.
3. State the external factors that affect photosynthesis.
4. Write a short note on the end products of photosynthesis.

5. Explain the two phases of photosynthesis.
6. What are the two possible reasons for opening and closing of stomata?
7. Explain carbon cycle with the help of an appropriate diagram.
8. Explain the internal structure of chloroplast with the help of labelled diagram.

(I) Give Reasons

1. Producers are important.
2. Plants have to be destarched before carrying out most experiments in photosynthesis.
3. Sodium bi-carbonate is added in the experiment to show O_2 is evolved in photosynthesis.
4. O_2 can be considered as a waste product of photosynthesis.

(II) Give the Full Forms

1. RuBP,
2. NADPH,
3. ATP,
4. Pi.

D. STRUCTURED/APPLICATION BASED

1. A portion of pond weed was kept in pond water as in the diagram. Bubbles evolved at the cut end of the stem. In dim light and dark no bubbles evolve :

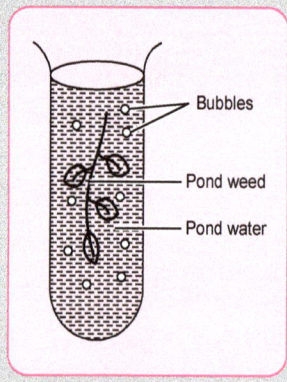

   (a) Name the gas which is evolved.
   (b) How can you confirm the presence of gas?
   (c) Why at some time we will find no bubble forming even though the plant is still in bright light?
   (d) What can you expect to happen if $NaHCO_3$ is added to the water?

2. The diagram given below demonstrates the importance of a factor necessary for photosynthesis. The star-shaped portion of the leaf exposed to light shown in the diagram appears blue when tested for starch, after the destarched potted plant was exposed to light for about 12 hours.

   (a) What is the aim of this experiment?
   (b) How will you test the presence of starch?
   (c) What are the factors necessary for photosynthesis?
   (d) What is the part labelled 'X'?
   (e) Define the physiological phenomenon that takes place in the given experiment.

3. The figure given below shows the apparatus used to perform an experiment to choose one of the conditions necessary for photosynthesis.
   (a) Name the condition.
   (b) List three (3) other conditions necessary for photosynthesis.
   (c) Give a balanced equation to explain photosynthesis.

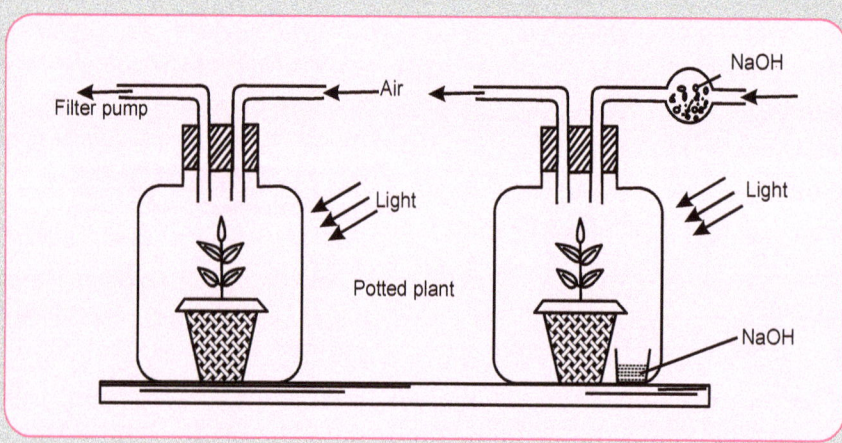

DO YOU KNOW ?

- More than half (70%) of the world's oxygen is produced by phytoplankton photosynthesis in the world's oceans.
- Thirty percent (30%) of the world's oxygen is produced in the rainforests.
- Photosynthesis produces about 155 billion tons of material each year.
- In 2005, scientists discovered that special bacteria deep in the ocean (where no sunlight could reach) were conducting photosynthesis using very faint light from hydrothermal vents. This could mean other life exists deep in the ocean or even on other planets!
- Researchers have discovered a sea slug that eats algae but does not digest it fully. Instead, the remaining algae continue to conduct photosynthesis inside the slug and contribute 79% to the energy of the slug.
- Photosynthesis is the reason, why conifers and other pine trees grow in a cone shape. This shape allows more needles to be exposed to the sun, which enables the tree to grow taller.
- One of the trees in Africa (the Tumbo Plant) has only two wide leaves but can live for over 1,000 years with little rain water.

7

THE CIRCULATORY SYSTEM

CHAPTER HIGHLIGHTS
7.1. Introduction
7.2. Fluids in Our Body
7.3. Blood–Vessels, Structure and Functions
    7.3.1. Physical Properties of Blood
    7.3.2. Functions of Blood
    7.3.3. Composition of Blood
    7.3.4. Cellular Elements of Blood
7.4. Blood Transfusion and Blood Groups
7.5. The Human Heart–Structure and Functions
    7.5.1. Chambers of the Heart
    7.5.2. Great Blood Vessels of the Heart
    7.5.3. Valves of the Heart
    7.5.4. The Passage of Blood through the Heart
    7.5.5. Blood Vessels
7.6. Blood Circulation–Main Blood Vessels
7.7. The Lymphatic System

7.1. INTRODUCTION

The circulatory system is a vast network of organs and vessels that is responsible for the flow of blood, nutrients, oxygen and other gases, and hormones to and from cells. Without the circulatory system, the body would not be able to fight disease or maintain a stable internal environment such as proper temperature and pH, known as *homeostasis*.

(a) All organs and systems of the body require circulating fluids and hence the circulatory system is vital for all of them.
(b) Oxygen from the air that is inhaled by the respiratory system needs to be transported to various parts of the body. Likewise, the CO_2 generated due to oxidation of carbohydrates at the cellular level needs to be transported to the lungs to be eliminated during exhalation.
(c) Nutrients obtained from the food by the digestive system needs to be transported to each cell in the body.
(d) The waste products (extra water, urea) generated by the body need to be transported to the excretory system for removal.
(e) Hormones secreted by the endocrine system need to be transported to its respective locations in the body.
(f) Heat is transported from active heat producing organs to others for maintaining homeothermy.
(g) All the above mentioned transportation and circulatory functions of the body are performed by the two major circulating body fluids in the blood and the lymph. These two fluids together constitute the circulatory system along with organs such as heart and the veins and arteries.

7.2. FLUIDS IN OUR BODY

The three essential fluids of our body are:
(a) Blood : present in the heart and blood vessels i.e. arteries, veins and capillaries.
(b) Tissue fluid : present between the cells of organs.

(c) Lymph : present in the lymph vessels and lymphatic organs i.e. tonsils and spleen.

Blood in human body flows through closed spaces called blood vessels. Such a system is called closed vascular system. Unlike humans, the blood flow in animals from heart to other body tissue spaces is through open spaces (without vessels). Hence, the blood circulation in higher invertebrates like annelids and arthropods is called open blood circulatory system (Fig. 7.1).

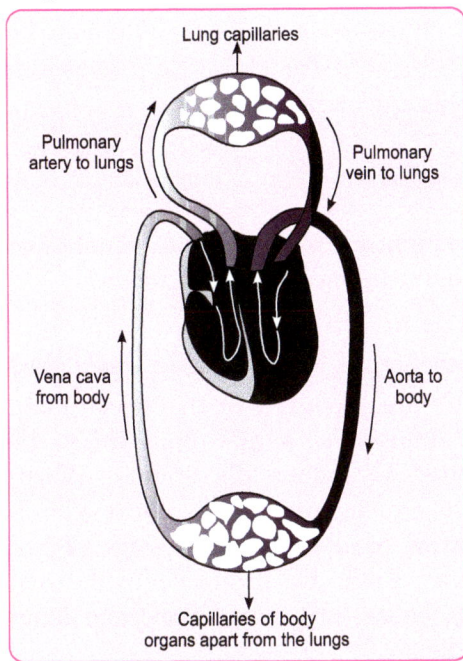

Fig. 7.1 : Diagrammatic representation of blood

7.3. THE BLOOD – VESSELS, STRUCTURE AND FUNCTIONS

7.3.1. Physical Properties of Blood

(a) The colour of blood from the artery is bright red and it is a little darker red from the veins.
(b) Blood is a viscous fluid connective tissue and is never stationary. It is in constant motion from the heart to the arteries and back to the heart through the veins. It constitutes about 6–10% of the body weight.
(c) The total volume of blood in an average adult is around 5–6 litres.
(d) Blood is slightly salty in taste and has pH between 7.3–7.45, i.e. it is slightly alkaline. It is a viscous fluid with viscosity five times that of distilled water.

7.3.2. Functions of Blood

The two main functions of blood are :
(a) Transport and (b) Protection.

(a) Transport
Blood transports the following substances :
(i) Digested foods like simple sugars, amino acids, vitamins, minerals, salts from the alimentary canal to the tissues.
(ii) Oxygen from the lungs by means of red blood cells in the form of an unstable compound called *oxyhaemoglobin* (formed from haemoglobin and oxygen) to the tissues where it breaks down as follows :
$$Hb + O_2 \rightarrow Hb.O_2$$
(iii) Transport of carbon dioxide from the tissues to the lungs either in combination with haemoglobin or as solution in the blood plasma.
$$Hb + CO_2 \rightarrow Hb.CO_2$$
Plasma proteins of the blood act as buffer and maintain pH of the blood and body fluids.
(iv) *Blood* transports excretory material from tissues to the liver, kidney or skin for removal or for conversion to harmless substances.
(v) *Hormones* secreted by *endocrine system* are carried by blood to their respective locations in the body.
(vi) Blood also aids in heat distribution for maintaining balance of body temperature.

(b) Protection
Blood offers the body protection in the following ways :
(i) By clotting during any physical injury: Clotting prevents excess loss of blood and also blocks the entry of harmful germs.
(ii) *White blood corpuscles* (WBC) present in blood protect the body by engulfing and attacking disease causing bacteria that may have entered the body.
(iii) Blood also produces *antitoxins* (for neutralizing harmful substances) and *antibodies* (for killing germs).

7.3.3. Composition of Blood

The blood consists of plasma and cellular elements like red blood corpuscles, white blood corpuscles and platelets (Fig. 7.2).

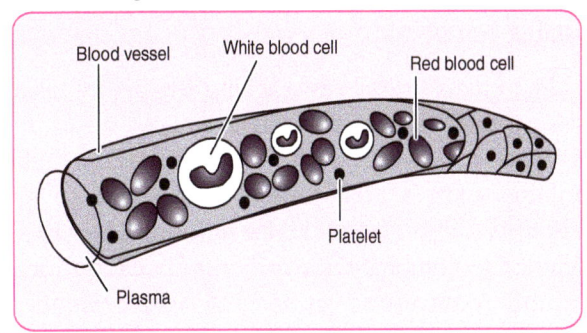

Fig. 7.2 : Composition of blood

(a) **Plasma :** It is the fluid part of blood and constitutes 55–60% of the blood. It is light yellow in colour and alkaline in nature. Composition of plasma is as follows :

Water: 90–92%

Proteins: 7–8%

Inorganic salts : Plasma contains 1% of inorganic salts like sodium chloride and sodium bicarbonate.

(b) **Other substances :** Small traces of other substances like glucose, amino acids, fibrinogen, hormones, urea, etc., along with small amounts of potassium, magnesium, phosphorus, calcium, iron, iodine are also found in plasma.

PROGRESS CHECK

FILL IN THE BLANKS

(1) _____ is present between the cells in the organs.

(2) The _____ secretes hormones that are carried to their respective locations by the circulatory system.

(3) Blood transports oxygen from the lungs by means of _____ in the form of an unstable compound called oxyhaemoglobin.

(4) _____ and _____ are the lymphatic organs of the body.

7.3.4. Cellular Elements of Blood

Cellular elements of blood are categorized as follows :

(a) Red blood corpuscles (RBCs)

(i) Red blood cells (erythrocytes) are the oxygen carriers of blood. Also known as RBCs for short, these are minute biconcave disc like structures that are flat in the centre and have a rounded, thickened periphery.

Red blood cells occur only in vertebrates. The shape and size of RBC vary in different vertebrates, but their function remains the same.

(ii) Their diameter is around 7μ 0·001 mm (μ stands for micron and 1μ = 0·001 mm).

(iii) Their small size and concave structure helps in providing a large surface area making them efficient oxygen absorbers and in travelling through extremely thin capillaries in the body.

Haemoglobin : A small respiratory pigment present in the colourless spongy body or stroma of the RBCs is called *haemoglobin (Hb)* and is the effective chemical constituent of the RBCs. Haemoglobin is made up of haemin, the iron containing part and globin, a protein. It combines with oxygen to form oxyhaemoglobin, an unstable compound.

The *oxyhaemoglobin* on reaching the needy tissues gives up its oxygen to the cells to be used for cellular respiration. Along with oxygen, haemoglobin combines with a little carbon dioxide too to give *carbamino-haemoglobin*. Haemoglobin also has a tendency to combine with carbon monoxide to form a stable compound called *carboxyhaemoglobin* (HbCO) which adversely affects the oxygen carrying capacity of the haemoglobin and can be fatal. This is a common reason of death of people working in and around furnaces in small rooms.

Life cycle of RBCs

(1) Formation of RBCs is called *erythropoiesis*.

(2) RBCs are produced in the spleen and liver in an embryo. In a new born infant there are around 6-7 million RBCs/mm^3. When a child starts growing, the RBCs are formed in red bone marrow of all bones till the age of 5 years. In adults, RBCs are produced in the marrow of long bones (ribs, breast bone and ilium of hip girdle).

(3) An adult male has around 5 million RBCs/ mm^3 while an adult female has 4.5 million RBCs/ mm^3.

(4) RBC count is affected by many factors. The count lowers by 5% during sleep and increases during high physical activity, pregnancy and emotional upsets. The count increases by nearly 30% in people living around 4,200m above sea level and more.

(5) RBCs have nuclei when they are produced but the nucleus is lost on maturity. Apart from the nuclei, mature mammalian RBCs are devoid of organelles like *mitochondria* and *endoplasmic reticulum*.

(6) The loss of nucleus makes the RBCs concave which increase their surface area to volume ratio and makes it more efficient in absorbing oxygen.

(7) The loss of mitochondria in RBCs serves two purposes:

(i) Mitochondria are responsible for respiration at cellular level. Absence of mitochondria will result in no consumption of oxygen by the RBCs. The total amount of oxygen that is absorbed is completely delivered to the tissues without being consumed.

➢ Absence of mitochondria also means full transport of glucose in blood plasma.

The loss of *endoplasmic reticulum* increases the flexibility of RBCs for their easy movement through narrow capillaries.

Life span of RBCs : The average life of an RBC is about 120 days. The break-down of old and worn out RBC is called *haemolysis*. The old and weak RBCs are destroyed in the spleen, liver and bone marrow. The haemin (iron part) is preserved in the liver and the protein part is converted to bile pigment called bilirubin for excretion. In an average adult, 1% (20,000,000) of the total RBCs are destroyed every day. Spleen is called the graveyard of RBC as in a normal adult man about 2–2·5 million RBCs are destroyed every minute in the spleen.

(b) White blood corpuscles (WBCs)

(i) White Blood Cells (leucocytes), unlike RBCs have a nucleus and do not contain haemoglobin. They are amoeboid in shape and can produce pseudopodia with the help of which they can exit through the capillary walls and enter tissues. This is called *diapedesis* (dia: across and pedesis: oozing out). They spend 90% of their time in the tissue fluid or lymph and just 10% in the blood.

(ii) There are 4000-8000 per mm3 of WBCs in blood. The ratio of RBC and WBC is 600 : 1. Abnormal increase in WBC count happens in case of acute infections, a condition known as *leucocytosis*. WBC contains mitochondria, golgi bodies, endoplasmic reticulum, etc.

(iii) WBCs can be broadly classified into two major categories (granular and non-granular) and are of five distinct types based on their shape and other characteristics (Fig. 7.3).

(iv) Granular WBCs have cytoplasm with granules and lobed nucleus. These form about 65% of total leukocytes.

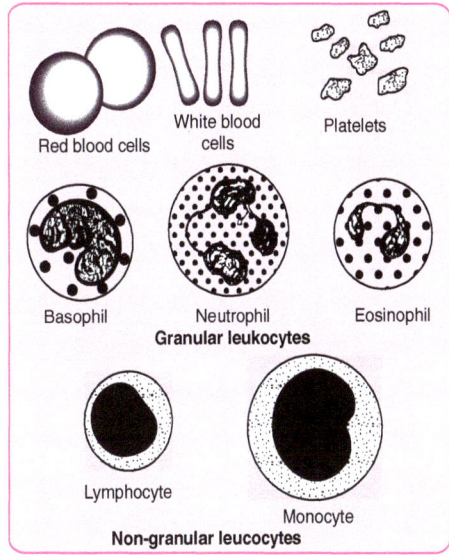

Fig. 7.3 : Kinds of WBCs

PROGRESS CHECK

FILL IN THE BLANKS

(1) Red blood corpuscles are formed in the _____ and the _____.

(2) _____ is a defence mechanism that protects us from disease-causing germs.

(3) _____ carry oxygen in the blood.

(4) _____ makes up 40-45% of the blood.

(5) The average life of an RBC is _____.

Neutrophils	Features	3-4 lobed nucleus.
		Cytoplasm is granular.
		Stain with neutral dyes. Their cytoplasmic granules take up both acidic and basic stains and appear violet or purple in colour in a stained blood slide.
		Comprises 62% of the total WBCs and are of two types, small and large lymphocytes.
	Function	Engulf bacteria.
		These are the chief phagocytic cells of the body and engulf microbes by phagocytosis and are called soldiers of the body.

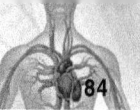

Eosinophils	Origin	In the Bone marrow.
	Features	Bi-lobed nucleus.
		Large Cytoplasm granules.
		Stain dark red with acid dye (eosin).
		Comprise 2-3% of the total WBCs and the count increases in allergies.
	Functions	Engulf bacteria.
		Release antitoxins.
		Associated with allergy.
		They have anti histaminic property.
Basophils	Origin	In the Bone marrow.
	Features	Large, distinctly lobed nucleus.
		Stain with basic dyes (methylene blue) appears blue in colour.
		Comprise 0-4% of the total WBCs.
	Function	Release chemicals for inflammation which dilate blood vessels.
		They secrete heparin and histamine and thus play a role in anticoagulation.
Lymphocytes	Origin	In the Bone marrow.
	Features	Smallest of WBCs.
		Single large nucleus.
		Comprises 30% of the total WBCs. Depending on size they are two types, small and large lymphocytes.
	Function	Produce antibodies and help in healing injuries.
Monocytes	Origin :	In the Bone marrow and Lymph glands (spleen, tonsils).
	Features	Single large nucleus that is kidney shaped, transforms into macrophages at the site of infection.
		Comprises 5-3% of the total WBCs.
	Function	Ingest germs.
	Origin	In the Bone marrow.

Functions of WBCs (Leucocytes) are as follows :

(1) **Phagocytosis** is a defence mechanism against disease causing germs. Most WBCs, especially the neutrophils and monocytes engulf bacteria and other particle like solid substances. Infection in the body increases the WBC count up to 50,000 per mm3 and this high count is also used to diagnose infection. Eosinophils and lymphocytes destroy toxins released by microorganisms.

(2) **Inflammation** is caused due to reaction of tissues to both injury and to invasion by germs. The visible changes due to inflammation are increased local heat, redness, swelling, pain etc. The WBCs, especially monocytes and neutrophils exit the capillary walls by diapedesis and fight against disease causing germs. They also act to destroy damaged cells by phagocytosis. Pus is an example of dead white blood cells massed together with dead tissue cells killed by bacteria.

(3) **Production of antibodies** by WBCs especially Lymphocytes, to kill or neutralize the germs or its poisons is one of the essential functions. Weakened germs or germ substances are introduced in the human body through vaccination. These germs cause the formation of specific antibodies that freely circulate in the blood plasma. When the particular

disease causing germs enter the body, they release poisonous substances called toxins that affect the body. The antibodies act against the toxins to neutralize them. The antibodies may continue to exist even after the toxins are neutralized and the person can be healed at a later period. In such a case, the person acquires immunity.

(4) Origin and life span of WBCs : The WBCs are produced in the red bone marrow, lymph nodes and sometimes even in the liver and the spleen. The average life of a WBC is around 2 weeks. The neutrophils live only for few hours and around 125 billion neutrophils are produced each day. The destruction of old WBCs is similar to that of the RBCs. The process of WBC formation is called *leucopoiesis*.

(c) Blood Platelets : "Platelets are the cells that circulate within our blood and bind together when they recognize damaged blood vessels," says **Dr. Marlene Williams**, Assistant Professor of Medicine and CICU Director for Johns Hopkins Bayview Medical Centre. "When you get a cut, for example, the platelets bind to the site of the damaged vessel, thereby causing a blood clot (Fig. 7.4). There is an evolutionary reason why they are there. It is to stop us from bleeding."

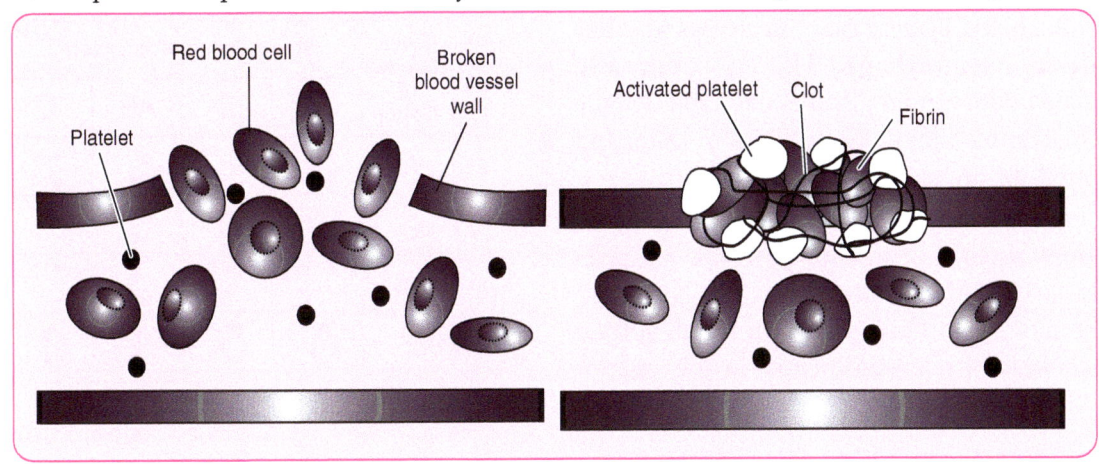

Fig. 7.4 : Blood clotting

(i) Blood Platelets *(Thrombocytes)* are minute oval or round structures that have no nucleus and float in the blood. They bud off from megakaryocytes in such a way that each platelet is surrounded by a membrane.

(ii) They are derived from megakaryocytes in the bone marrow. There are 200,000–400,000 platelets per mm^3 of blood in an adult. The life span of a platelet is 3-5 days. The old platelets are destroyed in the spleen by macrophages.

Function of platelets : Blood platelets are responsible for clotting of blood. Blood flows from a blood vessel in case of a physical injury like cut or bruising. The flow of blood discontinues after a while due to clot formation. At the site of the injury or cut, blood platelets release an enzyme, *thrombokinase*, which initiates the clotting of blood.

Blood clotting or coagulation occurs in a series of steps described below :

Blood clotting is a complex process which involves three steps completed over 2-5 minutes as otherwise the injured person can bleed to death from excessive blood loss due to failure of blood clotting. Blood, whenever it comes out of the blood vessels, quickly changes from a fluid state to thick jelly like material called clot and the process of separation of clot from the plasma is known as clotting or coagulation.

Following are the three steps involved in blood clotting :

(1) First, the thrombocytes (platelets) release a chemical compound called thromboplastin (or thrombokinase or Factor X) immediately at the site of injury. It can be shown in the form of reaction as follows :

$$\text{Platelets} \xrightarrow[\text{At the site of injury}]{\text{Release}} \text{Thromboplastin/Thrombokinase/X factor/Stuart factor}$$

(2) *Thromboplastin* released earlier converts the prothrombin present in the blood plasma to thrombin. Reaction for the same is as follows :

$$\text{Prothrombin} \xrightarrow{\text{Thromboplastin}} \text{Thrombin}$$

(3) *Thrombin* formed then converts the soluble fibrinogen present in the blood into fibrin which is insoluble in nature. Reaction for the same will be as follows :

$$\underset{\text{(Soluble)}}{\text{Fibrinogen}} \xrightarrow{\text{Thrombin}} \underset{\text{(Insoluble)}}{\text{Fibrin}}$$

Fibrin formed then forms a mesh-like structure which traps the elements of blood resulting into the formation of clot.

$$\text{Fibrin + Corpuscles} \longrightarrow \text{Clot}$$

All the above three steps are carried out in presence of calcium ions (Ca++) which is already present in the blood.

Blood clotting in test tube :

➢ Clotting of blood can also be observed if some blood is taken in a test tube. A clot will soon be formed and the serum released will collect on the surface. Failure of clotting of blood occurs when the blood platelet count decreases and this result in haemorrhage. This is commonly associated with certain diseases like viral dengue which accounted for many fatalities in Delhi and surrounding areas in 1996.

➢ It is believed that blood clotting depends upon exposure of blood to air. However, this has been found to be untrue. Clotting can also be caused by the movement of blood over a rough surface like cholesterol deposits present in the interior of a blood vessel.

7.4. BLOOD TRANSFUSION AND BLOOD GROUPS

Blood transfusion is the process of delivering blood or any of its components from an external donor into the body of a patient. The donor can be a normal healthy person whose blood is introduced into the veins of the patient. Before this is done, the blood type of the donor (healthy person) needs to be matched with the blood type of the recipient (patient).

The blood cells of the recipient may clump in case of incompatible blood transfusion. This is because the antigen from the blood of the donor attacks the antibody of the recipient's blood plasma. Thus, when blood from two different blood groups is mixed, clumping occurs due to antigen-antibody interaction. This is called clumping reaction or agglutination.

There are several systems to group a blood type, of which ABO and Rh systems are widely prevalent:

ABO system : Karl Landsteiner (1900) discovered this system according to which, human blood is classified into four types : A, B, AB and O.

Apart from donating blood to the person belonging to same blood groups as that of the donor, other possibilities may be :

It is clear from the table above that a person belonging to blood group O can donate blood to persons of any blood group and hence they are called universal donors. However, such universal donors can receive blood only from a person belonging to group AB. A person with blood group AB can receive blood from a donor with any blood group and such persons are universal recipients but can only donate blood to a person belongs to blood group AB. Person with antigen A belong to 'A' blood group, with antigen 'B' belong to 'B' blood group, person with both antigen A and B belong to AB blood group and with no antigen belong to blood group 'O' (Fig. 7.5).

Blood Group of Donor	Blood Group of Recipient			
	A	B	AB	O
A	✓	✗	✓	✗
B	✗	✓	✓	✗
AB	✗	✗	✓	✗
O	✓	✓	✓	✓

Fig. 7.5 : Blood donor and recipient chart

Rh system : The blood of most people contains a substance called *Rh factor* where Rh stands for *Rhesus*. This factor was first discovered in the common monkey. Human population is divided into Rh$^+$ and Rh$^-$ persons. When Rh$^-$ blood is donated to Rh$^-$ persons, transfusion is successful. Similarly transfusion of Rh$^+$ blood to Rh$^+$ persons has no problems. When an Rh positive person's blood is transfused into an Rh negative person, then the blood of the recipient starts forming antibodies against the Rh factor within a period of two weeks of transfusion. If the same transfusion is repeated, then the already formed antibodies will react with the newly transfused blood and can cause complications that may even be fatal. Due to this Rh factor, women can face problems during pregnancy.

An Rh negative woman may become sensitive if she bears an Rh positive child in her womb (happens if the husband is Rh positive). The first Rh positive child will face no problems but the second Rh positive child may have blood problems, sometimes fatal at the foetus stage as more antibodies are added in the mother's blood and a large no. of RBCs of the foetus are destroyed due to clumping. This causes haemolysis of foetus resulting in *erythroblastosis foetalis* or *jaundice* or *anaemia* in the new born.

7.5. THE HUMAN HEART - STRUCTURE AND FUNCTIONS

From the moment it begins beating until the moment it stops, the human heart (Fig. 7.6) works tirelessly. In an average lifetime, the heart beats more than two and a half billion times, without ever pausing to rest. Like a pumping machine, the heart provides the power needed for life.

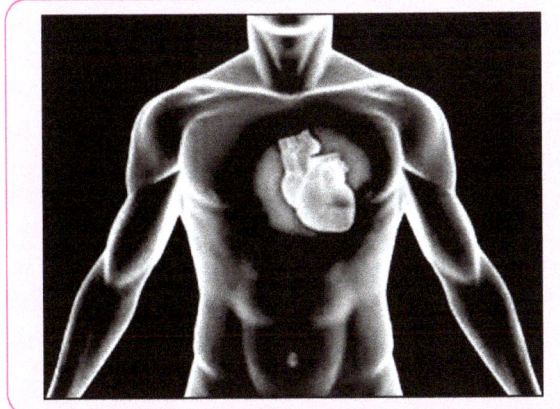

Fig. 7.6 : The Heart in our body

(a) Structure of the heart : The heart is a hollow, muscular organ enclosed in a membranous sac called *pericardium*. The wall of the heart is tri-layered - the *epicardium* (the outer layer), the *myocardium* (the middle layer) and the *endocardium* (the inner layer). The heart muscle, known as the cardiac muscle generates impulses that lead to its contraction that follows a specific rhythm. There are two types of muscle fibres in the heart. The *pacemaker* (also known as the *sinoatrial node*) occurs in the upper wall of the right atrium and is a specialized tissue. Its function is to control the movement of the heart muscles. Between the layers of pericardium, pericardial fluid is present which protects heart from injury and friction. It also keeps the heart moist.

(b) Location : It is situated in the thoracic cavity between the two lungs and above the diaphragm. It is slightly tilted towards the left of the midline in our bodies and almost two-thirds of its mass lies towards the left. During its working, the contraction of the heart is strongest towards this side, giving a feeling that the heart is situated on left hand side. The heart is anchored to its place by the pericardium (a bi-layered connective tissue membrane) and is enclosed by a bony cage.

In adults, the heart is about the size of a closed fist–12 cm in length and is 9 cm wide. It is protected by a double layered membranous covering, the pericardium, which protects the heart from mechanical injuries by means of the pericardial fluid contained in it. The pericardial fluid serves to reduce friction that may be caused by the beating of the heart.

7.5.1. Chambers of the Heart

The heart consists of four chambers, the two upper chambers called atria (singular-atrium) and two lower chambers called ventricles.

Auricles (The atria) : These are the two superior chambers of the heart, the right atrium or auricle and the left atrium or auricle (Fig. 7.7). The auricles are the blood receiving chambers and have thinner walls as compared to the ventricles. They are separated from each other by an inter-atrial septum. The main function of auricles is to receive impure blood from the body and pump it into the next ventricle.

Ventricles : These are two inferior chambers and are called the right and left ventricles. They are separated by an obliquely placed inter-ventricular septum. Between the auricles and the ventricles is a connective tissue which forms the valves. The ventricles perform the function of pumping pure blood to the various parts of body that is why the walls of ventricles are thick and muscular. They are also known as distributing chambers. Right ventricle supplies deoxygenated blood to lungs through pulmonary aorta.

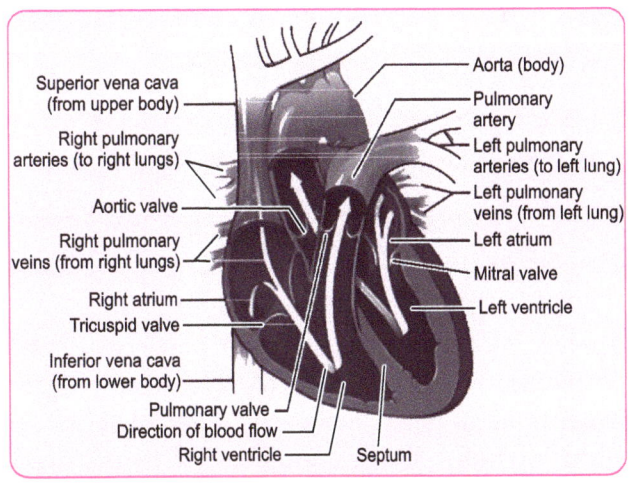

Fig. 7.7 : Internal structure of the human heart and the associated blood vessels

7.5.2. Great Blood Vessels of the Heart

The heart and the blood in our bodies have a special relationship. As a result, some major blood vessels enter and leave the heart. These vessels are called the great blood vessels. Blood vessels that enter the right atrium of the heart are :

(a) **Superior (Anterior) vena cava :** Carries deoxygenated blood from the head and upper body.

(b) **Inferior (Posterior) vena cava :** Carries deoxygenated blood from the lower regions of the body.

(c) **Pulmonary veins :** The left auricle receives two pairs of pulmonary veins, one from each lung, carrying oxygenated blood from the lungs.

(d) **Coronary sinus :** This carries deoxygenated blood from the heart wall. It consists of two coronary arteries supplying blood to the heart muscles. Blockage of the coronary arteries can result in *myocardial infarction* (heart attack). *Angina Pectoris* is the chest pain caused by insufficient blood supply to the heart muscle.

Blood vessels leave the heart and arise from the ventricles. There are two types of blood vessels :

(i) **Pulmonary artery :** Arising from the right ventricle, it carries deoxygenated blood to the lungs for oxygenation.

(ii) **Systemic aorta :** Arises from the left ventricle and takes oxygenated blood to all parts of the body.

7.5.3. Valves of the Heart

Valves are muscular curtain-like structures that permit blood flow only in one direction, and prevent back flow of blood. The difference in pressure across these valves regulates the opening and closing of the valves. There are two types of valves :

(a) **The atria-ventricular valves :** They separate the auricles and ventricles and let the blood flow from the auricles or atria to the ventricles. These valves are of two types:

(i) **The tricuspid valves :** The tricuspid valves (right atrio-ventricular valves) are positioned on the right side of the heart and have three cusps. It allows the blood from right atrium to right ventricle.

(ii) **The bicuspid valves :** The bicuspid valve (mitral valve) is positioned on the left side of the heart. The conical ends of the valves are attached to small conical extensions called papillary muscles on the insides of the ventricles with tendon-like fibrous cords called chordae tendinae. It allows blood to flow from left atrium to left ventricle. It is formed of two cusps.

(b) **Semilunar valves :** These valves have three half-moon-shaped pockets. They occur in the arteries that move out of the heart. They stop the blood from flowing back into the heart after the ventricles relax. These valves are also of two types :

(i) **The pulmonary semi-lunar valve :** This valve is situated in the opening where the pulmonary trunk leaves the right ventricle.

(ii) **The aortic semi-lunar valve:** This valve is situated at the opening between the left ventricle and aorta.

PROGRESS CHECK

NAME THE FOLLOWING

1. Heart is enclosed in a membrane sac.
2. They are known as distributing chambers.
3. Valves differentiate the auricle and ventricles.
4. Valve has three half moon shaped pockets.

7.5.4. The Passage of Blood through the Heart

Blood can be oxygenated or deoxygenated, depending upon the presence or absence of oxygen in it. Deoxygenated blood from all parts of the body enters the right atrium. Three veins carry this deoxygenated blood to the right atrium:

(a) **The superior vena cava or precaval or anterior vena cava :** It carries blood from different sections of the body superior to the heart (Fig. 7.8).

(b) **The inferior vena cava or postcaval or posterior vena cava :** It carries blood to different sections of the body inferior to the heart.

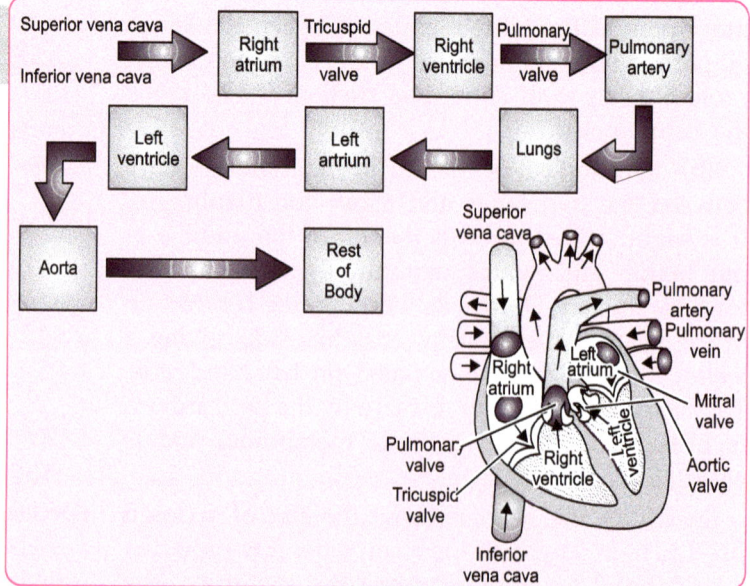

Fig. 7.8 : Diagrammatic representation of circulation of blood

(c) Coronary sinus : The walls of the heart receive blood through certain vessels. The coronary sinus drains the blood from these vessels.

Right atrium when filled with blood contracts due to which tricuspid valves open under pressure. The blood then gushes into the right ventricle.

Now, blood entering the right ventricle causes it to contract when filled fully. Due to this contraction of the right ventricle, the blood enters the pulmonary trunk but not in the right atrium, as the tricuspid valves shut down the aperture of the atrium.

There are two pulmonary arteries: the right pulmonary artery and the left pulmonary artery. These two arteries carry the blood to the lungs for oxygenation. A pulmonary semi-lunar valve stops the blood from flowing back into the right ventricle.

The oxygenated blood goes back to the heart through the pulmonary veins. These veins open into the left atrium.

The contraction of the left auricle leads to the movement of the blood into the left ventricle through the bicuspid valve which does not allow the back flow of blood.

The contraction of the left ventricle leads to the pumping of the blood into the aorta. This is the largest artery in the body. The aorta branches into vessels and carries blood to all body parts except the air sacs of the lungs.

Heart beat : The heart muscles contract and expand (relax) in a regular rhythmic fashion. The phase of contraction is known as systole and the phase of relaxation is called diastole. One diastole and one systole together constitute a heartbeat. The contraction and relaxation of the auricles and ventricles take place in a definite order. The auricles and ventricles do not contract simultaneously.

Cardiac cycle denotes the sequence of atrial and ventricular events which occurs once during each complete heart beat. It is completed in about 0·8 seconds.

If a stethoscope is placed on the chest, two distinct sounds – a LUBB and a DUP, can be heard in short succession. The 'LUBB' is produced by the closing of the tricuspid and bicuspid valves sharply at the start of the ventricular systole. The second sound 'DUP' at the ventricular diastole is produced by the closing of the semilunar valves at the roots of the aorta and the pulmonary artery.

The functioning of the heart may be divided into three phases.

I-Phase : The auricle contracts and the blood are pumped into the ventricle which is relaxing. The auricle is said to be in *systolic stage* while the ventricle is said to be in *diastolic stage.*

II-Phase : In this phase the ventricles contract while the auricles are relaxing. The blood is forced into the arteries.

III-Phase : In this stage, both auricles and ventricles are relaxing and the blood enters into the auricles.

Rate of heart beat : The rhythmic contraction and relaxation of the heart to pump out and receive blood is called the *heart-beat.* The rate of the heart beat varies from species to species. The smaller the animal, the higher is the metabolic rate and so greater is its heart rate. The heart rate is about 25 times per minute in an elephant and about 300 times per minute in a rat.

In a healthy adult, the normal heart beat at rest is about 70-72 times per minute. It increases during fever, exercise, anger and pain.

7.5.5. Blood Vessels

The circulatory system is composed of three main types of blood vessels (Fig. 7.9) :

(a) Arteries : Blood is transported away from the heart to the tissues by means of the arteries. The aorta divides and sub-divides into arterioles. Arteries are known as distributing vessels. All arteries except the pulmonary artery function as carriers of oxygenated blood. Pulmonary artery carries deoxygenated blood from right ventricle to lungs. The artery walls comprise three thick coats made up of muscles. The coat in the centre is elastic and composed of collagen. This coat exhibits the property of contractibility. When the ventricles thin, extra blood is accommodated and the arteries dilate to do so. The blood moves through the arteries due to the relaxation of the ventricles. We must remember that arteries occur deep inside our bodies and the flow of blood in the arteries occurs under pressure. Lumen of artery is without valves.

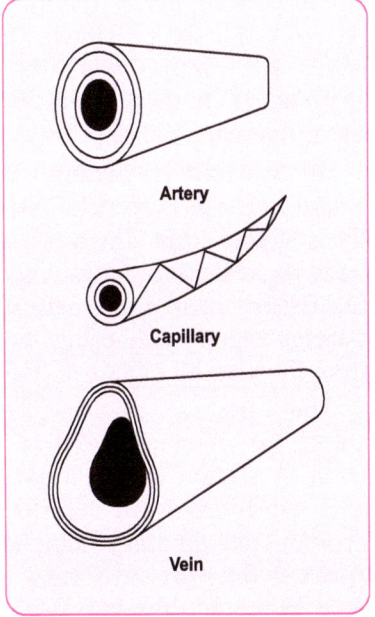

Fig. 7.9 : Main blood vessels

(b) Veins : Blood is transported to the heart through the veins. All veins except the pulmonary vein usually carry deoxygenated blood. Veins are collecting vessels. The walls of the veins also comprise

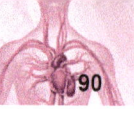

three coats. But these walls are thinner and they have the capacity of distending. In doing so they adjust to the amount of blood moving through them and the pressure under which they pass. There are valves present in the veins, primarily those in the limbs and they carry blood against gravity. Small veins are called venules, blood flows smoothly through them. They prevent the back flow. Veins are superficially situated and can be seen from the surface of skin.

(c) Capillaries : Capillaries are formed of only one layer of epithelial tissues. They are minute blood vessels and have a capacity to dilate. They form a network in the tissues. The surface area increases due to the thin walls and quick exchange of material between blood and tissue cells occur. Capillaries maintain continuity between arterioles and venules.

7.6. BLOOD CIRCULATION – MAIN BLOOD VESSELS

Blood circulation in humans is called double circulation because it enters and exits the heart twice with each heart beat. *Pulmonary circulation* is between the heart and the lungs and *systemic circulation* of blood is between the heart and the body organs (except lungs).

(a) Pulmonary circulation : The right side of the heart regulates the pulmonary circulation. This circulation begins at the right ventricle; blood is released into the pulmonary trunk. The blood then enters the vascular system of the lungs where it is oxygenated. It then enters the left atrium through the pulmonary veins.

(b) Systemic circulation : This form of circulation begins in the left ventricle. The blood is pumped into the systemic aorta. The aorta has branches to all the body organs except lungs. Oxygen gets diffused into the tissues from these arteries. The superior and inferior venae cavae bring the deoxygenated blood from the visceral organs to the right auricle.

The aorta can be classified into the ascending aorta, the descending aorta and the arch of the aorta. A section of the aorta divides into arterioles and subdivides into capillaries. The capillaries provide oxygenated blood throughout the body apart from the air sacs in the lungs. The deoxygenated blood flows back into the lungs through the systemic veins. Capillaries form venules and then veins. In systemic circulation, the veins flow into either the superior or the inferior vena cava or the coronary sinus. The veins drain into the right atrium.

Hepatic portal circulation : The veins that collect blood from different parts of alimentary canal, spleen and pancreas do not open directly into the inferior vena cava. But they join to form hepatic portal vein; it carries blood to liver and forms capillaries. These capillaries then rejoin to form a new vein called the hepatic vein. A portal vein is the vein which starts with capillaries and ends also in capillaries.

(i) Blood pressure : When blood flows it exerts pressure on the arteries. This pressure is created when the heart pumps blood. Every time the heart contracts fresh blood is pumped into the arteries. The pressure is then at its highest level and is called the systolic pressure. The opposite happens when the heart expands and this is called the diastolic pressure.

(ii) Pulse : It is the rhythmic contraction of heart which is felt in the arteries in the form of jerks. Pulse is the expansion and elastic recoil of an arterial wall. It takes place with each systole and diastole of the left ventricle. The pulse beats the strongest in the arteries that are nearest to the heart. We cannot locate it at all in the capillaries. It is very conspicuous in places near the surface of the body, the bones and firm tissues. We generally use the radial artery at the wrist to locate the pulse.

Ideally the intervals between beats should be of equal length. Pulse beats should also be of equal strength. If there is an irregularity in strength there may be a lack of muscle tone in the heart arteries. Pulse rate is same as the heart beat rate, 68 -72 times per minute.

7.7. THE LYMPHATIC SYSTEM

Lymph is a straw-coloured fluid. This fluid is carried throughout the body in vessels that are called lymphatic vessels and some structures and organs that contain *lymphatic tissues* or *lymphoids*.

(a) Working of the lymphatic system : Pressure from the heart leads to the seeping of the fluid through the porous walls of the capillaries. It transports nutrients to the tissues and draws in waste matter. These fluids are called tissue fluids or interstitial fluid and contain proteins, salts and waste matter. The salts and water pass back into the veins. The proteins cannot enter the venous system directly. The collection of proteins may harm the tissues around them. Proteins also have to move to different parts of the body where they may be needed for the development of the body and its refurbishment. Most of the fluids flow through a system of vessels that form the lymphatic system.

At their commencement the lymphatic vessels are microscopic, blind-ended vessels in areas between the cells. Lymph vessels are also called lymphatics. The lymphatics absorb the protein-laden filtrate like a blotting paper. In the intestine, they absorb an emulsion of fats that have seeped out from the capillaries. Tiny flap-like valves inside the lymph-

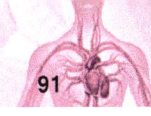

THE CIRCULATORY SYSTEM

walls stop any fluid from flowing back into it. The locomotion of the lymph relies on the movement of the muscles and our breathing movements. Lymph ducts grow around the muscles of our arms and legs. Their contraction and relaxation leads to the development of pressure on the lymph vessels. They also grow around the aorta and the powerful pulsations of the aorta are used by it to thrust the lymph forward. Exercise, deep breathing and massage can make the lymph move faster. The lymph has its own circulatory system. Through its circulatory system the lymph moves towards the heart and empties into the vena cava prior to entering the heart.

(b) Lymph nodes and glands : Lymph nodes and glands are formed in the body like beads. When lymph passes through the nodes it is shorn of foreign material which are captured by the reticular fibres inside the node. Lymph nodes are enlargements in lymph vessels.

An example of a lymphatic nodule is the tonsils which are situated in the posterior wall of the nasopharynx. They are strategically located at the from port of entry of microbes and this position stops the body being attacked by foreign matter. Tonsils produce lymphocytes and antibodies. The largest lymphatic tissue in our body is the spleen, about 12 cm long. It is situated between the fundus of the stomach and diaphragm and gives birth to antibodies, phagocytic bacteria and destroys worn out or damaged red blood cells and platelets. It also performs the function of storing blood and discharging it at times of emergency. Another lymphatic organ is the thymus.

(i) Lymph helps in the distribution of nutrients and oxygen to tissue cells.
(ii) It helps in the removal of nitrogenous waste and CO_2 from the tissue cells.
(iii) It absorbs fatty acids and glycerol.
(iv) Its lymphocytes destroy harmful pathogens.
(v) It serves to equalize body temperature.

Animation for Circulatory System
https://www.youtube.com/watch?v=L5XN9fcZoTg
https://www.youtube.com/watch?v=gn6QmETEm8s

Table 1 : Differences between Artery and Vein

Artery	Vein
1. Vessels which carry blood from the heart to various body parts.	1. Vessels which carry blood from the various body parts to the heart.
2. Arteries carry oxygenated blood from the heart except pulmonary artery.	2. Veins carry deoxygenated blood from the various body parts except pulmonary vein.
3. Arteries have thick elastic muscular walls.	3. Veins have thin non elastic walls.
4. Valves are absent.	4. Valves are present to prevent the backward flow of blood.
5. Blood flows under high pressure.	5. Blood flows under low pressure.

EXERCISE

A. VERY SHORT ANSWER TYPE

(I) True or False
1. Erythrocytes are the oxygen carriers of blood.
2. The blood moves in the body in a process of systemic, cerebral, and pulmonary circulation.
3. Human blood is classified into four types: A, B, AB and O.
4. The taste of blood is slightly sweet.
5. Blood is transported to the heart through the arteries.

B. SHORT ANSWER TYPE
1. What is diapedesis?
2. What is the function of the arteries?
3. What are lymphocytes?
4. What is fibrin?
5. What is the composition of blood?
6. What do you understand by the term 'pulse'?
7. What is haemoglobin?

C. LONG ANSWER TYPE
1. What are the functions of blood?
2. What are the three essential fluids of our body?
3. What are the valves of the heart? Explain.
4. What are the functions of WBCs?
5. What are the cellular elements of blood?
6. Write in detail about the chambers of the heart.

(I) Answer in One Word

Furnish the appropriate terms for the following :
1. A substance released by the platelets and injured tissue cells that break down at the site of the wound.
2. A stable compound formed by the combination of haemoglobin and carbon monoxide.

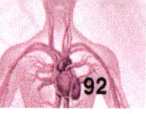

3. Minute oval or round structures that float in the blood.
4. This substance is produced when oxygen, haemoglobin combines with a little carbon dioxide.
5. The fluid portion of blood.
6. No. of RBCs in 1 ml of human blood.
7. The process by which WBCs engulf bacteria.

(II) **Define these Terms**
1. Pulse rate
2. Blood pressure
3. Pulmonary artery
4. Systemic circulation

(III) **Where are the following structures found and what are their functions?**
1. Mitral valve
2. Bicuspid valve
3. Pericardium
4. Platelets

D. STRUCTURED/APPLICATION BASED

1. The following figure shows a simplified plan of the circulatory system of human.
   (a) Name the blood vessels 1 to 7.
   (b) Name the chamber of the heart which
      (i) receives blood from vessel 1.
      (ii) pumps blood into vessel 8.
   (c) Name two substances which might be present in abundance in vessel 3 after a heavy meal.
   (d) Give two differences between the contents of the blood in vessels 1 and 8.

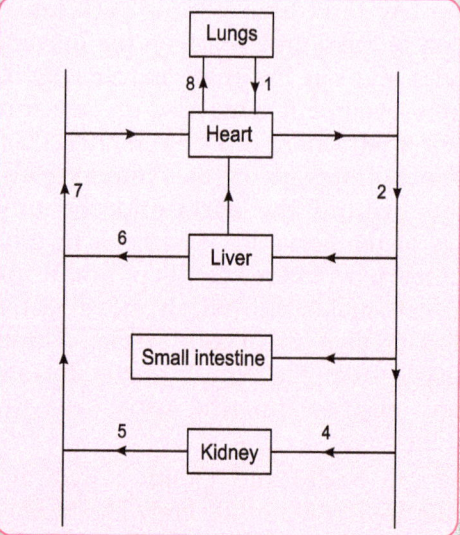

2. The figures given below are cross-section of blood vessels.
   (a) Identify the blood vessels A, B and C.
   (b) Name the parts labelled 1-4.
   (c) Mention two structural differences between A and B.
   (d) Name the type of blood that flows (i) through A, (ii) through B.
   (e) In which of the above vessels referred to in (4) above does the exchange of gases actually takes place?

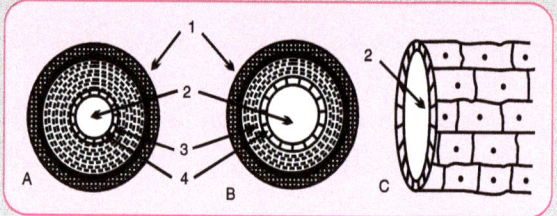

DO YOU KNOW?

➢ It takes 20 seconds for blood to circulate the entire body. Oxygenated blood leaves the aorta at about 1 mile an hour.
➢ The power output of the heart ranges from 1-5 watts per minute which is equivalent to the usage of a 60 watt bulb. It has been said that enough energy is produced in a day to drive a truck 20 miles.
➢ Human blood is colourless; it is the haemoglobin that makes it red.
➢ Due to the heart having its own electrical impulse, it will continue to beat even when removed from the body as long as it has an adequate supply of oxygen.
➢ On average, the human body has about 5 litres (almost 9 pints) of blood continually travelling through it by way of the circulatory system. A kitchen tap would need to be turned on all the way for at least 45 years to equal the amount of blood pumped by the heart in an average lifetime.

8

EXCRETORY SYSTEM

CHAPTER HIGHLIGHTS
8.1. Introduction
8.2. Wastes in the Body
8.3. The Excretory Organs
8.4. Structure of Kidney
8.5. Mechanism of Urine Formation
8.6. Constituents of Urine
8.7. Regulation of Urine Output
8.8. Functions of Kidney
8.9. Miscellaneous Useful Information

8.1. INTRODUCTION

Excretion is the process by which animals rid themselves of waste products and of the nitrogenous by-products of metabolism. Through excretion, organisms control osmotic pressure—the balance between inorganic ions and water—and maintain acid-base balance. The process thus promotes homeostasis, the constancy of the organism's internal environment.

The excretory system is a passive biological system that removes excess, unnecessary materials from an organism, so as to help maintain homeostasis within the organism and prevent damage to the body. It is responsible for the elimination of the waste products of metabolism as well as other liquid and gaseous wastes, as urine and as a component of sweat and exhalation.

During the metabolic activities in the body, large quantities of organic compounds are broken down which results in the production of carbon dioxide, water and other nitrogenous waste products. These waste products cannot be ignored as their accumulation can result in the death of an organism. All organisms, from the simplest to the most complex, are made up of cells. These cells carry out their life processes in the form of biochemical reactions that may result in the following :

(a) Production of toxic wastes in the body.
(b) Changes in the water content in the body.
(c) Creation of ionic imbalance in the body.

For an organism to lead a normal life, toxic wastes being produced in the body as a result of metabolic activity, must be removed continuously and various ions present in its body must also be regulated.

Some part of the food that we eat remains undigested.

Digested food: By-products of metabolism such as hormones and enzymes are secreted for the use of body. Rest of the by products which are not useful are excreted from the body through organs like lungs, skin and kidneys.

Undigested part of the food is removed from anus in the form of faeces.

8.2. WASTES IN THE BODY

There are several substances which are not used by the body, the removal of which from the body is essential, since otherwise they become toxic. Some such substances are :

(a) Carbon dioxide and water : Oxidation of food results in the production of carbon dioxide and water during the process of respiration. Carbon dioxide is exhaled through lungs but the water is not removed from the body. Instead it becomes a part of the rest of the water in the body.

(b) Nitrogenous wastes : These include urea, ammonia and uric acid produced in the liver from the remains of the tissues known as dead proteins which are then brought to liver. Extra amino acids are broken down in the liver to glucose, which can be stored and urea that needs to be excreted. Urea produced is excreted out through the kidneys because it is highly poisonous and accumulation of the same in the blood can be fatal.

(c) Mineral salts : Common salt (NaCl) and some water soluble salts such as sodium, potassium, calcium and magnesium are eliminated through the kidneys.

(d) Water : Excess water taken in with food and beverages is removed. The removal of such water is useful as it helps in dissolving the harmful material which otherwise cannot be excreted out of the body.

(e) Bile pigments : Haemoglobin from the dead cells is broken down to form bile pigments, also known as yellow bilirubin. After being extracted from the blood circulation, liver secretes it into the bile juice which reaches duodenum through the common bile duct. Bile pigments are modified in the intestine such that the part of resultant pigments gives yellowish-brown colour to faeces and the remaining pigments are excreted with urine.

(f) Vitamins and hormones : Excess of vitamins and hormones are eliminated from the body in urine.

(g) Drugs : Excess of drugs or their breakdown products are removed by the kidneys.

8.3. THE EXCRETORY ORGANS

The following organs serve as excretory organs (Fig. 8.1) in mammals :

(a) Kidneys : Kidneys play a vital role in the process of excretion and are responsible for removal of nitrogenous metabolic waste from the body in the form of urine.

(b) Sweat glands : Primary function of sweat glands is *thermoregulation (cooling)*. Sweat secreted by these glands consists of nitrogenous wastes in small quantities and is passed out only when cooling is required.

(c) Lungs : They help in the excretion of carbon dioxide during exhalation.

8.4. HUMAN EXCERETORY SYSTEM

(a) Kidneys : The excretory system in human beings (Fig. 8.2) consist of : (a) Kidneys, (b) Ureters, (c) Urinary bladder, (d) Urethra.

(i) External structure of kidney

Location : The pair of Kidneys is located one on either side of the backbone just above the waist and is protected by the last two ribs.

Shape : Bean shaped organs which are 10 cm long, 6 cm wide and 3 cm thick. Their inner concave sides face each other. The left kidney is usually placed a little higher than the right one.

Colour : They are reddish brown in colour.

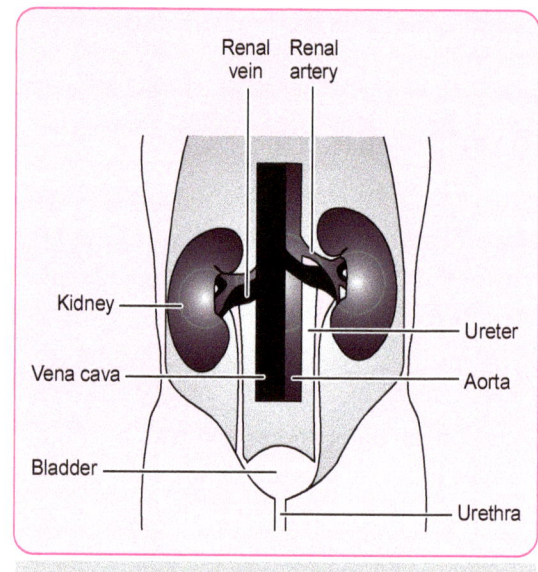

Fig. 8.1 : Urinary system

Weight : They weigh between 125 to 170 gms in adults (150 gm in adult male and 135 gm in adult female).

Kidneys are convex laterally and concave medially. On the concave side, there is a longitudinal notch called hilum.

Renal hilum : It is the point at which the ureter and renal vein exit the kidney and the renal artery enters the kidney.

Renal artery : Renal artery branches from the aorta. It carries deoxygenated blood to the kidney which is rich in toxic nitrogenous wastes.

Renal vein : Renal vein leaves the kidney and carries with it oxygenated/pure blood.

(b) Ureters : They are tubular structures emerging from the medial surface of each kidney. Each ureter is made up of smooth muscle fibres and connects the kidney to the base of the urinary bladder. It is responsible for transporting urine from the kidneys to the urinary blander. Muscles in the ureter walls produce peristalsis which helps in the onward passage of urine. Back flow of urine is prevented by valves present at the opening.

(c) Urinary bladder : It is a large, thin walled highly distensible muscular bag-like organ situated at the lower end of the abdomen. Its outlet is normally closed by a tight ring of muscle, called sphincter.

(d) Urethra : It is a muscular canal, which is guarded by a sphincter muscle. It relaxes at the time of urination under an impulse from the nervous system. In females, urethra carries only urine but in males urethra carries both urine and sperms.

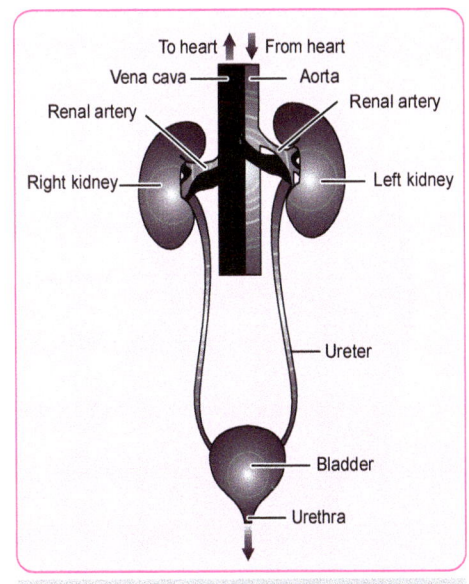

Fig. 8.2 : Human excretory system

PROGRESS CHECK

FILL IN THE BLANKS

1. Undigested part of the food is removed from anus in the form of _____.
2. Bile pigments are also known as _____.
3. Primary function of sweat glands is _____.
4. Kidneys are _____ laterally and _____ medially.
5. Outlet of urinary blander is normally closed by a tight ring of muscle called _____.

(ii) Internal structure of kidney

As shown in longitudinal section, the kidney consists of two distinct regions, the outer dark cortical region and the lighter inner medullary region. The medulla is made up of a finely striped substance arranged in conical pyramids, each apex projecting into the pelvis of the kidney.

Each kidney comprises of millions of complex structures called uriniferous tubules or nephrons. These are approx. 2 million in number if both kidneys taken together. These minute tubules are considered to be the structural as well as functional units of the kidney.

Structure of kidney tubule : Each kidney tubule or nephron is made up of the following parts :

(1) Malpighian body : It again consists of :

➢ **Bowman's capsule :** It is a hollow cup-like structure pressed deep on one side. Its internal space continues into the tubule. It receives the *glomerular capillaries*.

➢ **Glomerulus :** It is a knotted mass of blood capillaries that emerges out from Bowman's capsule. One end of glomerulus is attached to renal artery which brings deoxygenated blood and the other end comes out as a blood capillary, surrounds the tubule of nephron and finally joins a renal vein.

Thus we see that the *Bowman's capsule* and the Glomerulus together make up the *Malpighian body* or *Renal tubule* or *capsule*.

(2) Renal tubule : It consists of the following regions :

➢ **Proximal convoluted tubule (PCT) :** It is the starting convoluted part of the tubule and is permeable to water. It lies nearer to the Bowman's capsule in the renal cortex.

➢ **Loop of henle :** It is the middle, thin U-shaped part of the renal tubule and is a hair pin like structure. It is not convoluted. It has a descending and an ascending limb.

➢ **Distal convoluted tubule (DCT) :** *Ascending limb* on entering the cortex becomes convoluted and is known as distal convoluted tubule and leads to a collecting duct. As the name suggests, ('distal' means farther) it lies away from the Bowman's capsule. It is impermeable to water.

➢ **Collecting duct or tubule :** *Distal convoluted tubule* opens into the collecting tubule. These tubules then fuse to form a duct which receives the contents from numerous kidney tubules and pours it as urine in the pelvis of the kidney (Fig. 8.3).

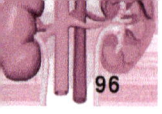

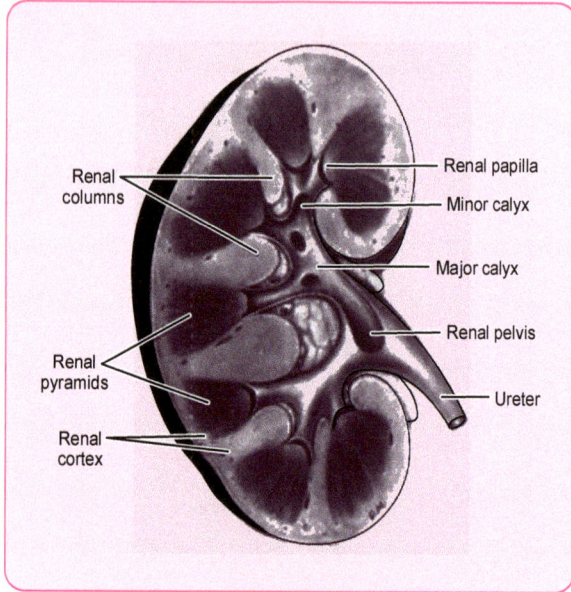

Fig. 8.3 : Longitudinal section of kidney

8.5. MECHANISM OF URINE FORMATION

A pair of renal arteries branch out from the dorsal aorta and enter each kidney present. Each renal artery then further divides into the several smaller vessels called as arterioles. The afferent arteriole supplies blood to Bowman's capsule and further sub-divides into a knot like mass of capillaries called *glomerulus* (Fig. 8.4). The capillaries of the glomerulus reunite to form efferent arteriole. They emerge from *Bowman's capsule*. After covering a short distance, they branch out into secondary capillary network known as vasa recta which surrounds the renal tubule and reunite together again to form a vein. The veins of this network unite again and again to form the renal vein which branches out from the median surface of the kidney to supply blood to the posterior vena cava.

The formation of urine is the mechanical aspect of excretion and involves two major steps, viz., *ultrafiltration* and *selective reabsorption*.

(a) Ultrafiltration or glomerular filtration : This process occurs in the malphigian bodies. Pressure of the blood flow is much greater when flowing through the glomerulus as compared to that flowing through the capillaries elsewhere. This is because the efferent arteriole (outgoing) is narrower than the afferent (incoming) arteriole (Fig. 8.5). This high pressure results in the filtration of liquid part of the blood from the glomerulus into the renal tubule. The liquid from the renal tubule after filtration consists of glucose, urea, uric acid, salts and a large amount of water and is called glomerular filtrate. This filtration under extraordinary pressure is called *ultrafiltration*.

During ultrafiltration, almost all the liquid content of blood consisting of plasma and other organic and inorganic products like glucose, amino acids, urea etc. passes into the Bowman's capsule from the glomerulus. The fluid entering the renal tubule is called the glomerular filtrate.

The thicker part of the blood left behind in the glomerulus after ultrafiltration then enters the efferent arteriole. It is thick, consisting mainly of plasma proteins, blood

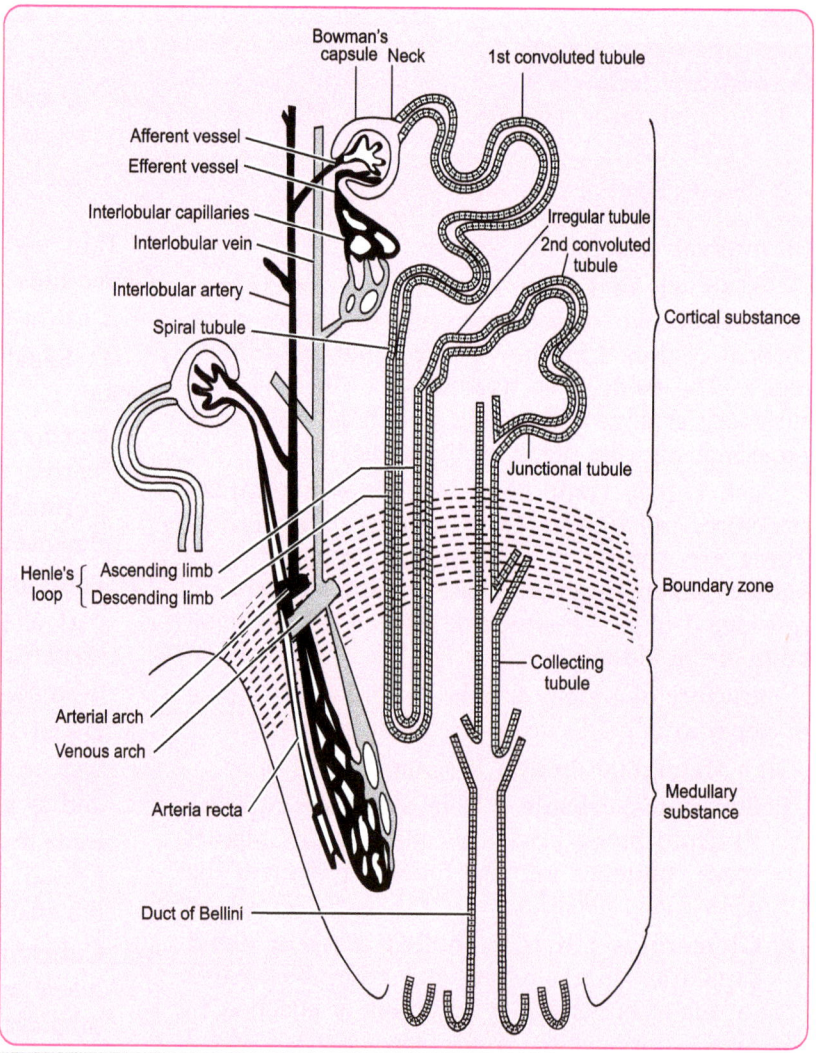

Fig. 8.4 : A single uriniferous tubule

corpuscles and a small quantity of water. As a result of ultrafiltration, almost all the substances that are dissolved in plasma like inorganic salts, certain proteins, some vitamins, amino acids, glucose are filtered out.

Ultrafiltration is the process in which filtration takes place under tremendous hydrostatic pressure.

(b) Reabsorption : During ultrafiltration even those substances which are valuable to the body

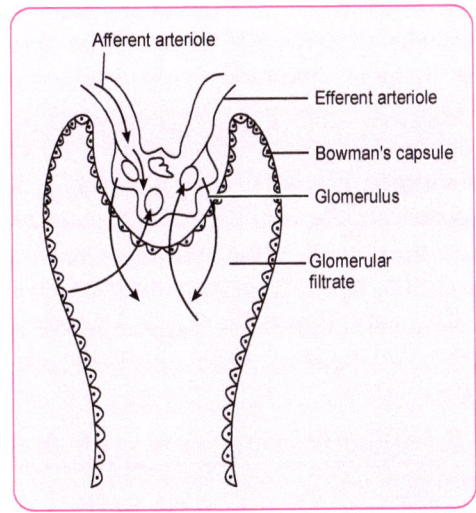

Fig. 8.5 : (a) Ultrafiltration in glomerulus

diffuse out. Almost all glucose, amino acids and some inorganic salts are reabsorbed from nephric filtrate in the proximal convoluted tubule. In the ascending limb active absorption of sodium chloride takes place without water. If blood contains excess water, the reabsorption of water is less and urine is dilute. But in case the amount of water in blood is less, more water is reabsorbed from the filtrate. Thus, the kidneys help in *osmoregulation*.

The liquid entering the renal tubule is extremely dilute and consists of useful materials namely glucose and some salts like sodium. While the glomerular filtrate passes down the tubule, selective reabsorption of water along with useful substances takes place. The reabsorption is termed as *selective reabsorption* as it takes place for maintaining the normal concentration of the blood.

(c) Tubular secretion : The cells of the tubular wall also secrete specific enzymes that help in the active transport of solutes. During the secretion, substances like K^+, H^+, NH_4^+ and creatinine are added to the filtrate. It helps in removal of toxic substances from the body and also helps in maintaining the pH of blood. Activity of tubular cells is involved in this passage thus it is called as *tubular secretion*.

Urine excretion : The liquid that passes into the collecting tubules is termed as final urine. Ducts formed by the fusion of collecting tubules release the urine into the renal pelvis from where it is passed into the ureter. Movement of urine from the ureter to the urinary bladder takes place due *to urethral peristalsis*. The back flow of urine is blocked by the valves formed by the ureter at the base of bladder. Simultaneous contraction of bladder and relaxation of sphincter muscles result in the removal of urine from the bladder. Micturition is defined as the expulsion of the urine from the bladder through the urethra. The colour of the urine is due to a pigment called *urochrome*.

Energy requirements of the kidney during urine formation are high due to a multitude of functions and hence the oxygen demand of the kidneys may be 6-7 times that of muscles.

8.6. CONSTITUENTS OF URINE

Urine under normal conditions consists of 95% water and 5% solid wastes which are in dissolved state. This percentage of solid waste may vary according to the intake of food and drink by an individual.

Generally, the chemical composition of urine is as follows :

Organic Compounds	Quantity (in g/L)
Urea	2.3
Creatinine	1.5
Uric Acid	0.7
Others	2.6

Inorganic Compounds	Quantity (in g/L)
Sodium Chloride	9.0
Potassium Chloride	2.5
Ammonia	0.6
Others	2.5

Persons suffering from urine disorders may pass out certain hormones and also some anti – bodies and excess vitamins. These are known as the abnormal constituents of urine. The abnormal constituents of urine may be due to the following conditions and consist of the following :

(a) Haematuria : Due to infection in urinary tract, kidney stone or tumour, blood is passed along with urine.

(b) Glycosuria : In this situation, excess glucose is passed with urine. It is found in individuals suffering from diabetes.

(c) Albumin : It is found when an individual is suffering from high blood pressure or when the bacterial infection increases the permeability of Bowman's capsule.

(d) Bile pigments : It is found in the urine of an individual suffering from *anaemia* or *hepatitis* or *liver cirrhosis*.

(e) Pus cells : Presence of pus cells in urine is called pyuria.

(f) Ketone bodies : Presence of abnormally high ketone bodies in urine is called ketonuria.

Physical properties of urine :

(a) Colour : Typically yellow-amber, but varies according to recent diet and the concentration of the urine.

(b) Smell : Generally fresh urine has a mild smell but aged urine has a stronger odour similar to that of ammonia.

(c) Acidity : The pH of normal urine is generally in the range 4.6–8.0, with a typical average being around 6.0. Much of the variation occurs due to diet. For example, high protein diets result in more acidic urine, but vegetarian diets generally result in more alkaline urine (both within the typical range of 4.6 – 8).

(d) Density : The density of normal urine ranges from 0.001 to 0.035.

(e) Volume : 1 to 1.5 litres per day but varies.

(f) Taste of urine : Normally, salty in taste.

It is sweetish in taste in individuals suffering from sugar diabetes whereas it is tasteless due to presence of water in more quantity.

8.7. REGULATION OF URINE OUTPUT

Anti–diuretic hormone (ADH) which is secreted by the posterior lobe of the pituitary gland regulates the concentration of urine by water reabsorption. Hypo-secretion of ADH leads to an increase in urine output. This condition is known as Diuresis and the substances that increase urine formation are called *diuretics*.

PROGRESS CHECK

NAME THE FOLLOWING

1. A hollow cup like structure of nephron.
2. Artery which brings deoxygenated blood.
3. Arteriole that supplies blood to the Bowman's capsule.
4. Expulsion of urine from the bladder along the urethra.

8.8. FUNCTIONS OF KIDNEYS

Given below are the functions performed by the kidney :

(a) Excretion : It removes the following from the body :

(i) Nitrogenous metabolic waste
(ii) Excess salts and vitamins
(iii) Bile pigments
(iv) Excess Water

(b) Osmoregulation : Osmoregulation is the process which regulates the concentration and osmotic pressure of blood by regulating the water content of blood plasma. It is an important process as excessive loss of water may cause dehydration whereas excess of water intake may dilute the body fluids.

Animation for Excretory System
  https://www.youtube.com/watch?v=lfGYd1wrTgE
  https://www.youtube.com/watch?v=XF_lF3J4ZKs

The vertebrate kidney is extremely flexible in its working. It excretes large amount of hypotonic urine when water intake is very high, while it excretes small amount of hypertonic urine when water is deficient and needs to be conserved.

(c) Regulates the pH value of the blood by modifying the rate at which the acid or alkaline phosphates are secreted. Apart from this, kidneys maintain proper amount of salt in the body, maintain homeostasis, produces erythropoietia which stimulates the production of RBCs.

8.9. MISCELLANEOUS USEFUL INFORMATION

One can lead a normal life even if one of the kidneys fails to function properly. However, failure of both kidneys can be fatal. In such cases, the patient has to resort to Dialysis. During dialysis, patient's blood is passed through the dialysis machine via radial artery in the arm in order to remove the excess salts and urea to purify the blood. This purified blood is then returned to the vein in the same arm. Patient is subjected to dialysis for about twelve hours twice a week in case of permanent failure of both kidneys.

EXCRETORY SYSTEM

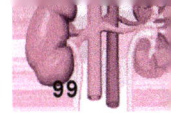

EXERCISE

A. VERY SHORT ANSWER TYPE

(I) Multiple Choice Questions

1. Outer region of the kidney containing Bowman's capsule is the :
   (a) Glomerulus
   (b) Proximal Convoluted Tubule
   (c) Loop of Henle
   (d) Distal Convoluted Tube

2. Which of the following organs removes bile pigments from the body?
   (a) Kidney
   (b) Skin
   (c) Lungs
   (d) Liver

3. Which of the following is impermeable in nature?
   (a) Loop of Henle
   (b) Glomerulus
   (c) Proximal Convoluted Tubule
   (d) Distal Convoluted Tubule

4. Which of the following is NOT excreted by kidney?
   (a) Nitrogenous metabolic wastes
   (b) Excess salts and vitamins
   (c) Excess water
   (d) Bile pigments

5. Urea is transported by :
   (a) Plasma
   (b) Blood
   (c) RBC
   (d) WBC

6. The kidneys resemble the contractile vacuoles of amoeba in :
   (a) Expulsion of excess water
   (b) Expulsion of glucose
   (c) Expulsion of urea and uric acid
   (d) Expulsion of salts

7. Glucose is reabsorbed in the kidney mainly by :
   (a) Bowman's capsule
   (b) Loop of Henle
   (c) Proximal Convoluted Tubule
   (d) Distal Convoluted Tubule

8. In the kidneys of mammals, Loop of Henle can be found in :
   (a) Medulla
   (b) Cortex
   (c) Pelvis
   (d) Pyramid

9. In the kidney the correct sequence of formation of urine involves the following processes :
   (a) Glomerular filtration, reabsorption, tubular secretion
   (b) Reabsorption, filtration, secretion
   (c) Filtration, secretion, reabsorption
   (d) Reabsorption, secretion, filtration

10. The function of the mammalian kidney is to excrete :
    (a) Excess salts, urea and excess water
    (b) Extra urea, excess water and excess amino acids
    (c) Extra urea, extra carbohydrates and extra water
    (d) Extra urea, extra salts and extra sugar

(II) Name the Following

1. The part of uriniferous tubule that consists of elements of Henle's loop and the collecting tubules.
2. The organic constituent of urine which is found in abundance.
3. The hormone that regulates the output of urine by the method of water reabsorption.
4. The capillary net around the renal tubule.
5. Substances excreted by kidney.
6. Functional unit of kidney.

B. SHORT ANSWER TYPE

1. Name an organ in the human body, other than the kidney, in which excretion takes place.
2. Filtration is an essential process in the formation of urine. In what part of the kidney does it take place?
3. Why is glucose normally absent from urine?
4. Where does filtration of blood take place within the kidney?
5. Where in the kidney is Bowman's capsule located?
6. Underline the area[s] of the kidney in which re-absorption takes place:
   Cortex, medulla, pelvis.
7. Suggest a treatment that may be used for a person whose kidneys are not carrying out their normal functions.

C. LONG ANSWER TYPE

1. Define excretion. Also list the substances that are excreted out from the body.
2. Explain the term dialysis in detail.
3. State the function of :
   (a) Loop of Henle
   (b) Sweat glands
   (c) Collecting tubule
4. Explain the term Ultrafiltration in detail.

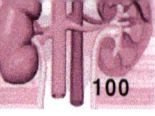

5. Explain tubular reabsorption and tubular secretion.
6. Explain the functions performed by Kidney.
7. A sample of urine was found to contain glucose. Would you consider this to be normal? Explain your answer.
8. Explain how one can lead a normal life if both the kidneys fail?

(I) Give Reason(s)

1. Frequency of urination is generally more in winter than in summer.
2. We feel thirstier in summer than in winter.
3. On a cool and wet day, a large quantity of dilute urine is passed out by most people.
4. Following a period of heavy exercise an athlete may produce only a small volume of concentrated urine.

(II) Draw Labelled Diagrams of the Following

1. Excretory system in man.
2. Nephron.
3. L.S. of human kidney.

D. STRUCTURED/APPLICATION BASED

1. Given along side is the figure of certain organs and associated parts in the human body. Study the same and then answer the questions that follow :
   (a) Name all the organ system shown completely or even partially.
   (b) Name the parts numbered 1 to 5.
   (c) Name the structure and functional unit of the part marked '1'.
   (d) Name the two main organic constitutes of the find that flows down the part labelled '3'.
   (e) Name the two major steps involved in the formation of the fluid that passes down the part labelled '3'.

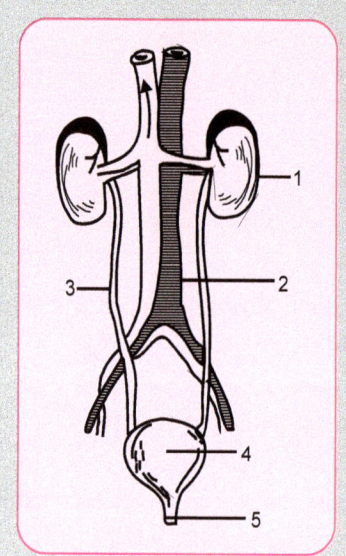

DO YOU KNOW?

- Your blood passes through the kidneys 300 times a day.
- A normal kidney contains 800,000 to 1.5 million nephrons.
- The nephrons clean all your blood in 45 minutes.
- Every day the nephrons send about six cups of urine to the bladder.
- We lose 1 litre of water by breathing and sweating.

9

NERVOUS SYSTEM

CHAPTER HIGHLIGHTS

9.1. Nervous System
9.2. Nerve Cell or Neurons—Unit of Nervous System
9.3. Major Divisions of Nervous System
9.4. Nerve Impulse and its Transmission
9.5. Central Nervous System (CNS)
    9.5.1. The Human Brain
    9.5.2. Brain Matter
    9.5.3. Parts of the Brain
9.6. Spinal Cord
9.7. Reflex arc and Reflex Action
9.8. Mechanism of Reflex Action
9.9. Reflexes
9.10. Peripheral Nervous System
    9.10.1. Somatic Nervous System
    9.10.2. Autonomic Nervous System
9.11. Sense Organs
9.12. The Eye and the Sense of Light
9.13. Structure of the Eyeball
9.14. Lens
9.15. Image Formation
9.16. Common Defects of the Eye and their Correction
9.17. Ear–The Organ of Hearing and Balance
9.18. Coochlea
9.19. Mechanism of Hearing and Balance
    9.19.1. Hearing Mechanism
    9.19.2. Balancing
9.20. Tongue and the Sense of Taste
9.21. Nose and Sense of Smell
9.22. Skin Receptors

We perform many activities consciously or unconsciously. When we eat our eyes help to locate the food, the nose smells it, hands bring the food to the mouth which masticates the food, teeth chew and the tongue helps to move the food into the digestive system. All these activities need to happen in a coordinated manner. The organ system in our body that helps in coordination and integration of body activities is the nervous system. The nervous system evolved as a means to sense and respond with absolute precision to changing conditions inside and outside the body. The information has to be exchanged between cells distant from each other, information about changes in the external environment has to be received and then transmitted to the cells situated far away in the body.

For control and coordination of the body, two types of systems have been developed in animals. These are :

(a) Nervous system : This system is made up of nerves which act by sending electrical signals as nerve impulses (Fig. 9.1). It is speedy and flexible to control. This system enables the organism to react accordingly to these changes. The changes in the environment are called stimuli and the organs which are associated to detect them are called receptors or sense organs. The reaction shown by a living organism is called response.

(b) Endocrine system : This system consists of ductless glands which control and coordinate the body by releasing chemical messengers, termed hormones, directly into the blood.

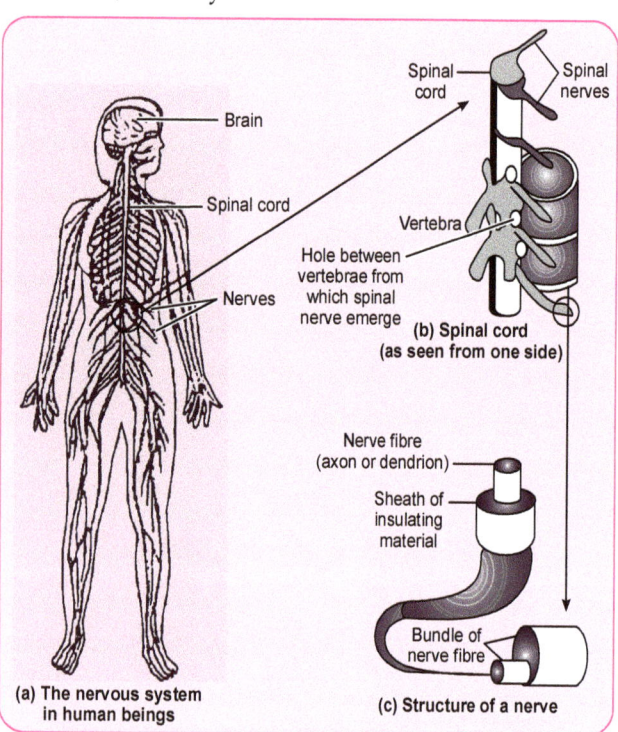

Fig. 9.1 : Structure of the human nervous system

9.1. NERVOUS SYSTEM

Nervous system is the main coordinating and integrating system of body activities.

Why is nervous system needed?

(a) Receiving external stimuli : It receives information of changes in the external environment by means of sense organs.

(b) Proper response : It initiates proper response to the external stimuli by the sense organs and carries them to the effector organs.

(c) Coordination : The nervous system conducts information and messages between different parts of the body. Thus it helps in coordination.

(d) Memory preservation and future guidance : It retains the previous responses as memory and uses these in interpreting and guiding future information.

(e) Internal coordination and homeostasis : It helps in maintaining the body balance by perceiving and responding to stimuli.

9.2. NERVE CELL OR NEURON—UNIT OF THE NERVOUS SYSTEM

The structural and functional unit of the nervous system is a highly specialized cell called the *nerve cell* or *neuron*. Each neuron consists of three principal parts (Fig. 9.2) :

(a) Cell body or cyton, (b) Dendrites, (c) Axon.

(a) Cell body (cyton or perikaryon) : The cell body has a large, central nucleus surrounded by granular cytoplasm. In the cytoplasm (also called neuro-plasm), *nissl granules* and *neurofibrils* are present. Cell organs like mitochondria, golgi apparatus, endoplasmic reticulum, microfilaments and microtubules are also present in the cytoplasm. There is no centrosome in the cyton because the nerve cells have lost the ability to divide.

(b) Dendrites : Several short, thread like branches called *dendrites* arise from the cell body. The dendrites conduct nerve impulses to the cyton.

(c) Axon : One of the branches grows very long in comparison to others. This branch is called the axon. The axon is covered by three layers :

 (i) Axolemma (the innermost layer).
 (ii) Myelin sheath or medullary sheath (the middle layer) shows gaps called Nodes of Ranvier throughout its length and has glistening appearance.
 (iii) Neurolemma the outermost white isolating sheath surrounding the axon.

The axolemma and neurolemma are continuous sheaths, whereas myelin sheath is not a continuous one. It is constricted at intervals. These constrictions are known as *nodes of ranvier*. The axon ends have swollen bulb-like ends which store *acetylcholine* (a neurotransmitter). These are called axon endings. Axon endings are closely placed near the dendrites of another neuron but are not connected to them. These gaps are called *synaptic clefts* or *synapses*.

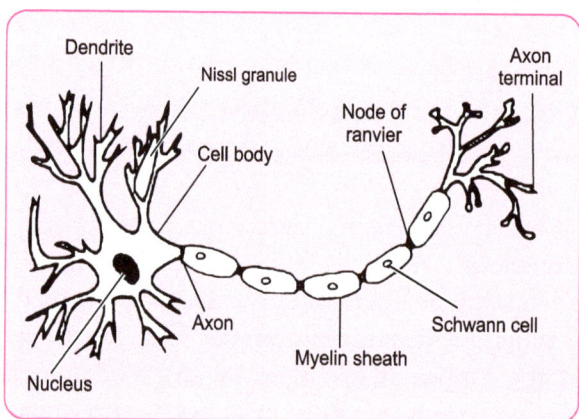

Fig. 9.2 : A generalized structure of a nerve cell or neuron

Major divisions of nervous system : The nervous system (Fig. 9.3) in human beings is divided into two main parts :

(a) Central nervous system.

(b) Peripheral nervous system.

The *central nervous system (CNS)* includes the brain and the spinal cord and is the site of information processing in the nervous system.

The *peripheral nervous system (PNS)* consists of nerves that coordinate between the CNS and different parts of the body. These nerves are divided into three groups :

(i) Sensory or afferent nerves : They carry sensory impulses from the sense organs to the central nervous system, e.g. the optic nerve arising from the eye and ending in the brain.

(ii) Motor or efferent nerves : These nerves carry messages from CNS to the effector organs like muscles or glands, e.g. nerve arising from brain and supplying the muscles of eyeball to rotate the eye.

(iii) Mixed nerves or association nerves : They connect sensory and motor nerves and process the sensory impulses coming from sensory nerves and pass them on to the motor nerves. Example: Spinal nerve.

The Peripheral Nervous System (PNS) consists of two subdivisions :

(i) Somatic nervous system : The somatic nervous system regulates voluntary activities and takes messages to the skeletal muscles.

(ii) Autonomic nervous system : The autonomic nervous system (ANS) though connected to the central nervous system (CNS), works somewhat independently to regulate involuntary activities. It has nerves and ganglia which connect the visceral organs and perform a variety of functions that are not under our control. It has two components :

(i) Sympathetic Nervous System (SNS)

(ii) Parasympathetic Nervous System (PSNS)

These two systems are antagonistic (opposite in function to each other).

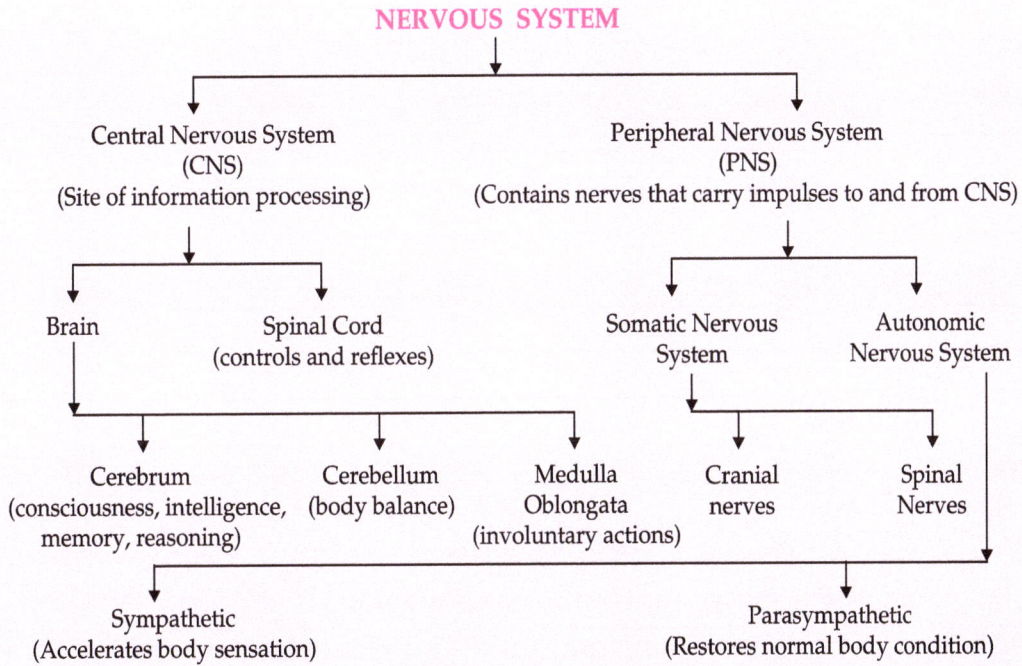

Fig. 9.3 : Organisation of the nervous system in human beings

9.4. NERVE IMPULSE AND ITS TRANSMISSION

The brain and spinal cord serve to coordinate information received as messages called *nerve impulses*.

A *nerve impulse* is an electrochemical charge that moves along a neuron to the next neuron in the series. The movement of the impulse is unidirectional. At one end, neuron is connected to a sensory receptor that receives the stimulus and converts it into electrochemical waves which are carried by the neuron. The fibre at this stage is said to *be excited*.

The events that take place during the conduction of an impulse along a nerve are described below:

(a) At resting stage–polarised state : At normal (resting stage) the outer side of nerve fibres carry more positive (+) charge due to more Na^+ ions outside the axon membranes. This is called *polarized* state (Fig. 9.4).

(b) At stimulated (excited) state-depolarisation : On receipt of a stimulus, the axon membrane at the place of stimulus becomes more permeable to Na^+

ions and as a result the Na⁺ move inside causing loss of polarity or *depolarization*. This region, thus becomes excited region. The region of depolarization moves forward to next area which in turn becomes *depolarized* (Fig. 9.5).

(c) Returning to normal state–repolarization : The previous area (which has received stimulus) becomes repolarized due to active transport of Na⁺ ions outside. This transport is achieved by 'Na pump' for which energy in the form of ATP is required. Thus conduction of nerve impulse is a wave of depolarization followed by *repolarisation* (Fig. 9.6).

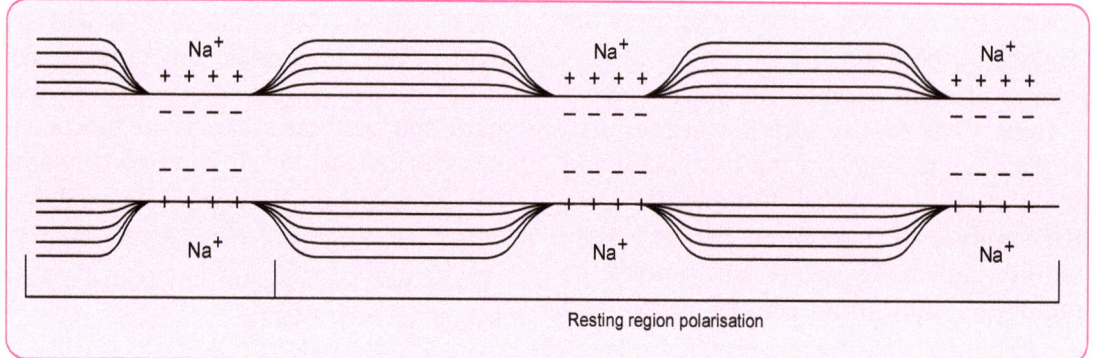

Fig. 9.4 : Resting region polarization

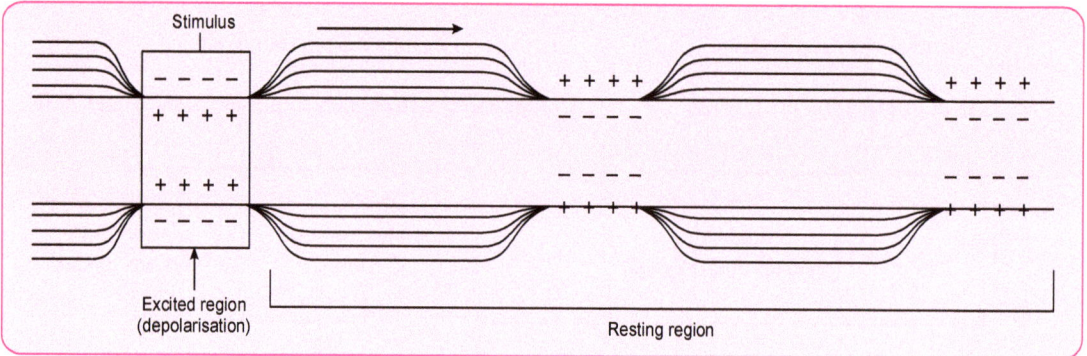

Fig. 9.5 : Excited region depolarization

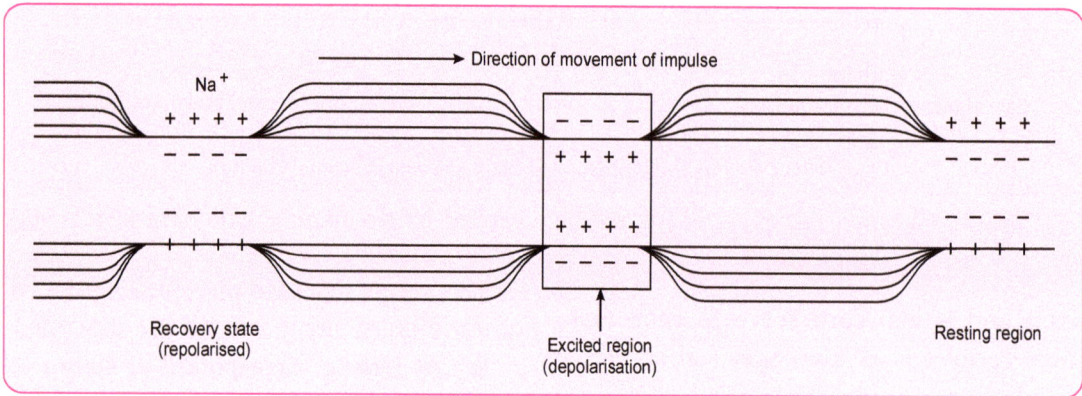

Fig. 9.6 : Repolarization

Chemical transmission of impulse at synapse : When an impulse arrives at a synapse, the chemical *acetylcholine* is released from the presynaptic bulb. It diffuses across the synaptic cleft and enters the dendrite endings and then initiates a new wave of *depolarization*.

PROGRESS CHECK

ANSWER THE FOLLOWING QUESTIONS

1. Name the nerves transmitting impulse to brain and spinal cord.
2. What is a synapse?
3. Define myelin sheath.
4. What are the functional units of nervous system?
5. Name the innermost layer of axon.
6. Name the receptor in the neuron.
7. Name the chemical in synapse.
8. Define Nodes of Ranvier.
9. What do you understand by polarized state?
10. Define mixed nerves. Give one example.

9.5. CENTRAL NERVOUS SYSTEM (CNS)

The central nervous system consists of the brain and the spinal cord.

9.5.1. The Human Brain

The human brain is highly developed and is situated in the cranium (brain box) of the skull. In an adult it weighs about 1.2 to 1.4 kg and is about 2% of the body weight. Approximately 80% of the brain is water and it consumes about 25% of the total requirement of oxygen of the body. The cranium protects the brain from injury.

The brain is covered on the outside by three membranes called meninges which continue backwards on the spinal cord. These meninges are:

(a) Duramater : The outer tough, protective layer is formed of fibrous tissue and is called *Duramater*.

(b) Arachnoid : Middle delicate membrane which gives the brain a web-like cushion.

(c) Pia mater : The inner thin transparent membrane, richly supplied with blood vessels.

Watery fluid which fills the space between meninges and also brain is cerebrospinal fluid. It acts like a cushion to protect brain from shocks.

The intervening space between the membranes is filled with a watery fluid called *cerebrospinal fluid* which cushions the brain from shocks.

9.5.2. Brain Matter

The nervous matter composing the brain is differentiated into :

(a) Gray matter forms the surface layer of the brain. It is formed of cell bodies of neurons.

(b) White matter lies on the inner side. It is formed of white *myelinated axons* of neurons that form nerve fibres.

9.5.3. Parts of the Brain

Human brain is divisible into three major parts (Fig. 9.7) : (a) Forebrain, (b) Midbrain, (c) Hind brain

(a) Forebrain : It is the anterior region of the brain. It has following parts:

(i) Cerebrum (governs intelligence, memory, consciousness and voluntary action).

(ii) Diencephalon (controls endocrine system mainly thalamus, hypothalamus, pineal gland).

(i) Cerebrum : It is the main part of forebrain.

(1) Cerebrum is the largest and the most prominent part of the brain. It is divided into right and left cerebral hemispheres.

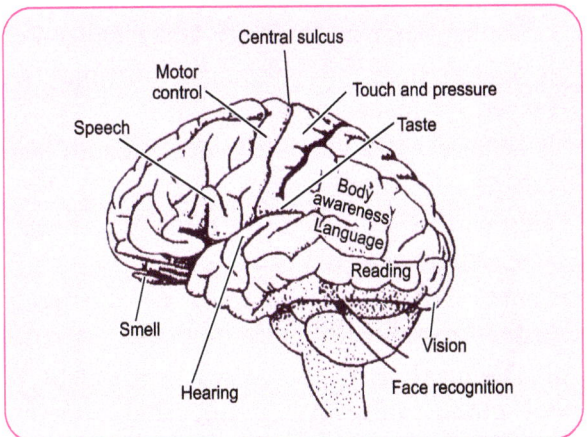

Fig. 9.7 : Parts of the Human Brain

(2) The two hemispheres are connected by a thick band of nerve fibres called corpus callosum

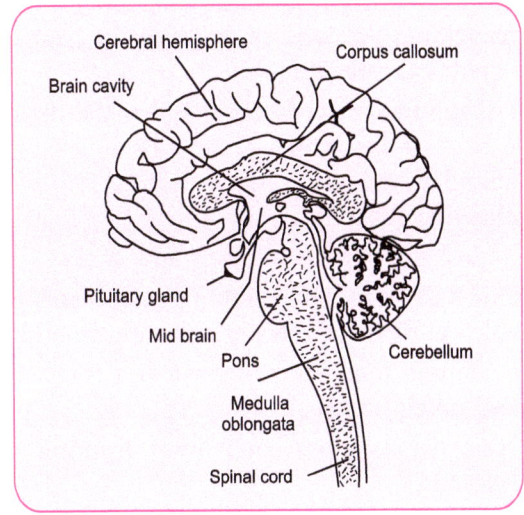

Fig. 9.8 : Brain in medial section

which helps in the transfer of information from one hemisphere to another (Fig. 9.8).

(3) Each hemisphere is hollow and its walls have two regions; outer cortex and inner region called *medulla*. Outer layer of cerebrum is cerebral cortex. It contains cell bodies of neurons and being grayish in colour, is called *gray matter*.

(4) It is convoluted and extensively covered with ridges and grooves. Ridges of these convolutions are called gyri and depressions are called sulci. These convolutions increase the surface area to accommodate more nerve cells.

(5) The number and pattern of convolutions are associated with the degree of intelligence.

(6) Inner region of cerebrum consists of white matter that has axons of nerve cells.

Functions
- Because of highly developed grey matter (cortex) it governs mental abilities like thinking, reasoning, learning, memory and intelligence.
- It also controls all voluntary functions, will power, emotions, speech.
- It enables us to observe things through sense organs.
- This part of the brain also controls feelings of love, admiration, hatred.
- Centres for subconscious mind are also located in the cerebrum.

(ii) Diencephalon : It mainly consists of the pineal gland, pituitary gland, thalamus and hypothalamus.

(1) Thalamus : It consists of two large ovoid masses and serves as a relay centre for sensory and motor impulses from spinal cord and medulla to various parts of the cerebrum. It regulates emotions and recognizes the sensory impulses of heat, cold, pain, light and pressure.

(2) Hypothalamus : Located below the thalamus at the base of the brain. It contains reflex centres for muscular and glandular activities. It performs the following function :
- Control the pattern of sleep and stress.
- Regulates hormonal secretions of pituitary gland which in turn controls various endocrine glands.
- It controls food intake, thirst and body temp. (thermoregulation).
- Optic nerves cross each other forming optic chiasma.

(b) Mid brain : It is a thick walled structure and constitutes a comparatively smaller portion of the brain. The midbrain or mesencephalon connects the anterior region of the brain to the posterior region and therefore all nerve fibres pass through this region. It also has four optic lobes which are centers of vision. It serves as a relay centre for auditory information to the thalamus.

(c) Hind brain : Hind brain has three main parts :

(i) Cerebellum (ii) Pons   (iii) Medulla oblongata

(i) Cerebellum : (Little brain)
(1) The cerebellum is situated in the dorsal region of the hind brain. Cerebellum is a much smaller area and is located at the base under cerebrum.
(2) There are no convolutions, but many furrows.
(3) It has an outer cortex made of gray matter and an inner section consisting of white matter.

Functions
- It maintains body balance and controls muscular activities.
- It makes the body movements smooth, steady and coordinated.
- It regulates and coordinates contraction of skeletal muscles. Proper coordination and timing of muscle contraction and relaxation is the responsibility of the cerebellum.

(ii) Pons : Pons forms the brain stem at the floor of hindbrain. It is in the form of a bridge of transverse nerve tracts extending from the cerebrum to the cerebellum. The Pons also connects the forebrain to the spinal cord.

(iii) Medulla oblongata : It is the third main part of the hind brain and is located at the base of the skull and is the lowermost part of the brain. It is continued as spinal cord in posterior region.

Functions
- It contains cardiac centre, respiratory centre, centres for swallowing, sneezing, coughing and vomiting.
- It controls involuntary functions like heart-beat, swallowing and breathing.

Cerebrum, cerebellum and medulla oblongata are the parts of the brain that are visible externally. Corpus callosum, thalamus and the hypothalamus are not superficially visible.

9.6. SPINAL CORD

Spinal cord is the posterior extension of the medulla oblongata running along the vertebral column. It is enclosed in a neural canal of vertebral column. In an adult human it is 42.45 cm long and 2 cm thick. It is a soft, whitish, slightly flattened, cylindrical tube with a narrow cavity called central canal. Like brain it is also protected by the *meninges, cerebrospinal fluid* and a cushion of *adipose tissue*.

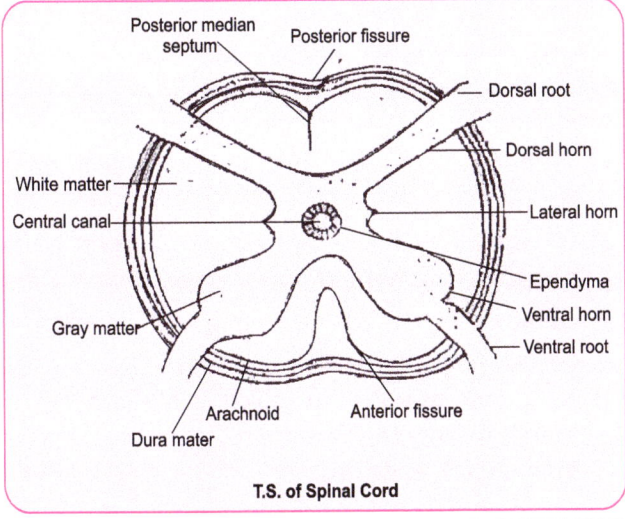

Fig. 9.9 : T.S. of spinal cord

In a transverse section of spinal cord (Fig. 9.9), the central canal can be clearly seen. This canal is filled with cerebrospinal fluid. Surrounding the canal are clusters of cytons which form the gray matter. In the peripheral part axons are concentrated and this area is called the white matter.

On each side of the spinal cord there are two horns, the dorsal and the ventral horn. A nerve joined to the dorsal horn picks up sensations from various organs. It is called the sensory nerve. From the ventral horn or root arises the motor nerve which takes the messages from spinal cord to the organs concerned.

Functions

- The spinal cord conducts, reflexes below the neck.
- It conducts sensory impulses from skin and muscles to the brain.
- It conducts motor responses from brain to the muscles of trunk and limbs.

9.7. REFLEX ARC AND REFLEX ACTION

There are certain body responses which are immediate and do not require any processing by the brain. These responses or actions are controlled by the spinal cord. These are called *reflex actions*.

A reflex action is defined as a spontaneous, automatic and mechanical response to a stimulus controlled by the spinal cord without involvement of the brain.

The pathway followed by sensory and motor nerves in a *reflex action* is called the *reflex* arc.

Components of a reflex arc : A reflex arc has four main components :

(a) *Receptor* or *sense organs* to perceive the stimulus.

(b) *Sensory* or *afferent nerve* that carries the message from receptor to the spinal cord.

(c) *Relay* or *association neurons* which transmit impulses from the afferent neurons to the efferent (motor) neurons.

(d) *Motor* or *efferent nerve* which carries the message from the spinal cord to the muscles or glands (effector organ).

9.8. MECHANISM OF REFLEX ACTION

If your finger touches a hot object, you withdraw your finger immediately. How does this happen?

The entire sequence of events that constitute a reflex arc are summarized as follows :

Thermal receptors in the skin of finger perceive the stimulus.
↓
It generates an electric impulse.
↓
Impulse is carried along by sensory neurons towards the spinal cord.
↓
Impulse travels through spinal nerves towards the spinal cord along the dorsal root.
↓
Impulse arrives at the nerve endings of sensory neurons in gray matter of the spinal cord.
↓
Nerve endings release neurotransmitters. This impulse passes across the relay or association neuron to the motor neuron.

> ↓
> Impulse travels along motor neurons away from the spinal cord along the ventral root.
> ↓
> The nerve endings of motor neuron then connect the biceps muscles of arms, which contract, pulling away the hand.
> ↓
> And the response is shown by hand by removing the finger.

9.9. REFLEXES

There are two types of actions :
(a) Voluntary actions and (b) involuntary actions

(a) Voluntary actions : These are actions which are performed consciously. For example, if you wish to play, or switch on T.V. to watch some programme. These are termed voluntary actions.

(b) Involuntary actions : Actions which occur unknowingly without our will. All involuntary actions are reflexes and involve some kind of sensory stimulation, e.g. immediate withdrawal of hand if it touches a hot iron.

Types of reflexes : There are two types of reflexes :
(i) Simple or natural reflexes.
(ii) Conditioned or acquired reflexes.

(i) Simple or natural reflexes : In this type of reflex, the brain is not involved. The receptor is stimulated which is conducted to the spinal cord by the affector. The effector neuron from the spinal cord conducts a response to the muscle or the gland. This causes an immediate reaction. It does not involve any thinking or reasoning. It is a natural response and will occur even in new-born babies. For e.g., blinking of eyes when strong light falls on the eyes. These are reflexes which do not require any previous learning experience. Such reflexes are inborn and inherited from parents.

Examples
(1) Withdrawal of leg if one suddenly steps on a nail.
(2) Closing of eyelid in response to a strong beam of light being flashed on the eyes.
(3) Blinking of eyelids in response to a foreign particle that approaches the eye.
(4) Knee jerk response in which if a sharp tap is made below the knee cap, then the leg is involuntary extended.
(5) Removal of hand if it touches a hot object.
(6) Peristaltic reflex to allow movement of food in the digestive tract.

(ii) Conditioned or acquired reflexes : These are the reflexes which develop due to some previous experience or training. They are not inborn and result due to some learning in one's life time.

Examples
(1) Watering of mouth (salivation) at the sight of tasty food.
(2) Tying one's shoelace.
(3) Applying brakes of your cycle when someone comes in front.
(4) Typing on the keyboard of a computer.
(5) Playing a musical instrument.

PROGRESS CHECK

ANSWER THE FOLLOWING QUESTIONS

1. What are the functions of cerebrospinal fluid?
2. Write the functions of spinal cord.
3. Why a person can die due to an injury to the medulla oblongata?
4. Define association neurons. What are their functions?
5. How are gyri and sulci related to intelligence?
6. Name the parts of hind brain.
7. Define corpus callosum.
8. Given below are some sensory capabilities of human brain. Name the parts of the brain governing these -

Sensory capability	Part of the brain
1. Memorizing	—
2. Thermoregulation	—
3. Body posture	—
4. Intelligence	—
5. Swallowing and coughing	—

9. A person received a serious blow to the head but appeared to be alright. However, after a few weeks, he developed loss of memory, will power and emotions, but no loss in sensory and motor functions. Which part (s) of the brain do you think may have been damaged?

9.10. PERIPHERAL NERVOUS SYSTEM

The peripheral nervous system (PNS) comprises the nerves that connect the central nervous system with different parts of the body. Peripheral nervous system is divided into two types–*somatic nervous system* and *autonomic nervous system*.

9.10.1. Somatic Nervous System

The somatic nervous system includes both motor neurons and sensory neurons. The fibres of motor and sensory neurons are bundled together into nerves, which are of two types :

(a) *Cranial nerves* connected directly to the brain. Example: Optic nerve (for eye), auditory nerve (for ears), mixed nerves (for face). There are 12 pairs of cranial nerves.

(b) *Spinal nerves* emerge from spinal cord. There are 31 pairs of spinal nerves. Each spinal nerve is a mixed nerve having both sensory and motor nerves. Of these, 8 pairs are present in the neck region, 12 pairs in the thorax, 5 pairs in the lumbar region, 5 pairs in the sacral region and 1 pair in the coccygeal region.

A typical spinal nerve originates from the spinal cord by means of two roots, a dorsal root and a ventral root.

The somatic nervous system regulates voluntary activities while the autonomic nervous system performs a variety of functions which are not under the control of an individual.

9.10.2. Autonomic Nervous System

The autonomic nervous system includes a chain of 22 pairs of ganglia which lie close to the spinal cord and are associated with the organs they control. ANS is a motor system consisting of neurons that control the functioning of many organs namely (Fig. 9.10) :

(a) Heart muscles

(b) Glands

(c) Smooth muscles (muscles of blood vessels, digestive, respiratory and reproductive tracts).

The ANS can stimulate or inhibit the activity of its target organs. The two divisions of ANS are the sympathetic nervous system and parasym-pathetic nervous system. The two systems are different in structure and function. The two systems send signals to the same organs but have opposite effect on their action, so they can be said to be antagonistic to each other in their function.

In general, sympathetic nervous system prepares the body for violent actions against unusual conditions. It is stimulated by the hormone adrenaline secreted by adrenal gland. Sympathetic response includes increased heart rate, diversion of blood flow away from the digestive system to arms and legs and extra glucose supply to muscles and nervous tissue where extra energy is needed.

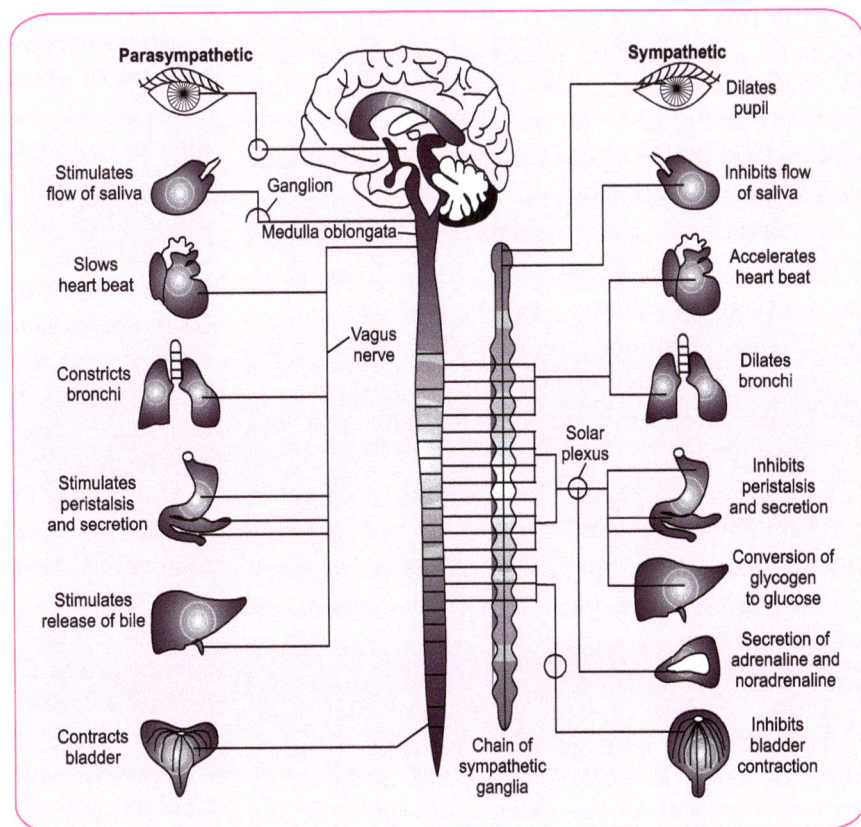

Fig. 9.10 : Autonomic nervous system showing sympathetic and parasympathetic nerves

Parasympathetic nervous system has inhibitory or calming effect on the body. This system stimulates smooth muscle contraction, increases intestinal motility and glandular secretions like salivation, gastric secretion etc.

PROGRESS CHECK

ANSWER THE FOLLOWING QUESTIONS

1. Define peripheral nervous system.
2. Differentiate between peripheral and central nervous system.
3. Name the various organs controlled by the autonomic nervous system.
4. Write the effect of sympathetic system on heartbeat, urinary bladder and absorption of food.
5. How does parasympathetic system work?

9.11. SENSE ORGANS

All living organisms respond to external or internal physical and chemical stimuli. We have special cells called receptors which receive stimuli from the environment. Eyes, ears, tongue, nose and skin are the major sense organs which are sensitive to light, sound, taste, smell and touch respectively. Each of these sense organs is directly connected with the brain.

SOME KEY TERMS

Stimulus : A physical event that affects an organism and excites the receptors to bring a change in the activity. Example, mechanical stimulus, (preserve and touch), chemical stimulus (taste, smell) and thermal (heat, cold). **Sensation :** A general state of awareness of stimulus.

Receptors : It is any specialized tissue or cell sensitive to a specific stimulus.

(a) **Mechano receptors :** respond to touch.
(b) **Chemo receptors :** receptors for taste of the tongue and smell of nose.
(c) **Photo receptors :** respond to light rods and cones in eye.
(d) **Thermo receptors :** respond to change in temperature of skin.
(e) **Exteroceptors :** specialized to detect sensory information from the external environment.

9.12. THE EYE AND THE SENSE OF LIGHT

Vision or sense of sight is the most vital of all body senses. We all respond to the light stimulus. Human beings have two eyes situated in the orbits on the front side of the head. Each eye is in the form of a ball called eyeball which measures about 2.5 cm in diameter. Each eyeball can be rotated with the help of six distinct sets of muscles.

Accessory structures of the eye

(a) **Eyebrows :** These are two arched and raised portions of skin above the eyes. They are thickly covered with coarse hair and are richly supplied with sebaceous glands. They protect the eye from *perspiration* and direct sunrays.

(b) **Eyelids :** They are folds of skin and muscles. The upper and lower eyelids have many important functions. They protect the eyes from excessive light and foreign particles, cover the eye during sleep and spread lubricating secretions over the eyeballs. The upper eyelid is more movable than the lower.

(c) **Eyelashes :** Each eye carries outwardly curved eyelashes. They prevent falling of particles into the eyes.

(d) **Sebaceous glands :** At the base of hair follicles of eyelashes are found sebaceous glands. These glands secrete a lubricating fluid into the hair follicles called *sebum*.

(d) **Lacrimal glands or tear glands :** These are a group of glands that manufacture and pour tears. A lacrimal gland is a compound gland located at the upper sideward portion of each eyelid (Fig. 9.11). Each *lacrimal gland* gives rise to 6 to 12 excretory lacrimal ducts which empty their secretion onto the surface of conjunctiva. From here, it passes to lacrimal canals and then into the lacrimal duct. From there a *nasolacrimal duct*

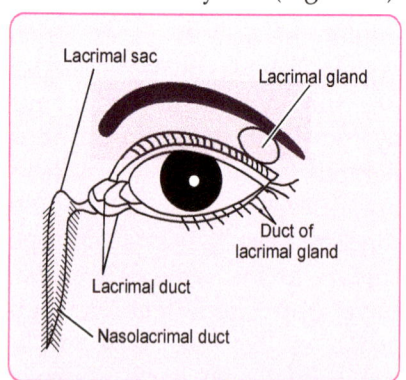

Fig. 9.11 : Location of lacrimal gland

conducts the secretion into the nasal cavity in the nose.

Tear or *lacrimal secretion* is a watery fluid containing salts, some mucus and a bactericidal enzyme called *lysozyme*. After being secreted it spreads over the surface of the eyeball and serves as a lubricant. It also cleans the front surface of the eyeball by washing away the dust particles. It also moistens the eyeball. The enzyme *lysozyme* contained in the tears kills the germs also. Tears also help in communicating emotions.

9.13. STRUCTURE OF THE EYEBALL

Eyeball is nearly spherical structure measuring about 2.5 cm in diameter. Only the front one-sixth of the eyeball remains exposed and the rest is enclosed in the orbit. Eyeball can be compared with a camera. Eyeball is composed of three layers: the outer sclerotic layer, the middle choroid and inner retina (Fig. 9.12).

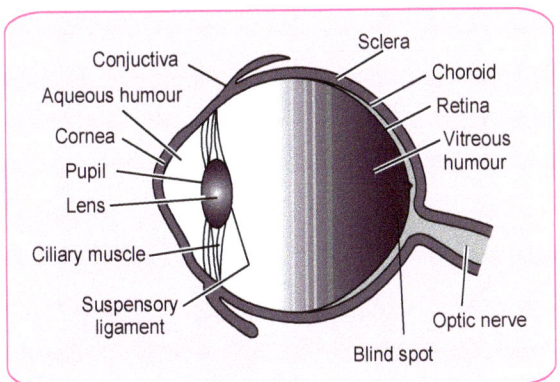

Fig. 9.12 : Vertical section of the human eye

(a) The sclerotic layer : Sclerotic layer or sclera is the outer tough coat of the eyeball made up mainly of collagen fibres. It can be divided into two regions. The posterior region called *sclera*, and the anterior region called *cornea*.

The *sclera* is a white coat of dense fibrous tissue that covers the entire eyeball except the cornea. It is also known as the white of the eye. The Sclera gives shape to the eyeball and also protects its inner parts.

The *cornea* is a transparent, fibrous coat through which the iris can be seen. The outer surface of the cornea is covered by an epithelial layer which is continuous with the epithelial layer of conjuctiva. The cornea receives nourishment from tears and aqueous humour.

(b) The choroid layer or ulva : The choroid layer is the middle layer of the eyeball and is composed of three parts–choroid, ciliary body and iris.

The choroid is a thin, dark brown membrane that lines most of the inner surface of the sclera. It has several blood vessels and a large amount of pigment. The choroid absorbs light rays so they are not reflected into the eyeball. The numerous blood vessels nourish the retina.

Iris and ciliary body : Behind the cornea, the choroid layer is modified to form iris and ciliary body.

Iris : It is a circular opaque disc of coloured tissue. It is the continuation of choroid and lies between lens and cornea. It has inner circular and outer radial muscles. These are arranged around a circular aperture called pupil. The light enters the eyeball through the pupil. The size of pupil is regulated by the muscles of iris so as to regulate the amount of light entering the eyeball.

In case of dim light : Radial muscles contract and the circular muscles relax. Hence, pupil becomes large and more light enters the eye (dilation).

In case of bright light : Circular muscles contract and radial muscles relax. Therefore, pupil becomes narrow and less light enters the eye (constriction).

Ciliary body : Along the margin of iris, choroid forms a ring like ciliary body. It is formed of smooth ciliary muscles having circular, radial and oblique fibres. Ciliary body forms ciliary processes into the eyeball.

(c) The retina : Retina is the third inner layer of the eye. It is located only in the posterior part of the eye. It is the light sensitive layer. It contains light sensitive cells called *rods* and *cones*.

The *Rod cells* are sensitive to dim light. They do not respond to colour. Rods contain pigment *rhodopsin* or *visual purple*. The rod cells are distributed throughout the retina.

The *cone cells* are sensitive to bright light. The cones are responsible for colour vision. Cones contain pigment *iodopsin*. Cone cells are mostly confined to the yellow spot or fovea centralis or macula.

9.14. LENS

The main body of the eye is divided into two parts by a biconvex lens which is a transparent, crystalline body. The lens lies just behind the pupil and iris. It is flatter at the front than at the back and is soft and slightly yellow in colour. It contains transparent lens fibres and an elastic lens capsule made of *glycoprotein*. There is no blood vessel in the lens. The lens is held in position by suspensory ligaments which are attached to the ciliary body.

The eyeball is divided into two cavities: *anterior cavity* (aqueous chamber) and *posterior cavity* (vitreous chamber).

The aqueous chamber is filled with a fluid called the *aqueous humour*. It is a thin and watery fluid. It keeps the lens moist and protects it from physical shock.

The posterior cavity is called the *vitreous chamber*. It is a large cavity. It lies between the lens and the retina. It contains a jelly like substance called the vitreous humour. It prevents the eyeball from collapsing and supports the retina.

Yellow spot and blind spot : Yellow spot is the area of best vision. It is also called the area centralis or fovea centralis. In this region, which lies on the optical axis of eye in retina, the cones are concentrated in centre and rods on the periphery. Because of the highest concentration of cones in humans, it is the region of highest visual activity. The image formed in this region is the brightest and sharpest.

Blind spot : It is the area of no vision. It is the area in retina below the yellow spot, where optic nerve and blood vessels leave or enter the retina. Because of the total absence of light sensitive rods and cones, it is unable to form an image; hence it is called blind spot.

9.15. IMAGE FORMATION

How do we see or how is image formed interpreted : Human eye works like a camera. The light rays enter the eye through the cornea and then pass through pupil, aqueous humour, the lens and vitreous humour before reaching the retina.

The diameter of the pupil changes to adjust to different intensities of light. In bright light, pupil constricts and in dim light, it becomes wider or dilates to allow more light.

Image formation on the retina : The formation of an image on the retina has four steps :
(a) Refraction of light rays.
(b) Accommodation of the lens.
(c) Convergence of the rays.

(a) Refraction of light rays : The eye focuses an image by refracting or bending the light rays using cornea and the lens. An upside down or inverted image is formed at the yellow spot on the retina. Most of the refraction of light occurs in cornea due to its curved surface.

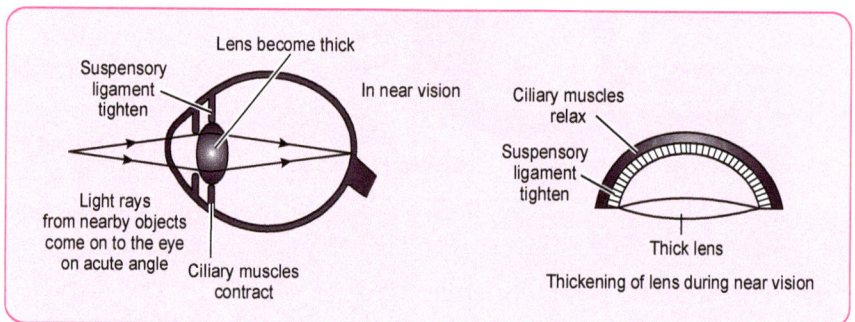

Fig. 9.13 : (a) Image formation on the retina in near vision

(b) Accommodation : In a normal eye, an object at a distance of 6 metres would be in perfect focus on the retina. The process of focussing by the eye at different distances is called *accommodation*. It is brought about by adjusting the curvature of the lens making it thinner or thicker.

In near vision the ciliary muscles contract by pulling the choroid forward towards the lens and tension is released on the suspensory ligaments. The lens becomes shortened, more convex and thickened due to its elastic nature (Fig. 9.13 a).

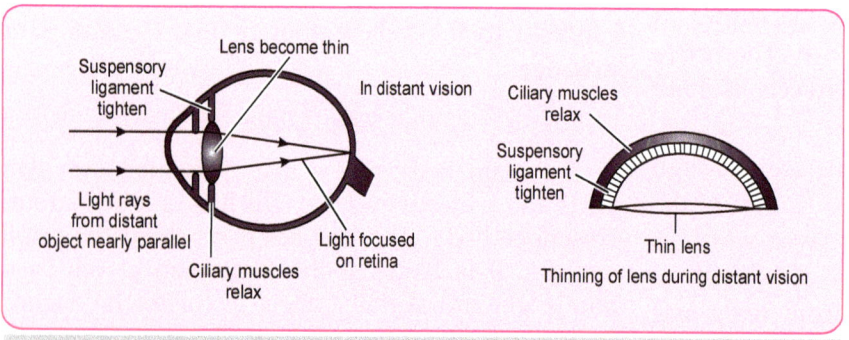

Fig. 9.13 : (b) Image formation on the retina in distant vision

In distant vision, ciliary muscles are relaxed and the lens becomes flatter or thinner due to stretching of the suspensory ligaments (Fig. 9.13 b).

(c) Convergence and binocular vision : We have two eyes but we see only one image of an object. This is known as binocular vision or stereo optic vision. While viewing objects, both eyeballs move towards the object. Thus, both the images fall on the corresponding points of both retinas at the same time and overlap with each other. This is known as convergence or binocular vision.

Photoreception : The image formed at retina stimulates photoreceptors. The light energy of the image formed at retina produces chemical changes in rods and cones which travel through optic nerve and reach the visual area of the cerebrum. At cerebrum the sensation of sight is interpreted.

How are the eyes adapted to bright light and dark?

When we are in a dark or dim light for a long period, then the rate of photo pigments (rhodopsin) formation by the rods is much faster than the rate at which they are broken down. Pupil dilates to allow more light to enter through retina to view objects in dim light. This is called dark adaptation.

When we are in a bright light for a long time, then the rate of rods breaking down is more, and the visual purple of the rods gets bleached, reducing their sensitivity. Further pupil constricts and size of pupil is reduced to reduce the amount of light to enter. This is called *light adaptation*.

9.16. COMMON DEFECTS OF THE EYE AND THEIR CORRECTION

(a) Myopia or short sightedness or near sightedness (Fig. 9.14 (a)) : A short sighted or near sighted person can see near objects clearly but not the distant objects. Image of near object is formed onto the retina but image of distant object is formed in front of retina and is blurred.

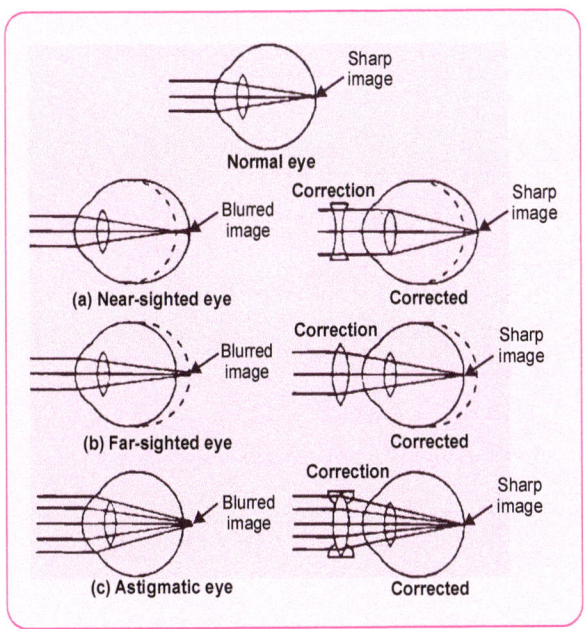

Fig. 9.14 : Image formation on retina in common side effects

Reasons : This defect may be because :
(i) Lens is too thick and convex.
(ii) The eyeball is too long because of dorsoventral flattening or both.

Correction of myopia or near sightedness (Fig. 9.14 (b)) : Myopia can be corrected by using a biconcave lens of appropriate power that diverges the light rays from distant objects before they enter the eye so that a sharp image is formed on the retina. The power of the glass is given as minus.

Long periods of reading, writing work or continuous work on computers can cause ciliary muscles to remain partly contracted and result in short sightedness. They may be inherited from parents also.

(b) Hypermetropia or far sightedness : A far sighted person can see distant objects clearly but not the near objects. The image of near objects is formed behind the retina. This results in blurred image.

Reasons : This defect may be due to :
(i) Lens is flattened or less convex.
(ii) Eyeball is too short.

Correction of hypermetropia or far sightedness : This defect is corrected by using biconvex lens of a suitable power so as to converge the light rays to form a sharp image on the retina. The power of the glasses is given as plus.

(c) Astigmatism (Fig. 9.14 (c)) : It is a defect in which some part of the object is seen clearly while others are blurred. It is caused due to the unseen curvature of the cornea or lens. This is corrected by cylindrical lens.

(d) Presbyopia : It is a condition found in older people who cannot see near objects clearly. Their lens loses flexibility because of the loss of elasticity of the ciliary body. This is corrected by *convex lens*.

(e) Cataract : It is a condition in which the lens turns opaque, increases in density and vision is cut down leading even to total blindness. It can be corrected by surgically removing the lens and by using highly *convex lenses* compensating for the missing lens; in a newer technique a small plastic lens is implanted behind the iris.

(f) Night blindness : It is a condition in which a person feels difficulty seeing in dim light, during night. This is due to the failure of the formation of pigment visual purple of the rods. Only rods function in dim light and in the absence of the pigments they cannot function. This is usually due to the deficiency of vitamin A which is required for the synthesis of the pigment.

(g) Color blindness : Some people by birth cannot distinguish between certain colours such as the red and green; this is a genetic defect. Males usually suffer from this defect, whereas it rarely occurs in females.

(h) Squint : In this defect, two eyes somewhat converge leading to what is called cross eye. An opposite condition appears when they diverge and is called the wide eye. Both conditions may cause double vision or diplopia. Surgery and suitable exercise can correct these defects.

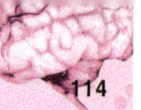

PROGRESS CHECK

A. STATE THE FUNCTION OF THE FOLLOWING PARTS OF THE EYE

1. Lens
2. Pupil
3. Cornea
4. Eyelid
5. Eyelashes
6. Iris
7. Choroid

B. NAME THE FOLLOWING

1. Coloured pigment present in rods and cones.
2. Enzyme present in the tears that kills bacteria.
3. The gland that forms tears.
4. The area of retina which is most sensitive for forming image.
5. The bony socket that encloses and protects eyeballs.

9.17. EAR–THE ORGAN OF HEARING AND BALANCE

Humans have two ears, one on each side of the head. Human ears are organs for senses of hearing and balance. The ear is a miniature receiver, amplifier and signal processing system.

Structure of ear : The human ear is divided into three parts (Fig. 9.15) :

(a) The external ear
(b) The middle ear
(c) The inner ear

(a) The external ear : It is also known as outer ear. It consists of an external visible part which is called pinna (or auricle) and an internal part the auditory canal.

The auditory canal is the passage leading to the ear drum (also known as tympanic membrane).

(b) The middle ear : The middle ear is a small air filled cavity. It is separated from the external ear by the ear drum (tympanic membrane) and from the internal ear by a thin bony partition which contains two small openings, namely oval window and round window.

The middle ear contains three tiny bones called ear ossicles. These bones are named as *malleus* (or *hammer*), *incus* (or *anvil*) and *stapes* (or *stirrup*) (Fig. 9.16).

The handle of malleus is attached to the internal surface of the eardrum. Its opposite end is connected with the incus.

Incus is the intermediate bone and it articulates with the head of stapes.

The flat part of stapes is attached to the margins of fenestra ovalis or oval window. Throughout oval window, the cavity of middle ear is connected with the cavity of internal ear. Directly below the oval window is another window, called round window.

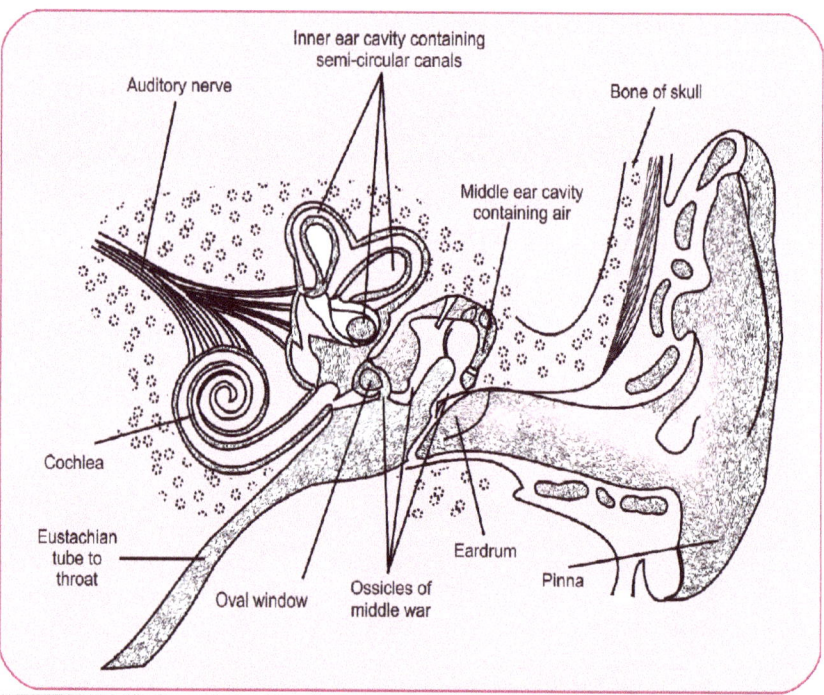

Fig. 9.15 : Various parts of human ear

The round window is covered by a thin membrane. The anterior wall of the middle ear contains an opening that leads to *auditory tube* (also known as *Eustachian tube*). This connects middle ear with the throat, thus any throat infection may reach the ear through the Eustachian tube. The Eustachian tube also helps in equalizing air pressure on both sides of the eardrum.

(c) The internal ear : The internal or inner ear is also known as membranous labyrinth. It has two main parts, cochlea and semicircular canals.

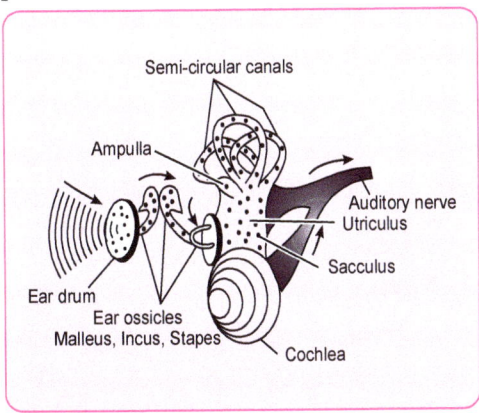

Fig. 9.16 : Internal structure of the human ear and course of perception of sound waves

9.18. COCHLEA

It is a hollow, spiral, shaped coiled chamber. It looks like a snail's shell. It consists of a bony spiral canal that makes about two and three quarter turns around a central bony core. Its inner spiral cavity contains three separate channels or canals that run parallel. These canals are separated by membranes. The median canal is filled with endolymph and the outer two canals are filled with a fluid called perilymph.

The middle canal contains a spiral organ called the Organ of Corti. This is the organ of hearing. It contains a series of nerve and hair cells which join the auditory nerve and help in hearing.

The hair cells of the spiral organ are very sensitive to sound. They can be damaged by exposure to high intensity noises such as those produced by jet engines, loud music etc.

The inner ear also contains three semicircular canals. These canals are arranged at right angles to each other in three different planes and are filled with endolymph. One end of each canal is swollen to form an ampulla. The ampulla contains sensory cells which help in balance of the body while moving. Nerve fibres arise from these cells and join the auditory nerve.

There is a short stem, known as vestibule which joins the semicircular canals and cochlea. It contains two small sacs, the utriculus and sacculus. These also contain tiny hair like sensory cells which help in static balance of the body at rest.

The external ear, middle ear and cochlea help in hearing. The sacculus, utriculus and the semicircular canals help in the sense of balance.

9.19. MECHANISM OF HEARING AND BALANCE

9.19.1. Hearing Mechanism

(a) Pinna collects and amplifies sound waves which enter the auditory canal. The sound waves strike the eardrum and cause it to vibrate.

(b) The Eustachian tube equalizes the pressure on each side of ear drum which allows them to vibrate freely.

(c) The vibrations in eardrum cause the bones of the ear ossicle to vibrate.

(d) Ear ossicles transmit vibrations from the eardrum to the denser fluid in the inner ear.

(e) The lever-like action of malleus and incus magnifies the vibrations of the stapes.

(f) The vibrating stapes transmit vibrations to the membrane of the oval window.

(g) Vibrations from oval window are transmitted to cochlea. This leads to vibrations in the fluid of cochlear canals.

(h) Vibration of fluid in cochlear canals triggers movement of sensory hair cells of organ of corti in cochlea.

(i) Movements of sensory hair cells is converted to a nerve impulse.

(j) Nerve signals are transmitted to the brain through auditory nerve and this result in hearing.

9.19.2. Balancing

The sensory hair cells in semi-circular canals are concerned with dynamic balance, i.e. while the body is in motion. Similarly, sensory cells in utriculus and sacculus are concerned with static balance with respect to the center of gravity.

Semicircular canals contain *calcareous particles* or *otoliths*. When the head is tilted from the normal position, the otoliths move towards the left and press the sensory hairs. The stimulus is picked up by the fibres of the auditory nerve and passed on to the brain. From the brain the necessary orders are sent through motor neurons to return the body to its normal position.

9.20. TONGUE AND THE SENSE OF TASTE (GUSTATORY SENSATION)

Tongue has chemoreceptors which are also called gustatoreceptors. The human tongue bears the taste buds on its upper surface. A taste bud is an ovoid body present in the papilla. The papillae make the surface of tongue rough (Fig. 9.17 a).

Each taste bud consists of taste receptors surrounded by supporting cells. The receptor cells are connected with the nerve fibres of sensory neurons and their free ends are produced into hair like sensory processes that project out of the taste bud through a pare.

Taste buds react to four primary tastes: Sweet, sour, salt and bitter (Fig. 9.17 b).

The receptors for each of them are located at different regions on the tongue. The tip of the tongue is more sensitive to salt and sweet, the sides to the sour and salt and back to bitter. All other tastes are a combination of these four tastes that are modified by accompanying olfactory sensations.

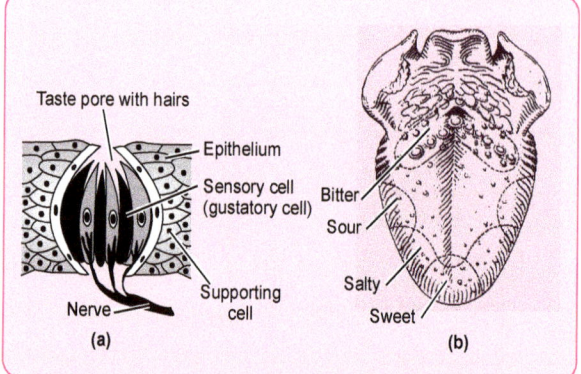

Fig. 9.17 : (a) Longitudinal section of a test papilla; (b) Location of the four types of taste receptors on the tongue

9.21. NOSE AND SENSE OF SMELL

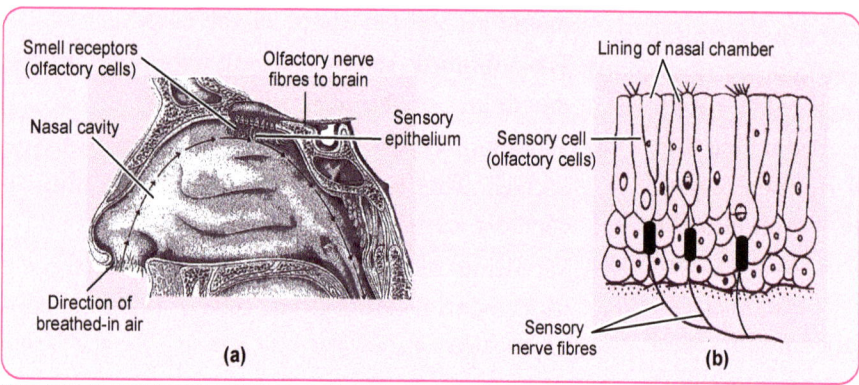

Fig. 9.18 : (a) Location of smell receptors in nasal cavity; (b) Location of sensory cells in nasal epithelium

The receptors for sense of smell or olfactory sense are located in the nasal epithelium of nasal cavity (Fig. 9.18 a). The sensory cells for smell have hair like projections called olfactory hairs (Fig. 9.18 b). These hairs react to odours in the air and stimulate the olfactory cells. The substance to be smelled is dissolved in the nervous secretion of the nose. The impulse from these cells is transmitted to the brain by the olfactory nerves and the brain decides the nature of smell (Fig. 9.17).

9.22. SKIN RECEPTORS

Our skin has many receptors, such as (Fig. 9.19) :

(a) **Free nerve endings** : These are distributed between epidermal cells. Most of these nerve endings are sensitive to pain.

(b) **Root hair plexus** : These are associated with hair and respond to touch.

(c) **Pacinian corpuscles** : They are located deep in dermis and are sensitive to strong pressure and vibration.

(d) **Ruffini corpuscles** : They respond to heat.

(e) **Meissner's corpuscles** : They are located in dermis just below the epidermis. They respond to touch.

(f) **Krause's corpuscles** : They are located in large numbers on the face and hands. They respond to cold.

(g) **Other receptors** :

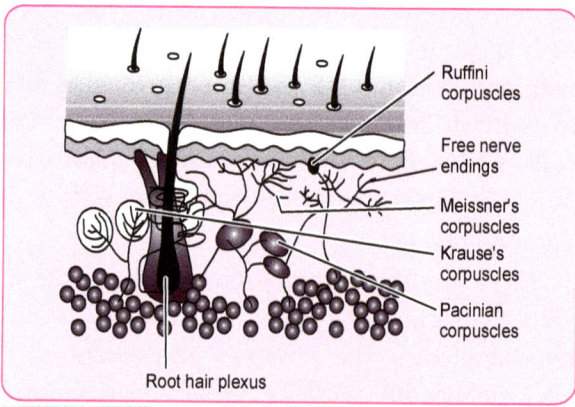

Fig. 9.19 : Corpuscles of skin receptor

(h) **Hunger :** Its receptors are located in the stomach wall.

(i) **Thirst :** Its receptors are located in the pharynx.

(j) **Fatigue :** Its receptors are located in the muscles.

PROGRESS CHECK

A. ANSWER THE FOLLOWING

1. What is the role of semicircular canals of internal ear?
2. Where is organ of corti located?
3. Define tympanum.
4. Differentiate between static and dynamic balance.

B. GIVE SCIENTIFIC NAMES FOR THE FOLLOWING

1. Eardrum
2. Internal ear
3. External ear
4. Oval window
5. Ear canal
6. Hammer headed bony piece of ear ossicles.

C. GIVE THE LOCATION OF THE FOLLOWING STRUCURES

1. Cochlea
2. Round window
3. Utriculus
4. Ear ossicles

EXERCISE

A. VERY SHORT ANSWER TYPE

(I) **Answer the Following Questions**

1. The eye defect caused due to the shortening of the eyeball from front to back.
2. The tube which connects the cavity of the middle ear with the throat.
3. The part of eye responsible for its shape.
4. The opening through which light enters the eye.
5. The part of eye responsible for change in the size of the pupil.
6. The ear ossicle in contact with oval window of inner ear.
7. Adjustment of eye in order to obtain a clear vision of objects at different distances.

(II) **Write in Logical Sequence**

1. Ear ossicles, oval window, tympanum, auditory canal, cochlea.
2. Yellow spot, conjunctiva, pupil, cornea, lens, vitreous humour, aqueous humour.

(III) **Match the Following Structures of the Ear with their Functions**

Column A	Column B
(1) Ear bones	(i) Detects soud vibrations.
(2) Eustachian tube	(ii) Detects change in position or movement.
(3) Eustachian tube	(iii) Amplify sound vibration.
(4) Semicircular canals	(iv) Protects eardrum from damage due to pressure differences on the two sides of eardrum.

(IV) **Given Below is a Table Consisting of a Set of Items Belonging to a Common Category. Complete the Table by Filling in the Category and the Odd Term :**

(Set, Category, Odd Term)

1. Malleus, cochlea, utriculus, Sacculus, semicircular canals ....
2. Myopia, hypermetropia. Xerophthalmia, astigmatism ....
3. Malleus, incus, stapes, sacculus ....

(V) **Mention the Functions of the Structures Given Below :**

1. Cerebrospinal fluid and ——
2. Pupil and ——
3. Cones and ——
4. Retina and ——
5. Cochlea and ——
6. Suspensory ligament of eye and
7. Organ of corti and ——
8. Otolith and ——
9. Eustachian tube and
10. Utriculus and ——

B. SHORT ANSWER TYPE

(I) **Differentiate between the following on the basis of Clues Given within Brackets**

1. Myopia and hypermetropia (cause).
2. Iris and pupil (function).

3. Cones and rods (sensitivity to light).
4. Sympathetic and parasympathetic nerve (function).
5. Cranial and spinal nerves (Number of nerves)
6. Yellow spot and blind spot (area).
7. Choroid and sclerotic layers (functions).

(II) Answer the Following Questions
1. What is sebaceous gland? Where is it located?
2. Write an account of structure and functions of cerebrum.
3. Name the three meninges which cover the brain.
4. Name the part of the brain associated with memory.
5. What is an axon?
6. What is the role of corpus callosum? Where is it found?
7. What is sympathetic nervous system?
8. Explain with an example the route of reflex.
9. Name the area of best vision in the eye.
10. Name the type of lens required to correct myopia.
11. Name the ear ossicle which is attached to the tympanum.

C. SHORT ANSWER TYPE
1. Draw the structure of a neuron and label the following on it–Nucleus, Dendrite, Cell body and Axon and name the part of neuron :
   (a) Where information is acquired.
   (b) Through which information travels as an electrical impulse.
2. Name the two main organs of our central nervous system. Which one of them plays a major role in sending command to muscles to act without involving thinking process? Name the phenomenon involved.
3. What is the function of cerebellum?
4. What is reflex action? Describe the steps involved in reflex action.
5. What is the role of brain in reflex action? What are the different types of reflexes?
6. Describe the common defects of vision, their causes and the methods of correcting them.
7. Draw a labelled diagram of the inner ear. Name the parts of the inner ear that is responsible for static balance in human beings.

D. STRUCTURED/APPLICATION BASED
1. The following diagram refers to the ear of mammals :
   (a) Label the parts 1 to 10 :
   (b) Name the structure which :
      (i) Converts sound waves into mechanical vibrations.

(ii) Converts vibrations into nerve impulses.
(iii) Responds to changes in position.

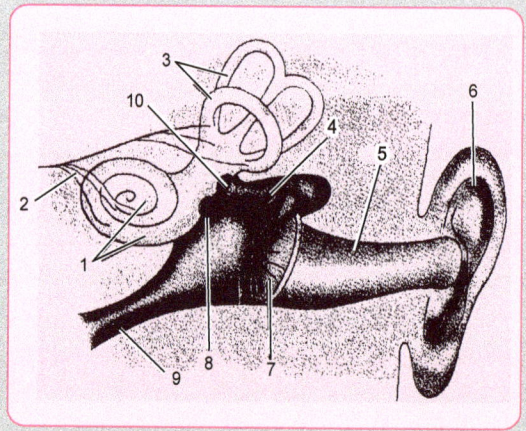

(iv) Transmits impulses to the brain.
(v) Equalizes pressure in the ear.

2. Given here is the diagram of a part of the human ear. Study the same and answer the questions that follows :

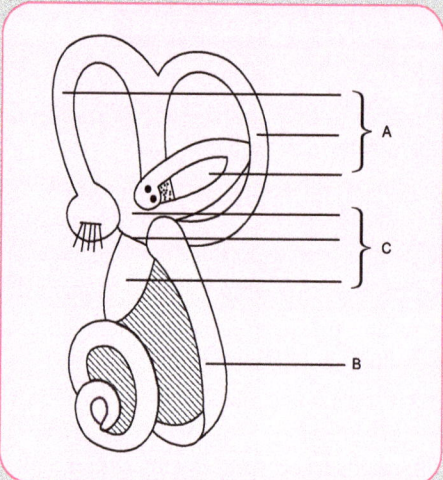

(a) Give the common name for malleus, incus and stapes.
(b) Name the parts labelled as A, B and C in the diagram.
(c) Name the audio receptor region present in the part labelled as B.

3. Given diagram is the vertical section of human brain. Observe it carefully and answer the following questions :

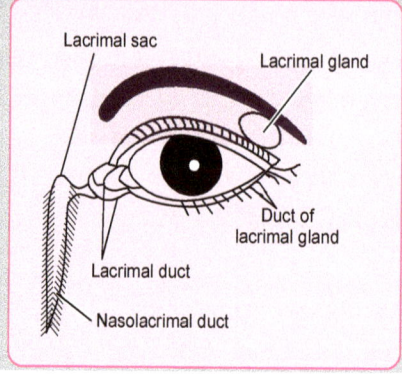

(a) Why there are elevation and depression in the brain?
(b) Label the areas 1–6.
(c) Which parts of the above diagram are responsible for :

(i) Vision.
(ii) Involuntary reaction.
(iii) Balancing the body.
(iv) Name the tissue which connects the two cerebral hemispheres.

DO YOU KNOW?

- The human brain alone consists of about 100 billion neurons on an average. If all these neurons were to be lined up, it would form a 600 mile long line.
- The human spinal cord, with an average length of 19 inches, consists of around 13,500,000 neurons. All the messages relayed between the brain and other parts of the body go via the spinal cord.
- The nervous system is able to transmit impulses at the speed of 100 meters per second. In fact, the speed of message transmission to the brain can be as high as 180 miles per hour.
- In a child, developing inside the womb, the neurons are known to grow at the rate of 250,000 neurons per minute. By the time of birth, the brain already consists of approximately 10 million nerve cells.
- In newborns, the brain is known to grow three times within the span of a year. As we grow older, the brain losses a gram every year.
- In humans, the right side of the brain controls the left side of the body, while the left side of the brain controls the right side.

10

ENDOCRINE GLANDS

CHAPTER HIGHLIGHTS
10.1. Need for Regulation of Body Activities
10.2. General Characteristics of Hormones
10.3. Endocrine Glands
10.4. Control of Hormonal Secretions

10.1. NEED FOR REGULATION OF BODY ACTIVITIES

Our nervous system controls and coordinates the functioning of different body parts and organs. Similarly our endocrine system brings coordination by means of chemical regulators called hormones.

The complexities of our bodily activities are extensive, thus, they require to be regulated in such a manner that every activity takes place at the right time in the proper order. For example, thyroxine which is present in most cells, stimulates the metabolic rate which proves essential for normal growth and development. While regulation carried out in this manner is conducted to some extent by the nervous system, it is also induced by chemical regulators known as hormones.

The major differences between hormonal control and nervous control are tabulated below :

Table 1 : The Differences between Nervous Control and Hormonal Control

Nervous Control	Hormonal Control
1. The nervous system controls and preserves the body's internal environment within physiological limits by impulses passing through neurons.	1. The endocrine system helps regulate and maintain various body functions by synthesizing and releasing chemical messengers called hormones directly into the bloodstream.
2. The nervous system is designed to send electrochemical messages to specific sets of cells like muscle fibres, glands and other neurons.	2. The endocrine system as a whole sends messages to cells in virtually any part of the body.
3. The nervous system directs muscles to contract and relax, glands to secrete more or less of their juices as required. Yet it does not stimulate growth.	3. It is responsible for our growth as it affects change in the metabolic activities of all our bodily tissues.
4. They act immediately. Neurons are prone to act within a few milliseconds.	4. They are slow-acting. This system uses hormones that can sometimes take minutes, hours, or even days to take effect and control events.

5. The effects of the nervous system are not long-lasting.	5. The hormonal effects may be more lasting and sometimes even permanent.
6. Nerves manage the nervous control.	6. Secretory cells control the endocrine system.
7. Localised, affects only particular muscle or glands called effector.	7. Generalized or widespread, influences many cells in different parts of the body.

A hormone is a chemical released by one or more specific cells or glands in the body and are carried to all parts by the blood but affects only one or more specific parts (target organ or cell) in the organism (Fig. 10.1). Hormones are chemical messengers or information molecules secreted by the endocrine glands.

The majority of the hormones are secreted by special glands known as endocrine glands (endo: inside, crine: separate) which means to 'secrete internally'; these comprise of a group of ductless glands that secrete hormones directly into the blood to be transported to the site of action. Since the endocrine glands do not have any ducts for transportation of their secretions, they are also called 'ductless glands'.

Hormones can also be produced within glands or organs which otherwise serve a different primary function, e.g. stomach and duodenum; Pituitary gland, thyroid gland, parathyroid, adrenal, pancreas, pineal and the thymus are the endocrine glands, present in the body.

Endocrine system : The endocrine system is a group of glands and organs that acts as the body's control system for producing, storing and secreting chemical substances called hormones.

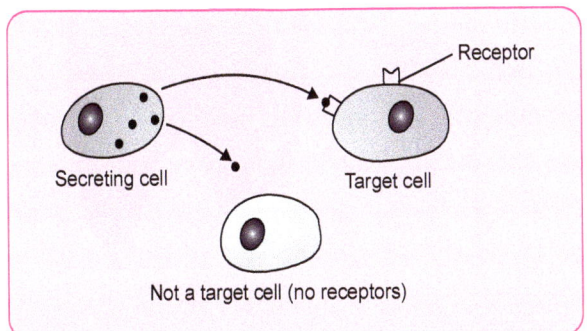

Fig. 10.1 : Hormones acting on target organs or cells

These hormones are directly secreted into the bloodstream to allow for chemical coordination in the body. In a coordinated manner they stimulate each other and work as a system of organs which is together called the endocrine system. The specific organs where the hormones act are called the target organs. The blood contains all the hormones, but the cells of the target organ pick up only the hormone specific to it ignoring all others, by means of a specific protein called *receptor*. The functioning of endocrine system is controlled by the nervous system. These two systems are together called the neuroendocrine system.

10.2. GENERAL CHARACTERISTICS OF HORMONES

(a) Hormones are substances secreted directly into the bloodstream and not into the lymphatic system.

(b) They are secreted in extremely small quantities. Amount of hormone secreted depends on the body's requirement.

(c) Chemically, hormones may be polypeptides (proteins such as insulin and their derivatives), amines (such as adrenaline) or steroids (such as testosterone derived from cholesterol).

(d) Hormones manage the physiological processes of the body by chemical means. They also have an effect on the enzyme systems of the body.

(e) Their hypersecretion or hyposecretion both might have severe consequences.

(f) Hormones do not stay in the body for long, i.e. they are not stored but are excreted from our system after use.

(g) Hormones effect the growth, differentiation and metabolic activities of the target cell.

(h) They have low molecular weight.

(i) Hormones are generally slow acting and take effect after a time lag, e.g. estrogen in ovary. However some hormones are quick acting too, e.g. adrenaline.

(j) The specificity of hormones varies widely.

(k) Hormones produced in one species generally show similar effect in other species too.

A hormone is a chemical secretion produced by specialized glands that manage and regulate the movement of certain cells or organs. It is manufactured by a particular tissue and transmitted by the blood stream to another, to cause physiological activity like metabolism or growth.

PROGRESS CHECK

FILL IN THE BLANKS

1. _____ cells control the endocrine system.
2. Hormones are secreted directly into _____.
3. Hormones manage the _____ processes of the body.
4. Hormones act on the specific organs called _____.

10.3. ENDOCRINE GLANDS

The chief endocrine (hormone producing) glands in our bodies have been shown in the figure below (Fig. 10.2) :

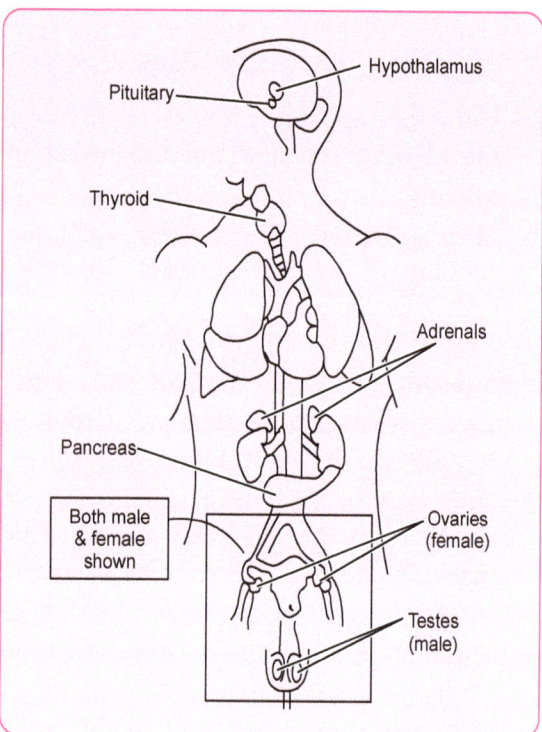

Fig. 10.2 : Endocrine glands present in human body

They are listed below

(a) Thyroid (b) Adrenal
(c) Pancreas (d) Pituitary
(e) Parathyroid (f) Thymus
(g) Gonads

Now, we shall have a look at the main functions of the above mentioned glands.

(a) Thyroid gland

Location : The thyroid gland is situated in the forepart of the lower neck, immediately below the *larynx* (voice box) and upper part of trachea in the neck.

Structure : The gland itself is bilobed, i.e. it is made up of two oblong lobes facing both sides of the *trachea* (windpipe) and attached by a thin band of tissue called the *isthmus*. It is highly vascular. The gland is reddish brown in colour and is shield shaped (Fig. 10.3).

Hormones secreted : Thyroxine and calcitonin are the two hormones secreted by this gland.

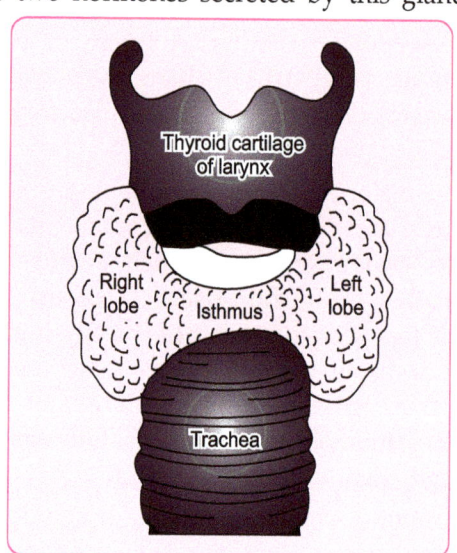

(a) : Front view

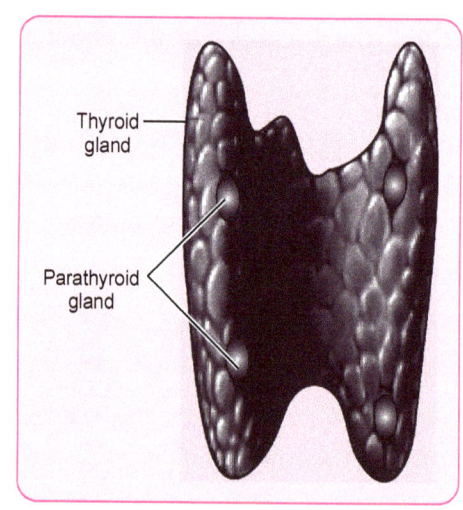

(b) : Back view

Fig. 10.3 : The Thyroid gland

Functions

(i) Thyroxine functions by increasing the action of mitochondria in the cells by getting attached to the cells' DNA (deoxyribonucleic acid), increasing the basal metabolic rate (the number of calories your body burns at rest to maintain normal body functions). Hence it acts as body's thermostat.

(ii) The amount of secretion of thyroxine is directly proportional to the metabolism rate, i.e. increase in the secretion leads to increase in the metabolism rate and vice-versa.

(iii) It influences the overall growth of the body.

(iv) It regulates the calcium and phosphate levels in the body.

(v) It also regulates the body temperature and mental development.

(vi) Thyroxine stimulates tissue differentiation, thus helping in metamorphosis of a tadpole into an adult frog.

(vii) Thyroxine also controls the physiology of excretion by kidney. It's deficiency results in decreased urine output.

Effects of under-secretion (Hypothyroidism) : Hypothyroidism is a condition in which the thyroid gland does not secrete enough thyroxine. This can result in three conditions–simple goitre, cretinism and myxoedema.

(1) Simple goitre : Simple goitre can arise when the thyroid gland is unable to generate enough thyroxine to meet the body's needs. The thyroid gland swells up and becomes larger, becoming visible as a swelling in the neck (Fig. 10.4). This usually occurs because of insufficient amount of iodine in food. We find this condition among people living in hilly regions where the soil has less quantity of iodine in it.

These regions are generally away from the sea coast. Thus, the food grown there is deficient in iodine as well. Addition of iodine to table salt can help in preventing the disease.

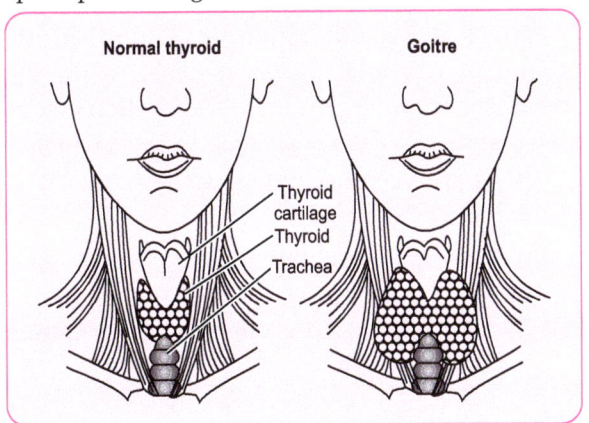

Fig. 10.4 : An individual suffering from simple goitre

(2) Cretinism : (in children) It is the consequence of insufficient secretion of thyroxin during fetal life or early infancy. This condition may also occur due to early atrophy (degeneration) of the thyroid gland. In this case, the brain and skeleton fail to grow and develop fully, resulting in mental retardation and dwarfism. The body temperature, blood pressure and heart beat are lower than normal. The patient is pot-bellied, pigeon chested and has a protruding tongue.

(3) Myxoedema : (in adult) A condition that occurs because of the under secretion of thyroxine in adults. It is characterized by a decreased metabolic rate, and symptoms may include slow speech, an enlarged tongue, puffiness of the face and hands, loss of hair, coarse and thickened skin etc. The patient lacks intelligence and initiative. The patient also suffers from low body temperature, slow heart rate, sensitivity to cold, dry hair and skin, muscular weakness, general lethargy and reproductive failure.

Effects of hyper-secretion : In this condition, the thyroid gland secretes too much of thyroxine. The condition is often referred to as an "overactive thyroid." Excess secretion of thyroxine may also result in the development of a goitre called exophthalmic goitre. An individual suffering from over-secretion of thyroxine shows increased metabolic rate, rapid heartbeat, shortness of breath, protruding eyes, goitre in the neck, nervousness, irritability, tremors and restlessness.

Calcitonin lowers the concentration of Ca and P in the blood by decreasing their release from the bones. It is secreted when concentration of Ca rises in the blood.

(b) Adrenal glands

Structure : Adrenal glands are triangle-shaped caps above the kidneys (Fig. 10.5). Each adrenal gland consists of two parts :

(i) Central medulla

(ii) A peripheral cortex

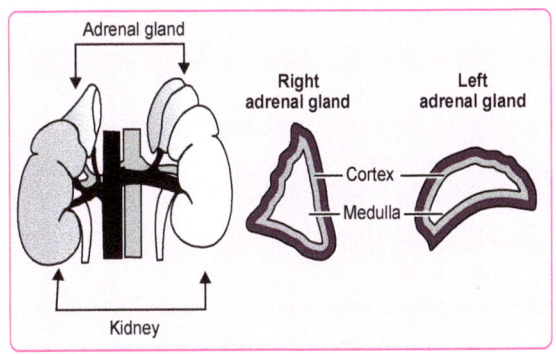

Fig. 10.5 : Adrenal gland

Location : It is positioned on top of the kidneys (ad: near, renal : kidney), is pyramid shaped and yellowish in colour.

(1) Adrenal medulla : The internal part of the adrenal gland is referred to as the medulla and it secretes adrenaline generally called epinephrine and noradrenaline (norepinephrine).

Adrenaline is a hormone produced by the adrenal glands during high stress or exciting situations. This powerful hormone is part of the human body's acute stress response system, also called the "fight or flight" response. This hormone is released into the blood in times of high emotional stress. The autonomic nervous system stimulates this gland via the nerve endings.

Functions of adrenaline hormone

- It works by stimulating the heart rate along with increase in blood pressure.
- There is increase of blood supply to the muscles while inhibiting it to the skin and visceral organs.
- More glucose is released into the blood via the liver.
- It prepares the body to face stress or danger. So adrenals are known as the glands of emergency.

(2) Adrenal cortex : The outer part of the adrenal gland is called the cortex and it produces the cortisone hormone. These cortical hormones are classified as :

(i) Glucocorticoid : Influences the carbohydrate, protein and fat metabolism.

(ii) Mineral corticoid : Influences mineral metabolism specially Na and K ions. Stimulates the kidneys to retain sodium and excrete potassium.

Functions of cortical hormones

- Increase the level of blood glucose concentration.
- Influence fat and protein metabolism.
- Allow for a balanced amount of salt and water in the body.
- Acclimatize the body to "stresses" like extreme cold or heat, burns, infections and so on.
- Some cortical hormones like androgen (in males), and estrogen (in females) behave like sex hormones. In case of an overgrowth of adrenal cortex in young children, it leads to premature sexual maturity.
- It controls reabsorption of sodium by kidneys and maintains Na^+ and K^+ rates in body fluid.

Effects of hyposecretion : Hyposecretion from adrenal cortex is responsible for *Addison's disease*. The symptoms of this disease are loss of energy, skin pigmentation, loss of weight, nausea, hypoglycemia (low blood sugar), sensitivity to cold and low threshold for pain, increased susceptibility to infections, increased urinary Na^+, vomiting, diarrhoea.

Effects of hyper secretion : Hypersecretion of adrenal cortex is responsible for *Cushing's syndrome*. The symptoms include obesity, hyperglycemia (higher blood sugar), osteoporosis, weakness, salt and water retention, rise in blood volume and blood pressure.

(c) Pancreas

Location : It is an abdominal gland located in the abdominal cavity close to the duodenum, behind the stomach, with its head pointed in the direction of the small intestine. It is yellowish in colour, about 15 cm long, weighs about 85 g and is a lobulated structure. It is both a duct gland as well as a ductless gland. So it is known as heterocrine gland. As a duct gland it secretes digestive juices which break down nutrients. These juices are poured into the duodenum, which is the beginning of the small intestine, for digestion. As a ductless gland it has Islets of Langerhans, for hormone secretion and are tiny clusters of cells scattered around the entire gland. They have 4 types of cells – alpha cells, beta cells, delta cells and F cells. These islets secrete three hormones- insulin, glucagon and somatostatin from three different types of cells namely beta, alpha and delta cells respectively.

(i) Insulin is a hormone secreted by the *beta cells* in response to the detection of increased blood sugar levels in the body. It stimulates glucose consumption by the body's cells. It stimulates deposition of extra glucose of the body as glycogen in the liver and muscles.

Effect of hypo secretion of insulin : Insufficient secretion of insulin results in diabetes (or diabetes mellitus or hyperglycemia). A diabetic person :

(1) Has high concentration of sugar in their blood (hyperglycemia- hyper: excess, glyce: sugar, emia : blood).
(2) Excretes copious amounts of urine loaded with sugar.
(3) Need to drink water often as much water is lost through urination.
(4) Loses weight and becomes increasingly weaker. Sometimes diabetes may result in loss of vision too.
(5) Catabolism of fats and proteins increases.
(6) Injuries take a lot of time to heal and may turn gangrenous.

We must understand that an insulin shot is not a cure but is a treatment meant to compensate the body with the hormone that is not being produced in the pancreas.

Hormones of Islets of Langerhans (in pancreas)

1. Insulin (from beta cells)	– Helps with glucose intake by body cells – Allows for extra deposits of glucose in liver and muscles

Insufficiency of this hormone causes diabetes mellitus

Overload of this hormone causes nerve cell starvation and brain coma

2. Glucagon (from alpha cells)	– Enables liver to convert glycogen into glucose
3. Somatostatin (from delta cells)	– Restrains the secretion of insulin and glucagon

Effect of Hypersecretion of Insulin

(1) Leads to lowered blood sugar levels (hypoglycemia, hypo : below) as metabolism of glucose increases.

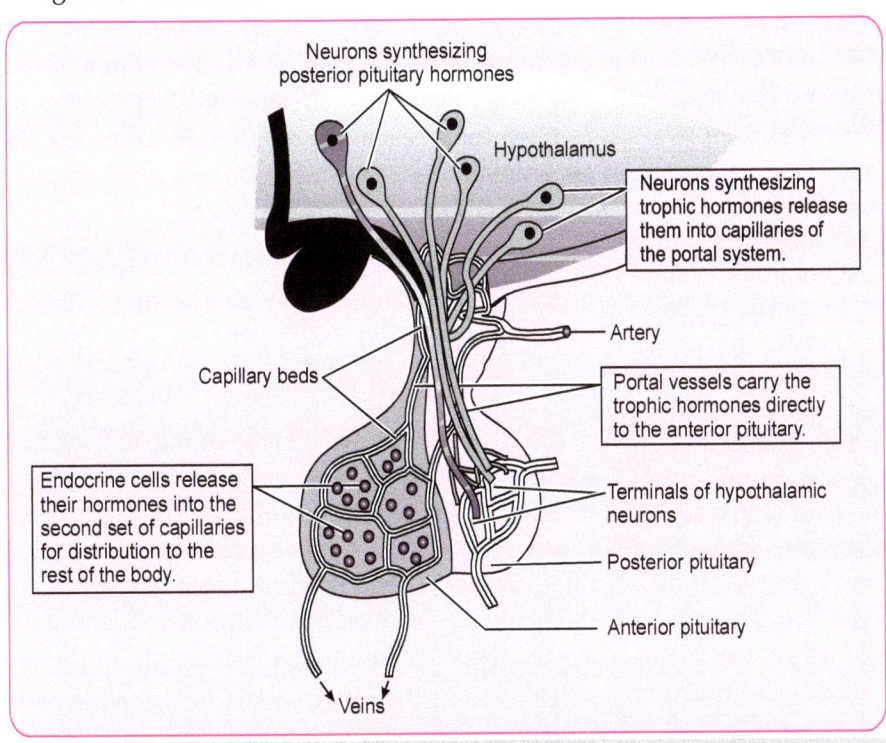

Fig. 10.6 : Pituitary gland

(2) The brain may enter into a state of coma if the insulin levels drop below a point even for a few minutes. This could also occur if a diabetic patient is given an overdose of insulin. In such cases, the patient might lose consciousness; this is called insulin shock or hypoglycemia and the patient should be given sugar candy or some sweet immediately.

(ii) **Glucagon,** the hormone secreted by the *alpha cells* raises blood glucose levels in the body. It causes glycogen in the liver to break down into glucose thus raising blood glucose levels.

(iii) **Somatostatin** is the hormone secreted by delta cells. It inhibits the secretion of insulin and glucagon.

Functions of Pancreas

➤ Glucagon speeds up the breakdown of glycogen into glucose in the liver and then releases it into the blood. Thus, it increases the blood sugar level.

➤ Insulin speeds up the transport of glucose to cells where the glucose is converted into glycogen thus lowering the blood sugar level.

(d) Pituitary gland (The master gland)

Structure : The pituitary gland is a small endocrine organ (about the size of a pea) It is located just below the hypothalamus (Fig. 10.6) and is divided into an anterior lobe and a posterior lobe, both of which are involved in hormone secretion.

This gland weighs only about one-half gram. In the posterior pituitary the frontal area is different as compared to the rest of the lobe and is called the intermediate lobe. This lobe is almost absent in human beings but is much larger and more functional in some lower animals. The pituitary gland is given the term *"Master Gland"* since it controls the functioning of almost all the other endocrine glands of the body.

Location : It protrudes from the base of the mid-brain and directs a multitude of important functions in the body.

Hormones from anterior pituitary : The major hormones secreted from the anterior pituitary lobe are :

(i) **Growth hormone (GH) :** It is a protein hormone vital for normal growth. It is synthesized and secreted by cells in the anterior pituitary and is also known as somatotropin (somatic: body, tropic: stimulating). Hyposecretion of GH during childhood leads to dwarfism (in spite of being fully developed, a dwarf retains the body proportions of a child). The growth of the body and long bones stops prematurely making the individual a dwarf. Excess secretion of this hormone during childhood leads to gigantism (the long bones in the body lengthen beyond normal which result in human giants up to 2.7 meters). When an excess of the growth hormone is secreted suddenly in an adult, an extra growth of bones in the face (particularly the jaws) and in the hands is noticed. Other noticeable symptoms include large nose and thick lips. This condition is called acromegaly (acro: height/extremity, megaly: large) guerrilla like appearance.

(ii) Thyroid stimulating hormone (TSH) : This hormone stimulates the thyroid gland to secrete thyroxin.

(iii) Adrenocorticotropic hormone (ACTH) : This hormone controls the activity of the adrenal cortex to secrete gluco corticoid and minerals corticoid.

(iv) Follicle stimulating hormone (FSH) : It stimulates sperm formation in male and growth of ovarian follicles in female.

(v) Luteinizing hormone (LH) : In males it produces testosterone and in female it causes ovulation and secretion of oestrogen. Both of these hormones are called gonadotropic hormones.

Hormones from posterior pituitary : The posterior pituitary secretes two hormones namely vasopressin and oxytocin.

(i) Anti diuretic hormone (ADH) : It is commonly known as arginine vasopressin or also called Vasopressin. The single most important feature of the antidiuretic hormone is to conserve body water by reducing the loss of water in urine. Antidiueretic hormone also raises blood pressure by causing the arterioles to constrict, thus promoting the reabsorption of water back into circulation. A deficiency of ADH causes diabetes insipidus (water diabetes) which is a condition characterized by extreme thirst and excretion of copious amounts of severely diluted urine. No glucose is lost in urine.

(ii) Oxytocin (oxys : sharp/quick, tokos: childbirth) : Oxytocin is released when the foetus stimulates the uterus and it enhances contraction of uterine smooth muscle to facilitate delivery. It is also known as birth hormone.

The below information, though not a part of the syllabus will help the students improve their subject knowledge :

(e) Parathyroid glands : These are small glands in two pairs. They are buried in the thyroid gland on its dorsal-posterior part. This gland secretes parathormone which serves to increase the blood calcium by taking the latter out of the bone. Mobilization of calcium and its proper amount in the blood is essential for muscular activities and other functions such as blood clotting.

(f) Thymus gland : This gland can be seen in the new-born child, close to the heart. It gradually becomes smaller with advancing years and in the adult it is degenerated. Thymus gland secretes thymosin and produces lymphocytes known as T-lymphocytes. The latter produce antibodies.

(i) Testes : Testes are the glands which are present only in males. Testes produce male sex hormone called *testosterone*. The function of testosterone is to control the development of male sex organs and male features such as deeper voice, moustache, beard and more body hair (than females).

(ii) Ovaries : Ovaries are glands which are present only in females. Ovaries produce two female sex hormones, oestrogen and progesterone. The function of *oestrogen* is to control the development of female sex organs, and female features such as feminine voice, soft skin and mammary glands (breasts). The function of *progesterone* is to control the uterus and changes in the menstrual cycle. It also helps in the maintenance of pregnancy.

Castration : Removal of the testes or ovaries from an animal.

Animation for Endocrine Glands
https://www.youtube.com/watch?v=NlNaidldt4M
https://www.youtube.com/watch?v=nNLsXKkLSTs

10.4. CONTROL OF HORMONAL SECRETIONS (FEEDBACK MECHANISM)

The excess or deficiency of hormones has a harmful effect on our body. For example, the deficiency of insulin results in diabetes whereas excess of insulin in the body can lead to coma. It is thus necessary that the hormones are secreted by the glands in our body in the precise quantities that are required for the normal functioning of the body.

This means that there should be some mechanism to regulate the production and release of hormones in the body. The timing and amount of hormones released by various glands are controlled by the 'feedback mechanism' which is in-built in our body.

For example, if the sugar level in the blood rises too much, they are detected by the cells of pancreas which respond by producing and secreting more insulin into the blood. And as the blood sugar falls below a certain level, the secretion of insulin is reduced automatically.

ENDOCRINE GLANDS

PROGRESS CHECK

NAME THE FOLLOWING

1. The hormone produced by adrenal medulla.
2. The hormone secreted by B cells of islets of langerhans.
3. Hormones help in intake of glucose by body cells.
4. Excess secretion of growth hormone during childhood leads to which disease.

Table 2 : Responses to Adrenaline

	Body Part	Effects of Adrenaline	Biological Advantage	Effect or Sensation
1.	Heart	• Beats faster • Blood pressure increases	Sends more glucose and oxygen to the muscles	Thumping heart
2.	Breathing centre of the brain	Faster and deeper breathing	Increased oxygenation of the blood; swift elimination of carbon dioxide	Feels breathless
3.	Arterioles of the skin	Constricts them	Small amount of blood reaching the skin allows for more blood available to the muscles	Person turns pale
4.	Arterioles of the digestive system	Constricts them	Small amount of blood available to the digestive system makes way for more of the blood to reach the muscles	Dry mouth
5.	Muscles of the body	Tenses them	Allows for instantaneous action	Tense sensation and shivering
6.	Liver	Conversion of glycogen into glucose	Makes available glucose in the blood for energy production	No sensation
7.	Fat deposit	Conversion of fats into fatty acids	Makes available fatty acids in the blood for muscle contraction	

Table 3 : Hormones Secreted by Pituitary Gland and their Actions

Source	Hormones and their Actions	
Anterior Pituitary	Growth Hormone (GH)	Works towards the growth of the body as a whole, especially of the skeleton Deficiency in childhood → Dwarfism
		Oversecretion in childhood → Gigantism In adult → Acromegally
	Tropic Hormones (Stimulates certain other endocrine glands)	**Thyroid Stimulating Hormone (TSH)** (Promotes the secretion of thyroxin in the thyroid gland)
		Adrenocorticotropic Hormone (ACTH) (Stimulates the adrenal cortex)
		Gonadotropic Hormones (Controls the actions of the gonads testes and ovaries)

		These are mainly of three types : **(i) Follicle Stimulating Hormone (FSH)** Stimulates the production of eggs in females and sperm formation in males **(ii) Luteinizing Hormone (LH)** Stimulates the creation of corpus luteum to enable the production of the female hormone progesterone, and the male hormone testosterone in the testes. **(iii) Prolactin** – Milk secretion
Posterior Pituitary	Antidiuretic Hormone (ADH) or Vasopressin	Boosts reabsorption of water from kidney tubules Deficiency : Diabetes insipidus (water diabetes)
	Oxytocin	Uterus contractions during child birth, stimulates milk ejection from breasts

10.4. THE HORMONES AT A GLANCE

The table below gives an overall general summary of the hormones of the four chief endocrine glands, their activities and various disorders occurring because of their undersecretion or oversecretion :

Endocrine Glands	Hormones Secreted	Principal Actions	Disorders	
			Underse-cretion	Overse-cretion
1. Adrenals (i) Adrenal cortex	(i) Mineralcorticosteroid (aldosterone)	Regulate plasma sodium and potassium concentrations	Addison's disease	Adrenal virilism Cushing's syndrome
	(ii) Glucocorticoids (cortisol, corticosterone)	Regulate carbohydrate, protein and lipid metabolism		
	(iii) Sex corticoids (adrenal androgens)	Stimulate development of external sex characteristics in males		
(ii) Adrenal medulla	Adrenaline	Causes stimulation of nervous system		
2. Pancreas (islets of Langerhans) (i) Beta cells	(i) Insulin	Lowers blood sugar level	Diabetes mellitus	
(ii) Alpha cells	(ii) Glucagon	Raises blood sugar level		
(iii) Delta cells	(iii) Somatostatin (Not in syllabus)	Inhibits the secretion of insulin and glucagon		
3. Thyroid	(i) Thyroxine	Promotes tissue metabolism, growth and differentiation	Simple goitre, cretinism in children and myxoedema in adults	Exophtha-lmic goitre (eye balls protrude, increased metabolism and restlessness)
	(ii) Calcitonin (Not in syllabus)	Promotes movement of calcium ions from blood to bones		

4. Pituitary (i) Anterior pituitary	(i) Growth hormone (GH)	(i) Body growth	Dwarfism	Gigantism in childhood, Acromegaly in adulthood and Pigmentation in skin
	(ii) Prolactin	(ii) Promotes lactation (milk formation and secretion)		
	(iii) Adreno-cortico-hormone (ACTH)	(iii) Stimulates secretion from adrenal cortex		
	(iv) Thyroid-stimulating hormone (TSH)	(iv) Stimulates thyroxine secretion		
	(v) Follicle stimulating hormone (FSH)	(v) In females, growth of Graafian follicles and oestrogen secretion		
	(vi) Luteinizing hormone (LH)	(vi) In males, spermatogenesis and testosterone secretion (vii) In females, ovulation, maintenance of corpus luteum and secretion of progesterone		
(ii) Posterior pituitary	(i) Vasopressin (ADH)	(viii) Increases absorption of water from kidneys, contraction of blood vessels causing rise in blood pressure	Diabetes insipidus	Elevation of blood pressure
	(ii) Oxytocin	(ix) Causes contraction of the uterine muscle during birth		

EXERCISE

A. VERY SHORT ANSWER TYPE

(I) Multiple Choice Questions

1. A gland which is both a duct gland as well as a ductless gland is :
   (a) thyroid   (b) pancreas   (c) pituitary   (d) adrenal
2. Cretinism is caused due to the undersecretion of :
   (a) corticoids   (b) insulin
   (c) calcitonin   (d) thyroxine
3. Which hormone in the pituitary gland promotes lactation (milk formation and secretion)?
   (a) luteinizing   (b) prolactin
   (c) oxytocin   (d) glucocorticoids

(II) Name the Following

1. The three hormones secreted by the adrenal cortex.
2. The hormone produced by the pancreas which lowers blood sugar levels.
3. The condition caused by the undersecretion of thyroxine.
4. The hormone secreted by the alpha cells of the islets of Langerhans.
5. The undersecretion of which hormone causes Dwarfism?
6. Name the gland which secretes the hormone Vasopresssin.
7. The hormone which maintains the corpus luteum and secretion of progesterone.

(III) Pick the Odd One Out

1. The conditions – goitre, beriberi, myxoedema, cretinism.
2. The hormones– alchohol, prolactin, growth hormone, vasopressin.
3. The sources of hormones –posterior pituitary, adrenal medulla, morphine, parathyroid.
4. The endocrine glands – thymus, insulin, thyroid, gonads.
5. Recognize the odd one in the following series and mention what the rest are:
   (a) calcitonin; blood; vasopressin; mineralocorticosteroids; _____; _____
   (b) FSH; GH; glucocorticoids; luteinizing hormone; _____; _____

(c) penicillin; insulin; oxytocin; thyroxin; _____ ; _____

(d) liver; muscles; hypothalamus; hyperglycemia; _____ ; _____

(e) gigantism; diabetes insipidus; meningitis; _____ ; _____

(IV) Match the Columns

Column I	Column II
1. Alpha cells of islets of langerhans	(i) Blood sugar level
2. Pigmentation in Addison's disease	(ii) Elevation of blood pressure
3. Adrenal virilism diseases	(iii) Adrenaline
4. Diabetes mellitus	(iv) Hypersecretion of thyroxin
5. Causes stimulation of the sympathetic nervous system	(v) Raises blood sugar level
6. Oversecretion of vaso-pressin	(vi) Pancreas
7. Exophthalmic goitre	(vii) mineralocorticosteroids
8. Negative feedback	(viii) adrenocorticotropic hormone

(V) Write the Full Forms of the Following

1. GH   2. LH   3. ADH
4. PRL   5. FSH

B. SHORT ANSWER TYPE

(I) State Whether True or False

1. Insulin is always described as an emergency hormone.
2. The pituitary gland is popularly called the 'master gland'.
3. The thyroid stimulating hormone is secreted from the alpha cells of the islets of Langerhans.
4. A person suffering from hyperthyroidism shows a marked increase in metabolic rate, shortness of breath, eyes are protruded.
5. Antidiuretic hormone regulates the activities of the testes and ovaries.

(II) Answer these Questions

1. What is the difference between endocrine glands and other glands?
2. Give three symptoms of diabetes mellitus.
3. Do you concur with the statement "All hormones are chemical regulators" Yes/no. Validate your answer.
4. What happens when the iodine level in our body is too low ?
5. What is the function of the antidiuretic hormone secreted by the pituitary gland ?
6. You are making your case before a judge and your mouth feels dry and you are panting. What is the reason behind these changes?
7. State the effects of the oversecretion of insulin.
8. What would an adult suffer from if there was hypersecretion from the thyroid?

(III) Explain the Following Terms

1. Endocrine gland   2. Hormone
3. Acromegay   4. Goitre

(IV) Give Reasons For the Following

1. Some women develop masculine voice.
2. Goitre is usually observed in people living in hilly regions.
3. Mouth dries up while making a public speech for the first time.
4. Pituitary gland is also known as the master gland.

(V) Name the Hormones Which are Responsible For the Following Conditions

1. Gigantism   2. Diabetes mellitus
3. Myxoedema   4. Exophthalmic goitre
5. Growth of beard in female

C. LONG ANSWER TYPE

1. Contrast the hormonal response with nervous response in our body systems as regards speed, transmission and the over-all nature of changes that take place.
2. Differentiate giving four points each between the activities of the hormones and that of the nerves as regards the regulatory mechanism of our bodies.

D. STRUCTURED/APPLICATION BASED

1. Shown alongside is a portion of the human body. Answer the questions :
   (a) Where in the body is this part located ?
   (b) State the names of the numbered parts.
   (c) State one main function of the parts labeled 1 and 2.
2. The diagram given below is an outline of the human body showing certain parts. Answer the following questions given.
   (a) Give the names of the parts which are numbered.

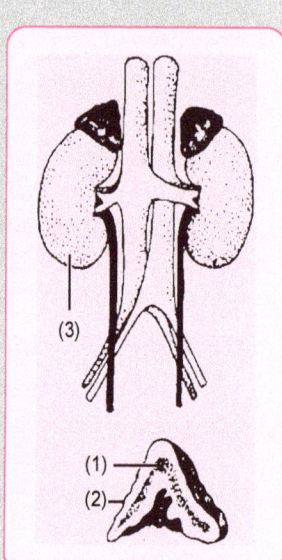

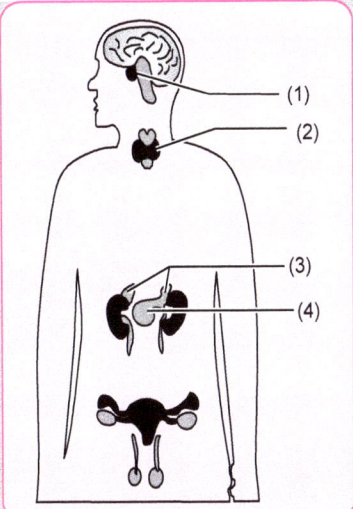

(b) What links all these part with respect to their role in the functioning of the body's systems?

(c) Give the name of the hormone secreted by the part numbered 3 in the diagram.

DO YOU KNOW ?

➢ The hypothalamus mak'es you aware of feelings like hunger and thirst. It also helps in maintaining body temperature.
➢ It aids the immune system by helping the body build resistance to disease.
➢ Human behaviour is also controlled by the endocrine system when it affects the nervous system.
➢ We must be thankful to the pineal gland for our sweet sleep. It secretes melatonin which regulates our sleep.
➢ There are 30 hormones in the human body.
➢ The secret behind your energy levels is Endocrine gland system.
➢ Endocrine system controls human behaviour.

11

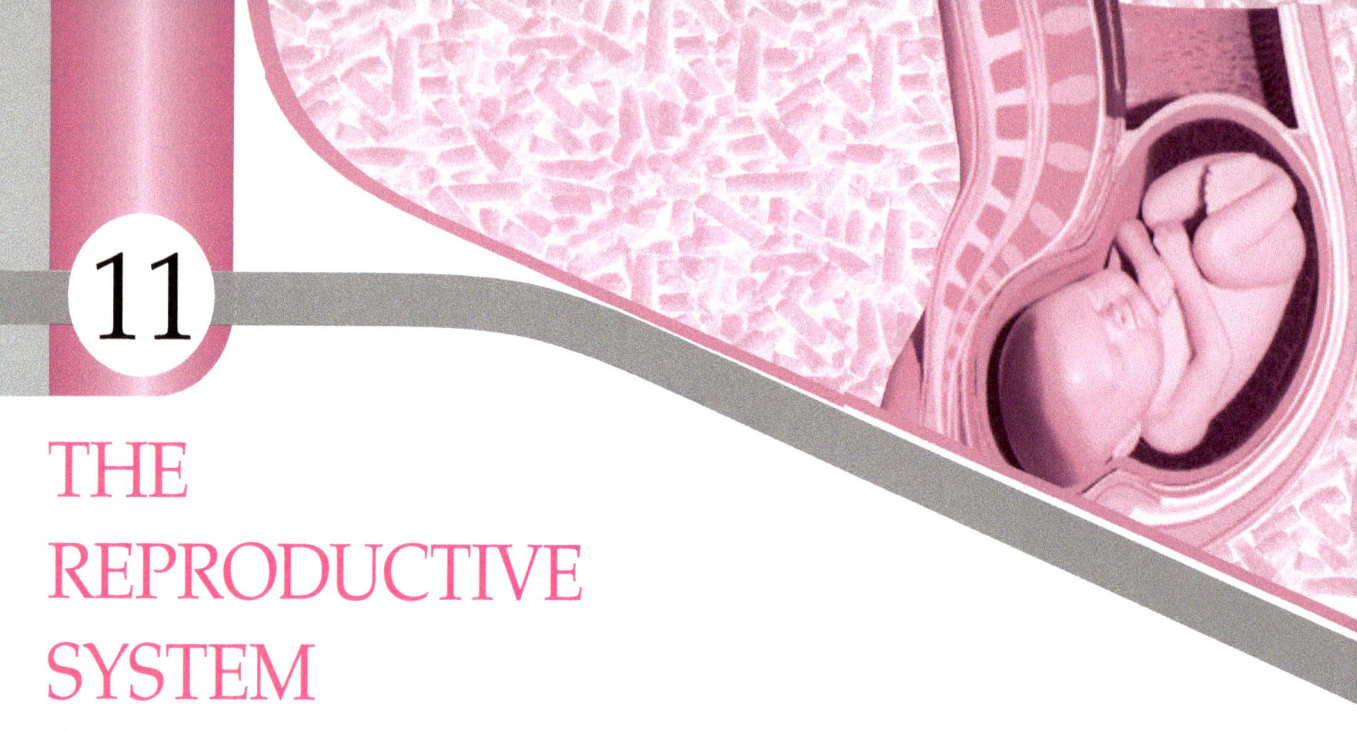

THE REPRODUCTIVE SYSTEM

CHAPTER HIGHLIGHTS
11.1. *The Reproductive System*
11.2. *Sexual Reproduction in Humans*
    11.2.1. *Male Reproductive System*
    11.2.2. *Female Reproductive System*
11.3. *Fertilization*
11.4. *Implantation*
11.5. *Placenta*
11.6. *Gestation Period*

11.1. THE REPRODUCTIVE SYSTEM

Reproduction is the ability of a living organism to give birth to its young ones similar to itself either by sexual or asexual means. In other words, reproduction is the process by which cell duplicates and passes the genetic material from one generation to another. Reproduction is essential for the survival of a species and continuity of life on earth.

Due to lack of specialized organs for reproduction, some living organisms reproduce asexually too.

Types of Reproduction

(a) Asexual reproduction : Asexual reproduction is a mode of reproduction by which offspring arise from a single organism, and inherit the genes of that parent only; it is reproduction which almost never involves ploidy or reduction. The offspring will be exact genetic copies of the parent.

Asexual reproduction is the primary form of reproduction for single-celled organisms such as the archaebacteria, eubacteria, and protists. Many plants and fungi reproduce asexually as well.

In asexual reproduction, male and female gametes are absent. Following are examples of asexual reproduction :

(i) Binary fission in Amoeba
(ii) Budding in Hydra
(iii) Spore formation in *Rhizopus*
(iv) Fragmentation in *Planaria*

(b) Sexual reproduction : It is the process in which the male and female gametes unite to give birth to a new organism. It occurs both in eukaryotes and prokaryotes. Sexual reproduction is the primary method of reproduction for the vast majority of macroscopic organisms, including almost all animals and plants.

Union of both gametes result in the formation of zygote which later develops into an individual. This process of union of male and female gametes is known as *fertilization*. In most animals, male and female gametes are present in two separate individuals. If both the gametes are present in the same animal, then the animal is known as *hermaphrodite* or *bisexual*. Whereas in plants, flower can be *unisexual* (either male or female gamete is present) or *bisexual* (both the gametes are present).

Secondary sexual characters : It is defined as the feature that helps in distinguishing between the male and female sex. Although these are not directly a part of reproductive system, they play an important role in attracting sex partners.

Table 1 : Differences between the Asexual and Sexual Reproduction

Asexual Reproduction	Sexual Reproduction
1. Does not require highly specialized organs.	1. Requires highly specialized organs.
2. Involves only one individual.	2. Involves two individuals.
3. Takes places by binary fission or cell division or budding.	3. Takes place by union of male and female gametes.
4. Faster process as compared to sexual reproduction only under favourable conditions.	4. Slower process as compared to asexual reproduction.
5. Gametes are not formed.	5. Gametes are formed.

11.2. SEXUAL REPRODUCTION IN HUMANS

Based on their function during the reproductive process, reproductive organs can be classified as follows :

(a) Primary reproductive organs
(b) Accessory reproductive organs

Primary reproductive organs are the organs that produce male and female gametes. In females, *ovaries* (produce eggs) and in males, *testes* (produce sperms) are the primary reproductive organs.

Accessory reproductive organs are the organs that help in the process of fertilization (union of male and female gametes).

11.2.1. Male Reproductive System

Male reproductive system consists of the following organs (Fig. 11.1) :

(a) Testes   (c) Accessory glands
(b) Sperm ducts   (d) Penis

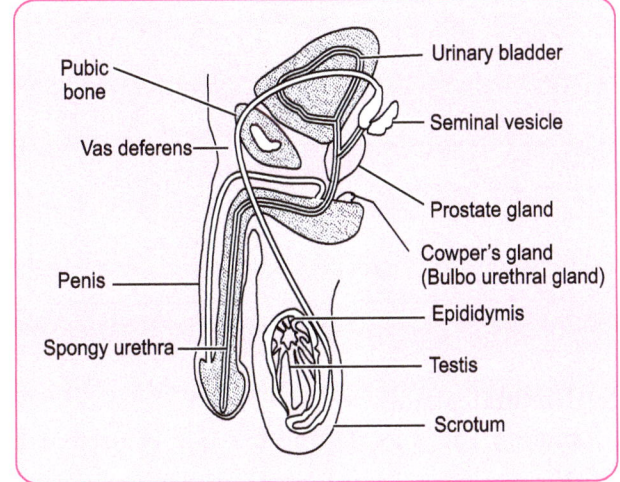

Fig. 11.1 : Male reproductive system in vertical section

(a) Paired testes

Location : These are a pair of oval glands that are enclosed in a thin walled loose cutaneous pouch called scrotum. Initially, at the embryonic stage, testes develop on the posterior wall of abdomen. But, before birth they descend into the scrotum. Testes cannot produce sperms if they do not descend into the scrotum. Such a condition can lead to sterility in males. The testes are located outside the abdominal cavity because sperm formation is very sensitive to temperature. Being outside the abdominal cavity, the temperature of scrotum is 1 to 3°C lower than the temperature inside the body. This provides an optimal temperature for the formation of sperms.

Structure : Each testis is enclosed in a dense fibrous covering the tunica albuginea and is internally divided into 15-20 sections known as lobules. Each lobule consists of *seminiferous tubules* (semini – sperm, ferrous – bearing) and interstitial cells (Interstitial – filling in between).

Seminiferous tubules : Production of sperms takes place here and the process is known as *spermatogenesis*.

Interstitial cells : They produce the male hormone, testosterone. They are present in between the coils of the seminiferous tubules. These cells are also known as *Leydig cells* and are responsible for development of secondary sexual characters in males.

Temperature regulation : Temperature plays a very important role in the production of sperms. Temperature in the testes is regulated with the help of contraction and expansion of the muscle fibres. Temperature should be 2 to 3 degree Celsius lower than the body temperature in order to be able to produce sperms. Muscle fibres contract if it is too hot and lead to the loosening of skin of the scrotum so that the testes are hanging down away from the body. Skin folds in such a manner in cold climate that testes are drawn closer to the body for warmth.

Functions : Production of sperms and secretion of male hormone known as testosterone.

(b) Sperm ducts

Location : From the rete testis, 15-20 fine ductules from the vasa efferentia arise which enter the *epididymis* (Fig. 11.2). *Epididymis* is about 6 meters long and is a highly coiled tube. *Epididymis* is divided into three zones:

(i) **Head :** Upper part which is wider and receives the vasa efferentia.

(ii) **Body :** This part temporarily stores the sperms undergoing maturation.

(iii) **Tail :** Here spermatozoa are stored temporarily before entering the vas deferens.

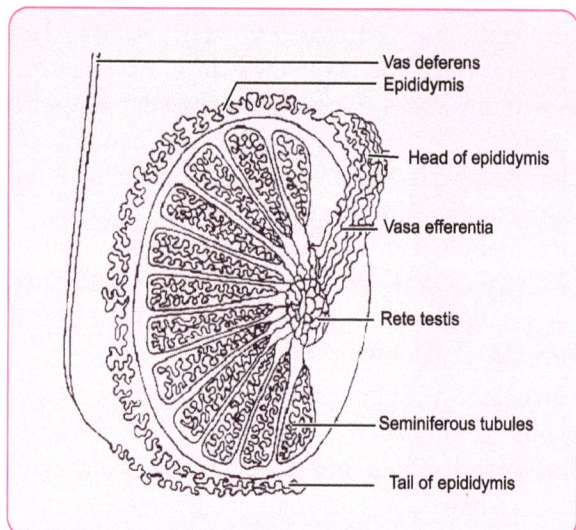

Fig. 11.2 : Longitudinal section of testis

Sperm ducts (vas deferens) start from epididymis and enter the abdominal cavity through the inguinal canal. It rises into the abdominal cavity and loops over the ureter of that side. Vas deferens is joined by the duct from the seminal vesicle to form the ejaculatory duct. The duct then passes through the prostrate gland and opens into the urethra.

Structure : They are each 30 centimeters long in humans and connect the left and right epididymis to the ejaculatory duct to provide a passage for the movement of sperms.

Function : It performs the function of transporting the sperms from the epididymis to the urethra.

(c) Accessory glands : Following are the accessory glands :

(i) Seminal vesicles

Location : They are present posterior to and at the base of the urinary bladder in front of the rectum (Fig. 11.3).

Structure : These are coiled pouch-like structures. A duct from each seminal vesicle joins the corresponding sperm duct before uniting with the urethra.

Function : They secrete a fluid which serves as a transportation medium for the sperms. The milky fluid that results from a mixing of this fluid with sperms is called semen. The sluggish sperms become more active by mixing with this secretion of the seminal vesicles.

(ii) Prostate gland

Location : It surrounds the urethra at the base of urinary bladder.

Structure : It is a single, bilobed doughnut-shaped gland.

Function : The fluid secreted by this gland is alkaline in nature and serves to neutralize the acidity of the female vaginal tract which would otherwise kill the sperms due to acidity.

(iii) Cowper's gland (Bulbourethral gland)

Location : It is present beneath the prostate gland on either sides of urethra. They have ducts that open into the urethra.

Structure : They are pea-sized ovoid glands, white in colour.

Function : It secretes a white, alkaline and viscous mucus which helps in the lubrication of tip of the penis.

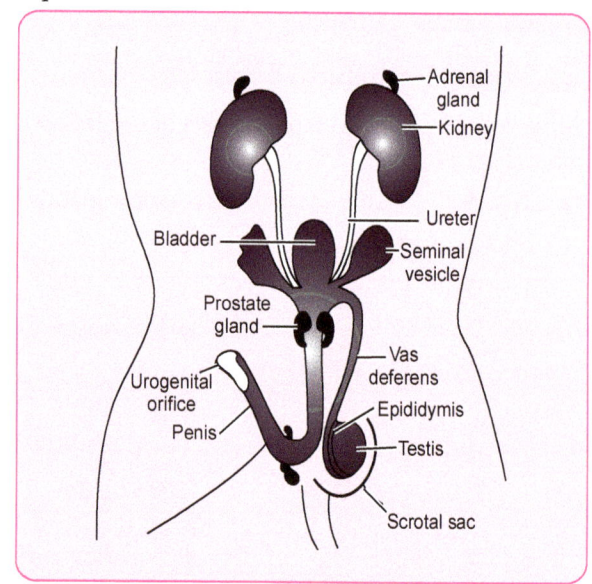

Fig. 11.3 : Male reproductive organs

(iv) Urethral gland

Location : It is located by the side of urethra in penis.

Function : It secretes fluid which performs the function of lubrication.

(d) Penis

Location : It is a muscular organ present in front of the scrotum. It is a copulatory organ.

Structure : It is cylindrical in shape (Fig. 11.4) and consists of erectile tissue and vascular spaces.

Function : Under the influence of sexual stimulation, large amount of blood flows into the penis which then enters into the vascular spaces. Due to this, penis enlarges and becomes rigid. Such a condition is called erection. During ejaculation, the smooth sphincter muscles which are present at the base of the urinary bladder close it, due to which urine cannot be expelled and semen cannot enter urinary bladder. Thus, it serves as a passage for both urine and semen. *Peristaltic contraction* of sperm ducts starts in males and the semen is discharged into the vagina. This is called *ejaculation*.

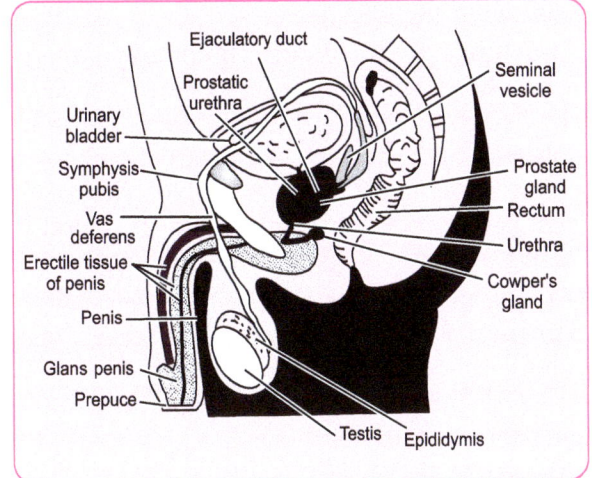

Fig. 11.4 : Lateral view of the male reproductive system

Semen is a milky fluid formed by the mixture of sperms and secretions from seminal vesicles, *prostate gland, Cowper's gland* and *urethral gland*. Its average amount per ejaculation is 2.5 to 5 ml which consists of 50-150 million/ml sperms. If the sperm count per ejaculation is less than 20 million/ml, it indicates that the male is sterile.

Functions of Semen

(i) Semen helps in transfer of sperms into the vagina.

(ii) It nourishes and activates the sperms to keep them active and mobile.

(iii) It neutralizes the acidity of urine in urethra of male and vagina of the female to protect sperms.

(iv) It facilitates the sexual act by lubricating the reproductive tract of the female.

Sperm : It is composed of the following zones :

(i) Head : It consists of a cap like structure at its tip, called an acrosome which is having a specialized lysosome. It facilitates the penetration by the sperm into the ovum by digesting its membrane. It has a large compact nucleus that consists only of condensed DNA and basic proteins. RNA, acidic proteins and nucleolus are absent.

(ii) Mid piece : It has abundant mitochondria which provide the energy which is utilized for locomotion. It has oxidative enzymes and provides energy for the movement of the sperm in the vagina.

(iii) Tail : Tail is long, slender and strengthened by axial filament. It projects posteriorly as end piece. It directs the sperm.

The head and middle piece of the sperm enter the ovum during fertilization.

PROGRESS CHECK

NAME THE FOLLOWING

1. Animal having both the gametes.
2. Process of sperm production.
3. Covering of testis.
4. Gland present beneath the prostate gland.

11.2.2. Female Reproductive System

Following are the parts included in the female reproductive system (Fig. 11.5) :

(a) Pair of ovaries
(b) Pair of oviducts (Fallopian Tubes)
(c) Uterus
(d) Vagina
(e) Vulva

(a) Pair of ovaries

Location : They are present in the pelvic cavity on either side of the uterus. They are held in position by a series of ligaments known as ovarian ligaments. Each ovary is attached to the broad ligament of the uterus by a mesentery, mesovarium. Second layer is known as *germinal epithelium* followed by tunica albuginea. The matrix is divided into cortex and medulla. Many ovarian follicles

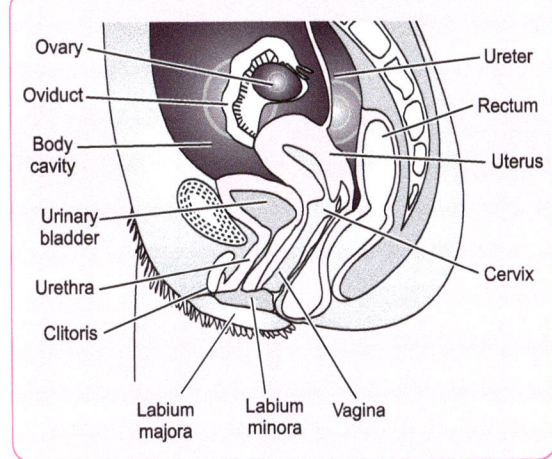

Fig. 11.5 : Side view of female reproductive system

(*Graafian follicles*) in different stages of development are present in cortex. Due to the rupturing of ovarian follicle, secondary oocyte is released and this process is known as ovulation (Fig. 11.6).

Structure : They are oval in shape and resemble unshelled almonds in size and shape.

Function : Produce mature ova by the process called oogenesis. The mature ova are discharged from the ovaries by the process known as ovulation. The ovaries secrete the female sex hormones oestrogen, progesterone and relaxin.

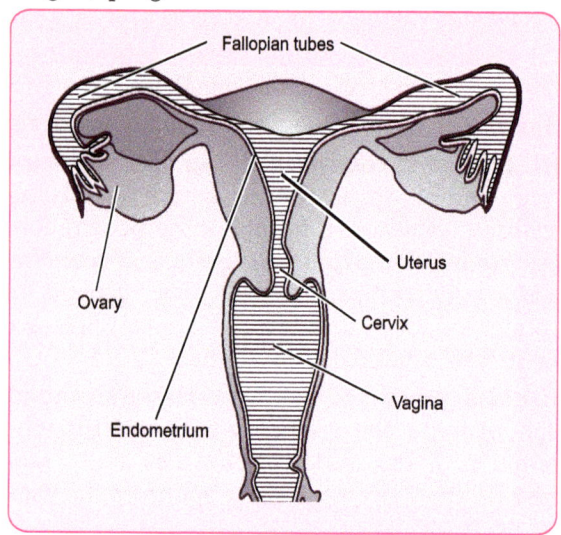

Fig. 11.6 : Front view of female reproductive organs

(b) Oviducts (Fallopian tubes)

Location : They extend from each ovary of the female mammals to the uterus on each side.

Structure : Each oviduct is tubular in shape and is 10-15 cm long. Each oviduct has a funnel-shaped opening known as *infundibulum* or *ostium*. This infundibulum has finger-like projections called fimbriae. Each oviduct is attached to the lateral end of the ovary. Walls of the oviduct are internally lined with ciliated epithelial cells. Infundibulum is followed by ampulla, then isthmus.

Function : It is able to push down the egg from the ovary into the uterus due to the muscular contraction of the walls of oviduct. This movement is known as *peristalsis*.

(c) Uterus

Location : It is present in the pelvic cavity above the urinary bladder and rectum.

Structure : It is a hollow pear-shaped muscular organ (7 cm × 5 cm). It can be divided into two regions, namely an upper wider portion (coming out from the two oviducts) known as fundus. Uterus has three layers, the outer wall *perimetrium*, middle layer is known as *ometrium* and inner layer is *endometrium*. Its upper broader portion is called *corpus uteri* (body of the womb) and the lower tapering and narrower part is called *cervix uteri* or neck of the womb.

The interior part of the uterus is known as the uterine cavity. The innermost layer of the uterus which is lined with secretary and ciliated cells is known as endometrium.

Function : Provides protection and nourishment to the developing embryo.

(d) Vagina

Location : It is present between urinary bladder and the rectum. It extends from the lower end of the uterus to the outside.

Structure : It is a tubular fibromuscular organ which is lined with mucus membrane. It measures about 7-10cm in length. There may be a thin folded membrane called hymen which partially closes the opening present at the lower end of vagina. The hymen is frequently ruptured during childhood due to heavy exercise. Vagina is the organ where the penis is inserted during coitus (act of copulation).

Function : It has smooth muscles that provide greater elasticity to the walls and thus provides passage for the baby at childbirth (parturition). The vagina serves as the birth canal.

(e) Vulva

Location : It is the external genitalia present in females.

Structure : Urethra and vagina are the two openings present in vulva. It has two small fleshy folds namely labia minora and labia majora which are equivalents of male scrotum. In the uppermost angle of vulva, infront of the urethral opening, there is a small cylindrical mass of erectile tissue which is sensitive in nature called *clitoris*. A pair of Bartholin's glands occurs one on either side of the vaginal orifice. These glands secrete a clear, viscid fluid which serves as a lubricant during copulation.

Ovulation : It is the process of rupture of the follicle resulting in the release of egg into the funnel of oviduct. Fimbriae of oviduct funnel then pick up the egg.

The remnant of the ruptured follicle persists for sometime in order to convert into a yellow mass of endocrine tissue called corpus luteum which secretes hormones oestrogen, progesterone and relaxin. At the time of pregnancy, corpus luteum continues to secrete the hormones till the time placenta is formed.

Puberty : It is defined as the period during which immature reproductive organs in boys and girls mature in order to be able to reproduce. In girls it is manifested by the enlargement of breasts and in boys by the enlargement of testis.

11.3. FERTILIZATION

Fertilization can be defined as the union of egg nucleus and sperm nucleus (Fig. 11.7). During mating, sperms are released by the male into the female vagina. Sperms are deposited in the vagina near the cervix of uterus. About 400 million sperms are released in a single ejaculation. These sperms swim with the help of their tail and travel through the cavity of uterus to reach the oviducts. If an ovum is present in the oviduct, fusion of ovum and sperm takes place when the lysosomal enzymes of the sperm cells digest the limiting membrane of the ovum. Once the sperm enters the egg, the entry of other sperms is restricted by a chemical barrier.

Thus, the fertilization can be defined as the fusion of the male gamete (sperm) and female gamete (ovum) to form zygote.

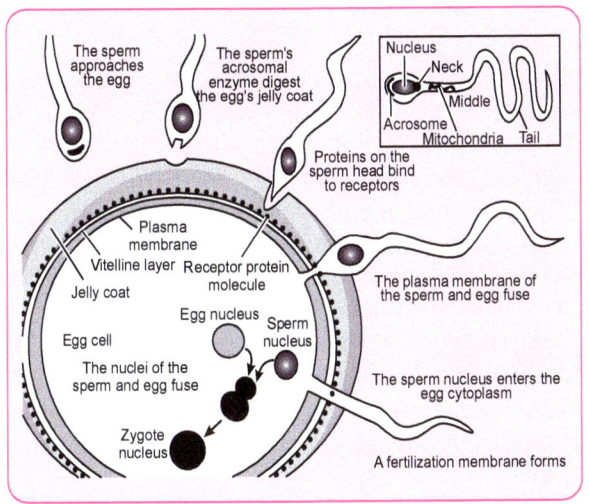

Fig. 11.7 : Process of fertilization

The life expectancy of sperm is usually 48 hours

Fraternal twins : Fraternal twins are formed when a woman's body releases two eggs during her cycle, and both are fertilized. These twins will come out looking very similar, but may possess completely different facial features, body types, hair types and even hair and eye colour.

11.4. MENSTRUAL CYCLE IN HUMAN FEMALE

In humans, female fertility period usually spans from an age of 12-13 years to 45-50 years. The onset of puberty in human females when she becomes mature enough to reproduce is called menarche.

Each month, reproductive system repeats a regular pattern of events, controlled by hormones

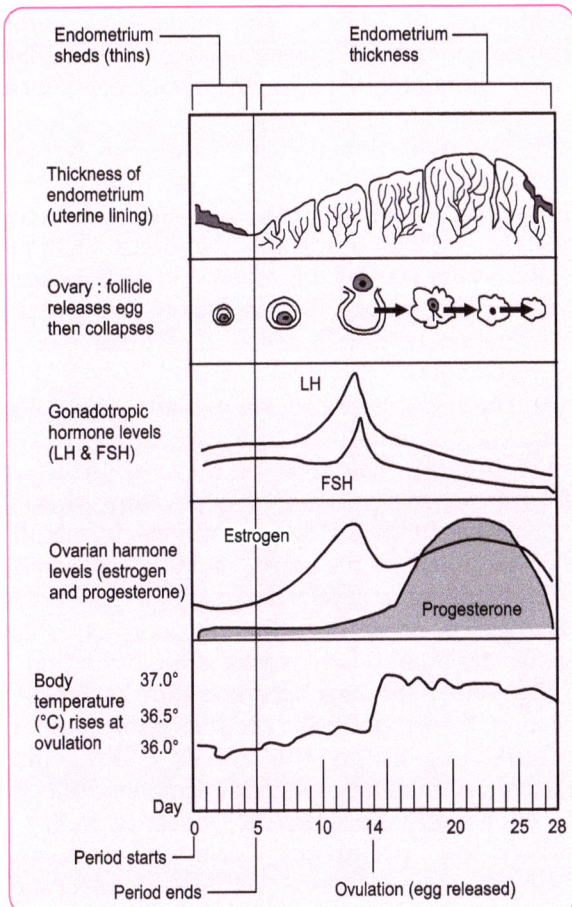

Fig. 11.8 : Menstrual cycle in human female

and this chain of events is known as *menstrual cycle*. The menstrual cycle is defined as the time from the first day of a woman's period to the first day of her next period. The average menstrual cycle time for women is 28 days. The menstrual cycle is divided into four phases :

(a) The menstrual phase : Day one of the menstrual phase is the first day of the menstrual cycle. In this phase, the cellular lining of the uterus is shed with blood flow. This menstrual blood (also known as menses) is shed from the lining of uterus, known as the endometrium. Menstrual blood is shed from the uterus through the cervix, vagina and out through the vaginal opening. This fluid may be bright red, light pink or even brown. A period usually lasts from three to seven days.

(b) The follicular phase : During this phase, generally from the 5th to the 13th day of the onset of the menstrual cycle, the hormone oestrogen causes the lining of the uterus to grow, or proliferate. The maturation of the Graafian follicle takes place. Graafian follicle is the final stage in the maturation of an ovum inside the ovary. This lining, called the endometrium starts to develop to receive a fertilized egg and to provide for the future development of embryo. The increase of another hormone, called the *follicle-stimulating hormone* (FSH), in turn stimulates the growth of ovarian follicles. Each follicle contains an egg.

(c) The ovulation phase : Ovulation happens when a mature egg (ovum) is released from ovarian follicle to the nearest fallopian tube during menstrual cycle. The egg then travels into the uterus. Ovulation usually occurs on day 14, when one of the ovaries releases a mature egg. If fertilization is to occur, it must happen within 24 hours of ovulation or the egg degenerates.

(d) The luteal phase : After ovulation, the follicle becomes a hormone producing structure called the corpus luteum. The cells of the corpus luteum produce oestrogen and large amounts of progesterone, with the latter hormone, stimulating the development of the uterine lining in preparation for implantation of a fertilized egg.

If there is no fertilization, the corpus luteum degenerates about two weeks after ovulation. If fertilization of the egg occurs within 24 hours of ovulation, then about five days after fertilization, the fertilized egg enters the uterus and becomes embedded in the lining. With implantation, cells that will eventually become the placenta begin to produce the "pregnancy hormone" or human chorionic gonadotropin (HCG). It interrupts menstrual cycle by providing continual stimulation of the corpus luteum to produce progesterone. This prevents the loss of uterine lining.

11.5. IMPLANTATION

Zygote formed as a result of fertilization undergoes cell division to form a small hollow ball of cells called blastocyst. Blastocyst now attaches itself to the root of the uterus in order to get nourishment from the mother. This process of attachment of the blastocyst to the wall of uterus, after 7-8 hours of fertilization is known as implantation.

11.6. PLACENTA

There is an intimate but temporary mechanical and physiological connection between foetal and maternal tissue for nutrition, respiration and excretion etc. of the foetus. This connection is known as placenta. The foetal surface is smooth and it is attached to the placenta by an **umbilical cord**.

Functions of Placenta :

(i) It connects the foetus with the uterus of mother.

(ii) It helps the excahnge of nutrients, gases and waste products between mother and the foetus.

(iii) It acts as an endocrine gland and secretes chorionic gon adotrophin hormone which maintains the pregancy.

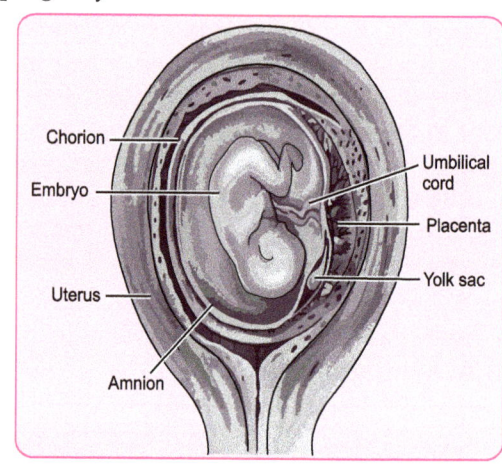

Fig. 11.8 : Placenta

11.7. AMINION

The mammalian embryo is protected by two sacs, the chorion and amnion. The amnion, which contains the amniotic fluid to protect the embryo from shocks. Amnion is a sac like structure which develops around the embryo even before the formation of allantois.

The main function of amnion is to protect the embryo from the physical damage or mechanical shocks.

11.8. GESTATION PERIOD

In human beings, the mothers carry the foetus for 280 days approximately which is known as gestation period. The gestation period is the time from conception to birth. **Parturition** is the process of expelling the fully formed young one from the mother's uterus at the end of gestation period.

Animation for Reproductive System

https://www.youtube.com/watch?v=a8fgm-zEYjQ

https://www.youtube.com/watch?v=yyuRhoAOjM8

PROGRESS CHECK

FILL IN THE BLANKS

1. Ovaries produce mature ova by the process of _____ .
2. Ovary is supported by the _____ membrane.
3. _____ secretes hormones oestrogen and progesterone.
4. _____ is external genitalia in females.

THE REPRODUCTIVE SYSTEM

EXERCISE

A. VERY SHORT ANSWER TYPE

(I) Multiple Choice Questions

1. Fertilization in human female takes places in
   (a) Vagina (b) Oviduct
   (c) Uterus (d) Vulva
2. The secretion of ADH is inhibited by
   (a) Emotion and stress (b) Nicotine
   (c) Alcohol (d) Morphine
3. One egg is released from an ovary in a human female every _____ .
   (a) 28 days (b) 48 days
   (c) 14 days (d) 38 days
4. Which of the following structures is found in both male and female bodies?
   (a) Scrotum (b) Uterus
   (c) Urethra (d) Testes
5. What is the function of the testes?
   (a) Mitosis (b) Meiosis (c) Oogenesis
6. What is the name of the hormone responsible for the development of masculine secondary sexual characteristics?
   (a) Follicle stimulating hormone
   (b) Oestrogen
   (c) Progesterone
   (d) Testosterone
7. What are the female gonads called?
   (a) Ovaries (b) Oocytes (c) Ova (d) Gametes

(II) Complete the Following Table by Writing the Name of the Structure or the Function of the Structure Given

Structure	Function
(1) Fallopian tube	(i) _____
(2) Umbilical cord	(ii) _____
(3) _____	(iii) Increases force during uterine contraction
(4) Placenta	(iv) _____
(5) Corpus luteum	(v) _____

B. SHORT ANSWER TYPE

(I) Name the Following

1. Testis in male is present in which structure?
2. What is the name of the tube that extends from ovary to uterus?
3. Name of the lower part of the birth canal.
4. Foetus in female mammals develops in which organ?
5. Name of the hormone secreted by graafian follicle.
6. Name the method of contraception in which the sperm duct is cut and ligated.
7. Thin walled sac of skin that covers the testes.
8. The permanent stoppage of the menstrual cycle in a women aged 50 years.

(II) Differentiate between the Following

1. Semen and sperm.
2. Implantation and gestation.
3. Graafian follicle and corpus luteum.

(III) Mention the Functions of the Following

(1) Testicles
(2) Corpus luteum
(3) Placenta
(4) Acrosome

C. LONG ANSWER TYPE

1. Explain the process of fertilization.
2. Explain Male reproductive system in brief.
3. Explain Female reproductive system in brief.
4. What is placenta? How is placenta beneficial to the foetus?

D. STRUCTURED/APPLICATION BASED

1. Given here are diagrams showing different stages in the process of fertilization of an egg in the female reproductive tract :

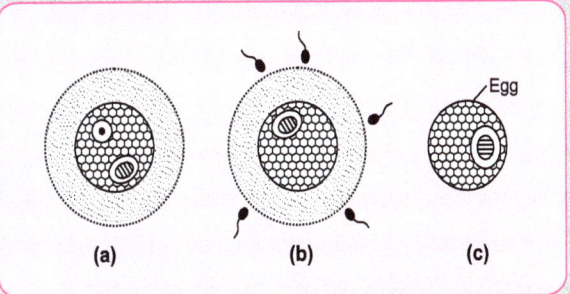

(a) Use the alphabets given below each diagram to show the correct order in the process of fertilization.
(b) Where in the female reproductive system does this process normally takes place?
(c) What is the biological term for the product of fusion?
(d) What is the chromosome no. of the egg and the fused product?
(e) Draw a neat labelled diagram of a mature human sperm.

2. The diagram given below is that of a developing human foetus in the womb. Study the same and then answer the questions that follow :

(a) Name the part labelled 1.
(b) Mention any two functions of the part labelled 2.
(c) Explain the role played by the part labelled 3.
(d) What is the normal gestation period (in days) of the developing foetus?

3. Study the diagram given below and then answer the questions that follow :
(a) Name the parts labelled 1 and 2. State the function of each part.
(b) State any one function of the amniotic fluid.
(c) Waht is the role of the umbillical cord in the development of the foetus.
(d) Name the part in the diagram which is endocrine in nature.

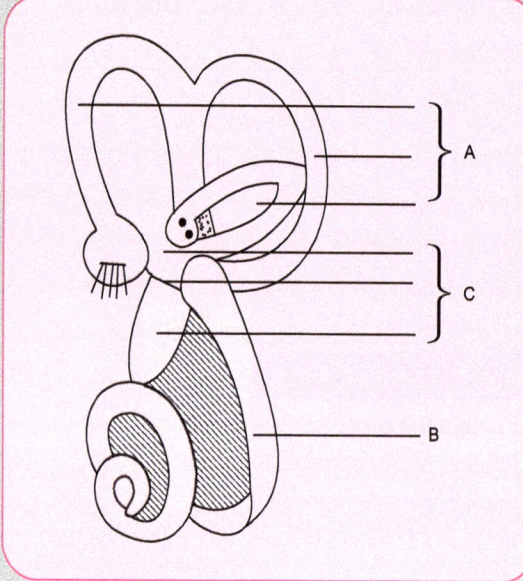

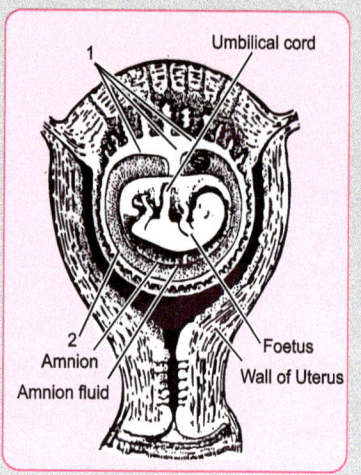

DO YOU KNOW ?

➤ The normal amount of menstrual flow during the entire period is about a quarter of a cup.
➤ Over the course of a lifetime, you release about 400 eggs in their mature form.
➤ The number of eggs that are still contained in the ovaries depends on how old you are.
➤ Human testes can produce 10 million sperm cells daily. This is enough to recopulate the entire earth in only 6 months.
➤ A pregnant woman's dental health influences the health of foetus.
➤ A woman is born with all the eggs she will ever have in her life, about 2 million.
➤ Males can produce about 1,000 sperm cells per second.
➤ You have the same receptors in your sperm, as you do in your nose. So once the sperm is released into the vagina, it hunts for the egg by its scent.
➤ During pregnancy, uterus will expand up to 500 times its normal size.
➤ Largest penis in the animal kingdom is that of the blue whale.
➤ Largest human cell is the female egg (ovum). Smallest human cell is the male sperm (spermatozoa).

12

POPULATION: THE INCREASING NUMBERS AND RISING PROBLEMS

CHAPTER HIGHLIGHTS
12.1. Population
12.2. Rising Population – A Global Threat
12.3. The State of Population Growth in India
12.4. Measures to Limit Large Families in India

12.1. POPULATION

A group of organisms belonging to a particular species residing in a geographically localized area and having ability to interbreed is termed as population. Simply put, population of a country is the sum total of the people who live in that country. If the population of a nation is to stay constant the number of births must be the same as the number of deaths. But often, natural calamities like floods, famines, earthquakes, epidemics, etc. lead to greater number of deaths than births.

Similarly, improvement in healthcare leading to reduced infant mortality and increased life expectancy leads to a rise in population. Mass movement of people from one place to another also influences the population of a place. Members of a population of a particular region have some common characteristics, share a common gene pool and are capable of interbreeding among themselves to produce fertile offspring.

The population of a nation plays a very important role in national development. Population is directly proportional to the use of natural resources. But, beyond that, the economic efficiency and productivity of the population is also important. Students should be familiar with the adverse effects of uncontrolled population growth, viz., increased pollution, indiscriminate consumption of natural resources, lowering of living standards, etc. We shall also briefly discuss methods of curtailing human population growth.

12.2. RISING POPULATION – A GLOBAL THREAT

Our country comprises only 2.5% of the land area of the world. India's galloping population growth influences its present national and regional development to a great extent. India's population crossed the 1 billion mark on 11th May, 2000. The fact that India has now a billion people reflects bleakly on the quality of life and the family planning measures that the government adopted since independence. Based on data from the Registrar General and Census Commissioner of India, the rate of increase in population is 1,55,31,000 per year.

The UNFPA (United Nations Population Fund) forecasts that India has a grim future if the population does not stop growing. The population report published by the organization states that lack of water for irrigation may lead to a 25% decrease in grain production. In sub-Saharan Africa and sections of the Indian sub-continent which houses about one-third of the population of the world, aquifers are on the way out and so is the per capita crop land.

In 1987, the United Nations ascertained that the population of the world was 5,000 million. The fact was that the population increased to double the figure from 1650 to 1850 and then quadrupled since 1850. The UN also ascertained that if the number of people continues to grow in this manner, then the population of the world will double by 2028. This phenomenon of sudden increase in the population is termed as population explosion.

The reasons behind rise in population are better living conditions, agricultural and technological developments and a decrease in the onset and outbreak of various diseases and epidemics. Alleviation of food shortages, better hygiene and sanitation and improved health care are all reasons for the sharp rise in world population.

Unfortunately, most developing and poor nations can ill afford this exponential increase in population. Third world nations like India, Indonesia, Mexico and Ethiopia experienced tremendous population growth by the year 2000. But, the populations of developed nations are likely to remain the same.

Overpopulation : It occurs when the population growth rate is considerably higher than the national income, thus, leading to the decline of per capita income.

This term was first coined by economist **B. Thomas Robert Malthus.** It was he who explained that population grows by geometrical progression while food production increases by arithmetical progression. Thus, it is imperative that a check be kept on population growth so that to ensure that food production and population grow at approximately the same rate.

The drawbacks of overpopulation : It is a natural conclusion that a large population would be beneficial to the economic development of the country. But, too large population could adversely affect the growth of the country because it would put pressure on the available resources. Due to this mismatch in resources and population, people are unable to benefit from the measures taken to boost the country's economy.

Apart from this, resources like food, land, water, energy, forest and mineral wealth are immensely pressurized. A way out of this situation is to distribute the rising national income among a greater number of people.

A brief discussion of the impact of overpopulation on various resources is given below :

(a) Food : The fact that population increases by geometric progression whereas food production increases by arithmetic progression results inadequate food supply for the people. This leads to undernourishment, malnutrition, starvation and famines. The burgeoning population will ultimately outpace the availability of food resources.

(b) Land : More and more land is being brought under cultivation and for housing and industrial expansion every year. Due to this excessive demand for land resources, availability of suitable land will be stretched to the limit. We will till and farm more and more land so that we can grow more food. As the population grows, the vicious cycle is repeated.

(c) Forests : Forests are natural resources which are of the greatest importance. Forests not only supply us with timber, pulp and medicine but also ensure the maintenance of our ecological balance and keep the stability of the climate intact. Due to increasing need for land, forests are being cut indiscriminately. Thus, large scale deforestation has become one of the most serious consequences of increasing population and has led to drought, soil erosion, flood and extinction of several animals and plants species.

(d) Water : When the population reaches alarming proportions, proper hygiene and sanitary conditions cannot be maintained. Rivers, ponds, lakes are polluted and the availability of clean and pure drinking water is under strain. Due to this, health is also indirectly affected.

(e) Energy : Coal and petroleum are fossil fuels. These are non-renewable resources. A rise in population leads to a rise in energy consumption. If the rate of consumption continues at the present rate the petroleum reserves may be depleted within the next 150 years and coal within a few more decades.

(f) Minerals : As population is directly proportional to the utilization of minerals, increasing use of minerals will lead to exhaustion of minerals. According to one estimate, copper reserves will exhaust in about a hundred years time.

12.3. THE STATE OF POPULATION GROWTH IN INDIA

The increase in population in India has continued from the first quarter of the century. There was a brief drop in the population due to the onset of famines and epidemics. Thereafter, the population has risen rapidly. By 1991, the population had reached the gigantic proportion of 844 million. The population is expected to jump by 16 million every year. If the present trend continues, India is going to be the most populous country much before 2050. Every sixth person in the world is an Indian, but in terms of land area, India has just 2.42 percent of total land area of the world.

The period between 1951 and 1981 has been called the period of population explosion.

Important terms related to population

(a) **Birth rate or natality**: It is defined as the number of children born per 1000 living persons per year.

(b) **Mortality or death rate**: It is defined as the number of deaths per 1000 living persons per year.

(c) **Growth rate of population**: It is calculated as the difference between the birth rate and death rate. It is positive if the birth rate is more than the death rate and it is negative otherwise. It is represented by the growth curve.

(d) **Sex ratio**: It is defined as the number of females per 1000 males. This ratio has declined over the years.

(e) **Population density**: It is defined as the size of the population in relation to unit area at given instance of time. It is calculated by the formula, $D = N/S$, where D = density of population, N = No of individuals, S = unit of space.

(f) **Demography**: It is defined as the statistical study of human population covering all aspects and parameters.

PROGRESS CHECK

FILL IN THE BLANKS

1. _____ and _____ are fossil fuels.
2. Population grows by _____ expression.
3. Growth rate of population is increased by _____.
4. _____ is the statistical study of population.

Reasons for the growing population: The increasing population is a measure of the the survival rate or the difference between the birth and death rates.

Following are the reasons for rapid increase in the population:

(a) **Famine and flood relief measures**: Natural calamities result in great loss to human life. The steps being taken by the government to reduce such accidental deaths have started yielding results. Better transportation and food storage facilities have led to the betterment of food distribution facilities. Import of food grains at the right time and international co-operation between nations leads to better food availability and the avoidance of starvation deaths.

(b) **Improved medical facilities and public health measures**: Medical advancements and widespread availability of health services brought about by International health organizations have reduced the incidence of epidemics and diseases. The mortality rate has also come down. This also leads to population growth.

(c) **Public health programmes**: Public Health Programmes have led to better water supply and sanitation facilities. Free milk is being provided to children of poor households in municipal schools. The general health of the people has shown a marked improvement, leading to higher survival rates.

(d) **Lack of education**: A large part of the population is illiterate, ignorant and superstitious. People are not aware of the functioning of the reproductive system. This ignorance directly results in avoidance of birth control measures and contributes to over population.

(5) **Religious and social customs**: Because of prevailing social structure too, many people are reluctant to accept the family planning programmes.

12.4. MEASURES TO LIMIT LARGE FAMILIES

When we live in a world with only limited space, society does not develop freely. So, it is important to educate people about the necessity of small families and persuade them to stop raising large families.

(a) **Family planning**: Family planning and welfare programmes have been receive great stress from the Government of India. It has undertaken a huge campaign on war footing to create awareness among the people. The message of 'small family, happy family' is being broadcast by all public media and means of mass communication (Fig. 12.1). At many public places, the inverted red triangle, the symbol of the Family Planning program is well-displayed. Social workers and volunteers

Fig. 12.1: A stamp demonstrating family planning

undertake trips to faraway towns and villages to increase awareness among the people about birth control measures that can help delay the conception of children. Methods include the use of *contraceptive pills, intra-uterine devices* (IUDs) and condoms and surgical methods like vasectomy for males and tubectomy for females.

(b) Enforce restriction on marriage age : The Government must increase and strictly enforce the minimum marriage age for both boys and girls. A low marriage age leads to a high birth rate. The government has a difficult job on its hands as it is difficult to alter what the people have believed for ages.

(c) Awareness or education : It is necessary to educate people to accept small family norms, its benefits and to create awareness about population explosion and its impact on the family. There should be family planning education at senior school level.

(d) Birth control techniques : Birth control techniques involve the prevention of fertilization made possible by the use of contraceptives (pills, devices, jellies) and several other means.

Following are the birth control techniques

(i) Contraceptive pills : Many birth control pills are available nowadays that prevent the release of the egg from the ovary.

(ii) Barrier methods

(1) Condom : It is used by men to prevent the sperms from entering in the Vagina. It is made of latex. It protects both male and female from *sexually transmitted diseases (STD)* and *Acquired Immuno Deficiency Syndrome AIDS.*

(2) Diaphragms : It is a cap-like thing which prevents the sperms from entry into the uterus. But, the only difference is that it is used by females. It is fitted deep inside the vagina on the mouth of uterus.

(3) Spermicidal agents : These are chemicals which kill the sperms that are present in the vagina near uterus.

(iii) Intra-uterine devices : Lippe's loop and copper-T are the two intrauterine devices that are fitted inside the uterus. It prevents the implantation of the blastocyst.

(iv) Surgical methods : This includes vasectomy in males and tubectomy in females.

(1) Tubectomy : In this, the abdomen is opened and fallopian tube is tied with a nylon thread to close the passage of the egg. It is performed by making a small hole in the abdomen.

(2) Vasectomy : In this procedure, a small cut is made in the scrotum and a small piece between the two ligatures of vas deferens is removed. It is considered safer if the husband gets operated as it neither affects the manliness nor it reduces the pleasure of intercourse.

PROGRESS CHECK

NAME THE FOLLOWING

1. Prevents the release of egg from ovary.
2. Cap like thing, prevents the entry of sperm into uterus.
3. Two surgical techniques that can be used to prevent pregnancy.

EXERCISE

A. VERY SHORT ANSWER TYPE

(I) Name the Following

1. The government of India's message for a happy family.
2. Methods of regulating birth rate.
3. A surgical method of sterilization.
4. Lack of proper food intake.
5. The difference between birth and death rate.
6. Average number of births per unit time.
7. Statistical study of human population of a region.

B. SHORT ANSWER TYPE

1. What natural calamities lead to greater number of deaths and births?
2. What do forests supply us with?
3. What was the population of India in 1991?
4. Name three fossil fuels.
5. Which period was called the period of population explosion?
6. Suggest some method of fertility control of men.
7. Which is the most thickly populated area..

POPULATION : THE INCREASING NUMBERS AND RISING PROBLEMS

C. LONG ANSWER TYPE

1. What are the resources that are put under pressure due to population growth?
2. What are the reasons for the growing population?
3. What are the results of the rise in population?
4. What are the different methods of birth control?

(I) Explain
1. Death rate and birth rate
2. Birth control techniques

(II) Define the Following Terms
1. Demography
2. Population density
3. IUD
4. Vasectomy
5. Death rate

DID YOU KNOW ?

- The fertility rate in India (children born per woman) in 2011 was 2.6.
- The child sex ratio 0-6 years (females per 1000 males) in 2011 is 914. In 2001, it was 927.
- The literacy rate in India in 2011 was 74%. In 2001, it was 65%.
- In India, the population over 65 years of age in 2011 was 5 percent. This rate for the world was 8% in the same year.
- From 2001 to 2011, India added 181 million people to its population, equal to the total population of Brazil.
- India will overtake China as the world's largest country by about 2020.
- There are 53 Indian cities which are home to atleast one million people, 18 more than the last census (2001). The number of Indian towns has increased by 2,774.
- India's rural and urban populations have increased by similar amounts in the last decade, 90.47 million and 91.00 million respectively. However, the respective growth rates were 12.18 percent and 31.80 percent.

13

AIDS TO HEALTH

CHAPTER HIGHLIGHTS
13.1. *Need to Keep Healthy*
13.2. *Immunity and Immunization*
   13.2.1. *Local Defense System*
   13.2.2. *Immune System*
   13.2.3. *Kinds of Immunity*
   13.2.4. *Antibodies*
13.3. *Vaccination and Immunization*
13.4. *Antitoxins*
13.5. *Antiseptics and Disinfectants Prevent Catching of Disease*
13.6. *Antibiotics – Penicillin and Others*
13.7. *Sulphonamide Drugs*
13.8. *First Aid*

13.1. NEED TO KEEP HEALTHY

Health is of virtual importance to each one of us. Keeping healthy has two aspects :

(i) Personal health and hygine that ensures the individual safeguards himself from infections.

(ii) Community heath means public health, i.e. ou surrounding should kept clean.

Man has always felt the need to remain healthy and unhindered by diseases. This can be tackled on two levels, first by safeguarding and promoting the health of the individual and secondly that of the community as a whole. Though it's not wholly possible to quantify the health of a community, health professionals infer it from mortality rates, illness, disability figures, etc. An individual's health on the other hand means their 'fitness'- the facility to perform and live a fruitful life.

Health promotes a sense of well-being and motivation for life. There is a clear connection between staying fit and good health. A thorough grounding in the various types of diseases, the measures to curb and cure them and consistent health checks are factors that significantly promote good health. Awareness and knowledge of administering First Aid proves indispensable when in emergency situations like accidents, burns, fractures, poisoning etc.

World Health Day : World Health Day is celebrated every year on 7th April globally to draw attention on important health issues facing the world every year.

13.2. IMMUNITY AND IMMUNIZATION

Immunity : It is simply the capacity of the body to resist attacks from disease causing microbes and other pollutants.

Our bodies are constantly open to such attacks through the skin, mucous membranes of sensitive organs like the eyes, nose or urinary and genital tracts or even through the food we eat or the air we breathe.

Stopping these harmful elements from entering our bodies is the first line of defense built-in into our systems. However, even if some of these manage to invade our bodies, our bodies are capable of fighting them and rendering them harmless.

Immunization : It is defined as the method by which an individual's immune system is reinforced against diseases through the use of inoculations like vaccines and serums.

Think of viruses, bacteria, and parasites as hostile, foreign armies that are not normally found in your body. They try to invade your body to use its resources to serve their own ends. Doctors often use the word 'foreign' to describe invading germs or other substances not normally found in the body. The immune system is your body's defense force which helps keep invading germs out, or helps kill them if they do get into your body.

The body's defense system works at two levels.

(a) Local defense system : This system acts as an obstruction to germs at their various entry points. It includes :

(i) Defensive mechanical barriers
(ii) Ejected, if they enter
(iii) Protective secretions which kill germs
(iv) WBCs which help in fighting against germs.

(b) Immune system : It comes into play after the damage is done and the germs are already inside the body tissue.

13.2.1. Local Defense System

(a) Defensive mechanical barriers : The body's external defense against pathogens is called the first line of defense of this system.

(i) Skin : Skin acts as the body's first line of defense. The various layers of skin block-off bacteria like a force field. Keratinocytes present in the skin perform the function of forming a barrier against environmental damage such as pathogens. Bacteria from the air or from direct contact with infected objects remain on the surface of our skin because they can't get in. When the skin is broken, or germs find a way in through the mouth, nose etc., we fall sick. Thorough washing with soap and water helps to disinfect the skin. Clotting of blood at the site of an open wound also serves to prevent the entry of germs into the body.

(ii) Hair : Body hair serves the purpose of cutting off the germ's passage inwards and up to the skin. Hair in the nasal cavity traps dust containing the germs.

(iii) Mucus : It is a viscous substance that lines the epithelial layer of organs and contains antiseptic enzymes. For example :

(1) The mucus layer along the inner walls of the stomach shields its cell linings from the highly acidic environment within it.

(2) Cervical mucus present in the female reproductive system prevents infection. The pathogens are destroyed by chemicals present in the mucus.

(iv) Stomach acid : Stomach acid kills bacteria and parasites that may have been swallowed with food.

'Friendly' (beneficial) bacteria : Beneficial bacteria growing on your skin, in your bowels and other regions in the body such as the mouth and the gut stop harmful bacteria from taking over completely.

(b) Ejected, if they enter : The bodily mechanisms of coughing, sneezing and vomiting are direct means of expelling from the digestive and respiratory systems what the body deems unwanted and alien. Urine flow flushes out pathogens from the bladder area. Even the unsightly appearance of pus means that the body's infection fighters are working.

(c) Protective secretions which kill germs : Secretions like tears, sweat, nasal mucus and saliva all have a specific and important role to play in helping us stay healthy. They possess properties that destroy harmful bacteria and germs. Tears in the eyes have lysozymes to kill bacteria entering the eyes. Sweat, saliva and nasal secretion also have lysozymes. Hydrochloric acid present in gastric juice and bile secreted by hepatic cells also check bacterial growth.

(d) WBCs (white blood cells) which detect and attack germs : White blood cells (WBCs), or leukocytes, are a part of the immune system and help our bodies fight infection. They circulate in the blood so that they can be transported to an area where an infection has developed. Leukocytes are of two basic types :

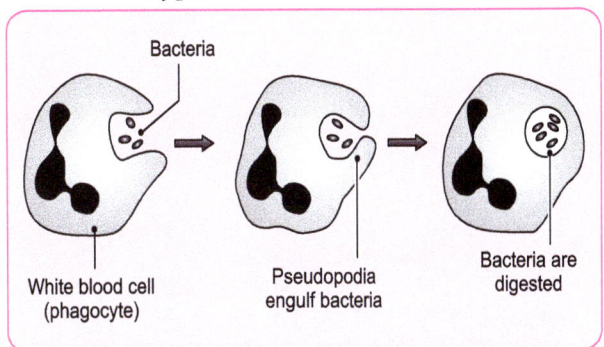

Fig. 13.1 : Engulfing of bacteria by white blood cells (phagocytosis)

(i) Phagocytes : Cells that consume invading organisms are termed as phagocytes. They squeeze out of the blood capillaries by diapedesis and destroy the bacteria or germs by engulfing them (phagocytosis) (Fig. 13.1).

(ii) Lymphocytes : Cells that help the body to remember and identify what has previously attacked it and aid the body in destroying them are termed as Lymphocytes. Lymph fluid is made up of white blood cells, which helps the body to fight diseases.

Merits of local defense system

(1) Reaction is instantaneous and immediate.

(2) The remedy they provide does not hinge on previous contact with infection.

(3) They are able to fight against a plethora of bacteria, microbes, viruses, toxins and parasites that invade our body.

13.2.2. Immune System

The principal behind the immune system is to keep contagious microorganisms, such as certain bacteria, viruses, and fungi, out of the body and to eradicate any contagious microorganisms that do invade it. This system is made up of an intricate and vital network of cells and organs that help the body to fight infection. It comes into play when the pathogens have already reached the protective barrier sand have infiltrated the deeper tissues and other organ systems.

When this happens, blood and the other body fluids perform the function of destroying foreign or unwanted substances. The fluids in our bodies have certain proteins called antibodies which react with the invading pathogens and antitoxins and counter their poisons. By doing this, it keeps the body secure against disease (immunity).

13.2.3. Kinds of Immunity

Immunity can be grouped into two main categories, namely innate and acquired immunity (Fig. 13.2).

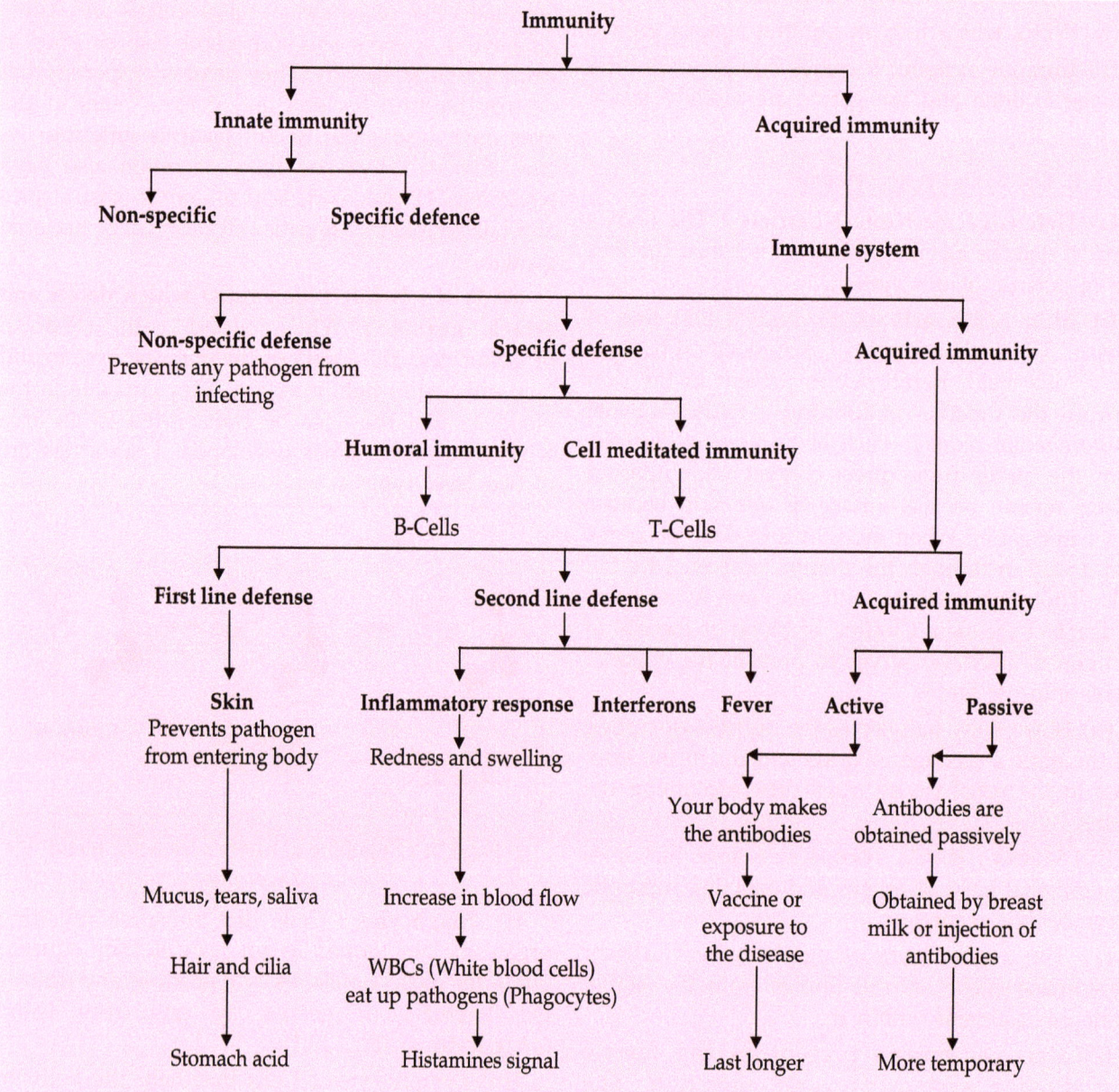

Fig. 13.2 : Kinds of Immunity

(a) Innate immunity : This immunity is by the virtue of the genetic composition of the individual. It is present in the body even when there is no external stimulus or prior infection. It is further classified as follows :

(i) Non-specific innate immunity : It is the level of natural resistance to all disease and infection in a general way. For example, vegetation acquires various highly infectious diseases which do not affect human beings. This is true even for some animal specific diseases.

(ii) Specific innate immunity : In this case, we find a natural immunity only to a specific type of pathogen. It is a phenomenon where a certain race or particular individuals do not contract certain infectious diseases. For example, Africans and Indians are less likely to contract leprosy than Europeans, Japanese or Chinese. This is not because of nutritional, climatic or economic causes but is in fact due to an inherent natural immunity within a particular race.

(b) Acquired immunity : Immunity to a particular disease that is not innate but has been acquired during one's lifetime.

It could be the product of :

Either

A prior infection (actively acquired immunity) e.g., Once a person has contracted "mumps", he is highly unlikely to suffer from it again.

Or

"Ready-made" antibodies supplied from outside (passively acquired immunity) e.g., Antitoxin is used to counteract the effect of a scorpion sting which is made up of antibodies created in a horse.

(i) Actively acquired immunity : The process by which the individual's body develops resistance due to previously having contracted the disease or from an antigen (chemical found on the surface of the disease causing germ cell) which enters the body naturally, (ii) naturally acquired active immunity or is administered externally, as in vaccinations, (artificially acquired active immunity). In both cases, lymphocytes in the body react in two ways :

(1) They create antibodies which circulate freely in the blood and lymphatic system, isolate the pathogens and destroy them.

(2) They generate killer cells which contain specific receptors for unwanted antigens present on attacking germs. Actively acquired immunities prove long lasting and are carried out through 'memory' lymphocytes.

(ii) Passively acquired immunity : This consists of immunity administered to an individual not by the functioning of his own body but from an external source by means of "readymade" antibodies. This immunity can be again of two types :

(1) Naturally acquired passive immunity : If antibodies produced by an individual are naturally transferred to another individual, the latter develops immunity. In this process recipients acquire immunity without the involvement of their own immune system and transfer of antibodies takes place naturally; this is referred to as "natural acquired passive immunity". For example: Immunity acquired by babies through natural transfer of antibodies from mother via placenta and breast milk is the best example of this type of immunity.

(2) Artificially acquired passive immunity : In this case, the antibodies are produced in the blood of an animal by injecting a safe amount of the germ into the animal's body. The animal's body creates antibodies in its blood. This blood is then refined, tested for purity and made into a serum (containing antibodies). This antiserum is then injected to treat patients. When a patient is suffering from a poisonous snake bite they are injected with antivenin to treat it.

Table 1 : Differences between Active and Passive Immunities

Artificial Immunity	Passive Immunity
1. Generated within our own bodies.	1. Administered from outside.
2. Brought on by infection or when the individual has had contact with immunogens. (like vaccines and allergens)	2. Received through readymade antibodies.
3. Offers long lasting and efficient protection.	3. Does not offer long lasting and efficient protection
4. Immunity takes place only aftersome time has elapsed (time needed while the antibodies are being produced).	4. Instantly effective.

13.2.4. Antibodies

An antibody is a protein molecule produced by lymphocytes in response to a foreign substance or antigen. They have the following characteristics :

(a) They are *proteins* falling under the category of immunoglobins.
(b) They are created by specialized lymphocytes in the presence of antigens (chemical substances found on the germ cells). These lymphocytes mainly concentrate in the lymph nodes and spleen and also in the blood being pumped all over the body. *Lymphocytes* originate in bone marrow and are termed as *B-lymphocytes*.
(c) The body has the ability to create infinite varieties of different antibodies.
(d) Antibodies are specialized i.e., a particular kind of antibody will react against only one specific kind of antigen.
(e) An antibody identifies its particular antigen and then attaches to it thus rendering it harmless. Later, it is destroyed and emitted from the body.
(f) Particular antibodies are present in the blood of certain individuals from birth itself. These individuals do not contract the particular disease against which they have been fortified with antibodies even if these germs have infiltrated the barriers and escaped the phagocytes.
(g) A persons immunity due to antibodies when exposed to antigens, is of either a short duration (as in a cough, diarrhea) or for a longer duration (as in influenza, mumps, etc.).

HIV and AIDS

HIV is a virus which is most commonly passed on by sexual contact. HIV attacks cells of the immune system. Untreated, the immune system weakens so that the body cannot defend against various bacteria, viruses and other germs. This is when AIDS (commonly now called late-stage HIV infection) develops. However, early detection and treatment with antiretroviral therapy (ART) means that people living with HIV can lead active, healthy lives, although they may get side-effects from the treatment.

13.3. VACCINATION AND IMMUNIZATION

Vaccination is the process by which antigens are introduced in order to stimulate the immune system of an individual to build up an adaptive immunity to a disease. Vaccines can check or mitigate the effect of infection by deadly pathogens. In scientific terms the process is called prophylaxis and the substance introduced into the body is called a *vaccine*.

Vaccines are administered into the body by injecting or orally. (e.g., typhoid vaccine) Once it enters the body, the vaccine stimulates the WBCs to generate antibodies against pathogens of that particular disease.

Small pox, the first disease for which a vaccine was developed in the eighteenth century, was generally associated with the terms vaccine and vaccination. But, these terms are now used in a general sense.

Four categories of vaccines

(a) **Killed germs** : Like WC/rBS vaccine for cholera, Havrix vaccine for Hepatitis A, and TAB vaccine for typhoid, Salk's vaccine for polio.

(b) **Attenuated virus** : Meruvax vaccine against rubella, varicella vaccine used against the viral disease commonly known as chickenpox.

(c) **Living fully poisonous germs** : To prevent the spread of smallpox, people were vaccinated with cowpox which is similar to the smallpox virus. As opposed to smallpox where several pustules develop, the cowpox virus causes only a single pustule. When infected, the body (most often) identifies the similar smallpox virus because of its antigens thus, enabling it to fight the smallpox disease easily. Fortunately this virus has been eradicated as of 1979, due to vaccination campaigns all through the 19th and 20th centuries.

(d) **Toxoids** : Researchers have found that they can treat toxins such that they are inactivated by the use of formalin, a solution consisting of formaldehyde and sterilized water. On receiving a vaccine containing a harmless toxoid our immune system learns how to fight off the natural toxin. Vaccines used against diphtheria and tetanus are examples of toxoid vaccines. Researchers are trying to create a vaccine against the AIDS virus.

Immunization : It is defined as the method of developing resistance to disease producing germs or their toxins by introducing killed germs or germ substances to induce the production of specific antibodies.

Great efforts have been made for immunization against various common infectious diseases in India. These efforts have been on a mass scale with the aim of reaching the entire population. The National Immunization Schedule is as follows :

AIDS TO HEALTH

Table 2 : National Immunization Schedule

Age	Vaccination
3-12 months	DTP-3 doses at intervals of 4-6 weeks. Polio (oral) – 3 doses at intervals of 4–6 weeks
BCG (Intradermal)	
9–15 months	Measles vaccine – one dose
18–24 months	DTP – Booster dose Polio (oral) booster dose
5–6 years	DT against diphtheria and tetanus, booster dose
Typhoid (TAB) vaccine-	2 doses at an interval of 1–2 months
10 years	Tetanus toxoid – booster dose Typhoid vaccine booster dose
16 years	Tetanus toxoid – booster dose
Typhoid vaccine booster dose	
Mothers (during pregnancy)	

(i) **Immunized previously :** One booster dose of tetanus toxoid preferably 4 weeks before the expected date of delivery.

(iii) **Non-immunized :** Two doses of tetanus toxoid, the first dose between 16 and 24 weeks and the second dose between 24 and 32 weeks of pregnancy.

Abbreviations
DTP = Diphtheria, Tetanus and Pertusis (Whooping cough)
DT   = Diphtheria and Tetanus;
BCG = (Baccillus of Calmette and Guerin) Tuberculosis

PROGRESS CHECK

ANSWER THE FOLLOWING

1. Define the term immunization
2. Give four characteristics of antibodies.
3. Name the following :

(a) Immunity provided not by one's own body but from an outside source is called...............
(b) Chemicals found in the blood which acts against germs or their secretions are called...............
(c) The system which is the body's defense against disease is...............

13.4. ANTITOXINS (ANTIBODIES)

Toxins are poisonous substances created within living cells or organisms, e.g. snake venom, scorpion sting poison, etc. The term was coined by organic chemist **Ludwig Brieger**.

Antitoxins are antibodies produced within the body which possess the facility to defuse and counter a specific toxin from entering inside and harming the body. They are produced within the bodies of certain animals, plants, and bacteria. While they prove highly efficient in neutralizing toxins, they destroy bacteria and other microorganisms as well. Currently the term being used is "antibody" rather than "antitoxin".

Antibody is a blood serum protein produced in response to the injected antigens.

The remedy for a person suffering from Hepatitis B is to inject the patient with antibodies produced from an outside source. In such a case, antibodies are developed by introducing a safe amount of the germ into the bodies of horses, rabbits etc. The animal's body then develops antibodies against the germ. The blood of the animals is clarified and made into a serum which is used to treat patients. This treatment with antibodies cultivated in another host is called *passive immunization*. The Serum Institute of India and the Haffkine Institute are developing various such antisera.

13.5. ANTISEPTICS AND DISINFECTANTS PREVENT CATCHING OF DISEASES

Antiseptics : Antiseptics are antimicrobial chemical substances that are applied on the surface of living tissue/skin to lessen the likelihood of infection. As they are very dilute and mild they do not adversely affect the skin or body. Boric acid, hydrogen peroxide, surgical alcohol, sodium bicarbonate, phenol etc., when diluted act as efficient antiseptics. A few antibiotic creams provide the same benefits.

Disinfectants : Certain strong chemicals are also sometimes applied or sprinkled to areas and locations where germs are likely to thrive and multiply. Such chemicals are called Disinfectants. Commonly used disinfectants are Ethyl alcohol, chlorine, Lysol, DDT mixture, thymol, peracetic acid, lime, etc.

Precaution : Since disinfectants are strong chemicals, they should not come in contact with human skin. Extreme heat and boiling water serve the purpose of killing germs and hence may be referred to as physical disinfectants.

Deodorants are mistakenly thought to have antiseptic or disinfectant properties but in reality have neither. All they do is disguise bad odours.

Table 2 : Differences between Antiseptics and Disinfectants

Antiseptics	Disinfectants
1. Mild and dilute pathogen destroying chemicals.	1. Concentrated pathogen destroying substances.
2. Does not injure the skin and body.	2. Can cause injury to the skin and body.
3. Applied on one's body.	3. Used in areas where germs are likely to thrive, e.g. toilets, hospitals, etc.
Example : Boric acid.	**Example :** DDT

13.6. ANTIBIOTICS – PENICILLIN AND OTHERS

Antibiotics are chemical substances produced by some micro-organisms, and can kill or inhibit the growth of other micro-organisms.

One of the earliest antibiotics discovered was Penicillin in 1929, yet it was actually used on patients only in the 1940. The term "antibiotics" was coined much later by Selman Waksman in 1942.

Discovery of penicillin : The bacteriologist **Alexander Fleming** working in London in 1928 accidentally discovered penicillin. He discovered that a laboratory culture of *Staphylococcus* had been contaminated by a blue-green mold and that the bacteria closest to the mold had dissolved. He proceeded to grow the mold in a pure culture and realized that this mold contained a substance that destroyed a variety of disease-causing bacteria. Fleming gave this bacteria destroyer the name Penicillin in 1929. As this substance would become an efficient killer of bacteria, it was first administered to laboratory animals and produced affirmative results without causing any harm to the animals.

When penicillin was used on humans in the year 1940 it proved to be effective against a number of infections. Especially, when used in the treatment of *gonorrhea*, a sexually transmitted disease, it produced excellent results. Physicians would sometimes prescribe a combination of penicillin and sulpha drugs, called *"pentidsulph"*. Subsequently, a host of other antibiotics like *neomycin, clarithromycin, ampicillin, amoxicillin* have been discovered and continue to be used successfully to treat several infectious diseases.

Antibiotics are also used for the prevention of infection during the vulnerable period just after surgical operations.

Sources of antibiotics : Penicillin is made from a mould *Penicillium notatum* which is very like the mould that often grows on oranges, lemon and other citrus fruits. Some high yielding *Penicillium chrysogenum* strains are being used to aid in the commercial mass production of penicillin; but it also being produced synthetically.

Streptomycin, a very widely used antibiotic is synthesized by *bacterium streptomyces*. This drug is widely used as it is effective against a wide variety of diseases.

Today, large quantities of antibiotics are being made synthetically instead of through cultures of micro-organisms.

Uses of antibiotics

(a) Principally, antibiotics are used in medicine to treat diseases that are caused by bacteria.

(b) A few antibiotics are used as food preservatives, chiefly in fresh meat and fish.

(c) Some antibiotics are introduced into animal feed so as to prevent internal infections.

(d) Antibiotics used on plants target pathogenic bacteria and other prokaryotic microbes (e.g., phytoplasmas).

How is it?

Readers may wonder how exactly the antibodies kill the germs. The below are two examplesPenicillin: Penicillin is an antibiotic that kills bacteria by interfering with the cell wall of the micro-organism. It causes this by inactivating an enzyme essential for the cross connection between bacterial cell walls. Streptomycin: Streptomycinis a protein synthesis inhibitor. It binds to bacterial ribosomes and eventually inhibits synthesis of protein and so finally causes death of microbial cells.

13.7. SULPHONAMIDE GROUP OF MEDICINES

From ancient times, man had felt the need to discover newer and better drugs to treat diseases. In the past, he had ventured to use the naturally available plant and animal products which produced positive results. He has also ventured to use chemicals to make medicines. Chemotherapy is a good example of such a chemically produced drug.

Salvarson is a medication that was first used in 1910 to cure syphilis and trypanosomiasis. It was the first contemporary chemotherapeutic agent, but its major drawback was that it frequently proved poisonous for the patient as well.

Sulphonamides or Sulpha drugs are a group of synthetic antimicrobial agents discovered in 1930 that showed positive results against various bacterial diseases. Sulfonylureas and thiazide diuretics are two such sulpha drugs. These drugs are produced synthetically and they function by interfering with the metabolism of bacteria which results in their death.

Today, sulphonamides are seldom used and when they are, it is in combination with other antibiotics for treating specific illnesses.

PROGRESS CHECK

FILL IN THE BLANKS

1. Antibodies produced in response to injected germs are called _____
2. Lysol is a _____
3. Term antibiotic was coined by _____
4. Penicillin was discovered by _____

13.8. FIRST AID

We know that health related emergencies occur in our lives with alarming frequency.Some such emergent situations are listed below:

(a) Severe cuts on the body
(b) Broken bones and fractures.
(c) Particles entering the eye
(d) Unexpected unconsciousness
(e) A heart attack
(f) Burns of various degrees
(g) Consuming poisonous material
(h) Drowning mishaps
(i) Bitten or stung by poisonous animals or insects
(j) Electric shock

In all the above cases, one must be trained to give initial treatment that can keep the patient alive before a doctor can arrive. Whatever care can be provided before definitive medical treatment is possible and the patient is taken to the nearest available hospital must be performed. This is known as First Aid. The following are some such treatments:

(i) Bleeding : If someone is bleeding, it is important to elevate the affected part so as to minimize gravitational outflow of blood. Rinse the area that has been cut with clean water, press gently at the area using clean cotton wool, and apply a mild antiseptic to the injury.

(ii) Fractures : When dealing with fractures, place the victim in a comfortable position and loosen or take off any clothing material from the affected part. Make sure not to move the part/parts that have been fractured. If the arm of the patient is fractured then tie a sling to rest the arm in it.

(iii) Eye : If some foreign substance enters the eye one must be careful not to rub the eye. Instead rinse carefully by sprinkling water into the eye.

(iv) Unconsciousness : If someone loses consciousness, one should lay the person down in a comfortable position, loosen the clothes and give him space to breathe fresh air.

(v) Heart attack : In this situation, immediately lay the person down flat and horizontally, and allow him to breathe fresh air.

(vi) Burns : If the burns are minor they need to be washed immediately with slightly cold water for a few minutes. One should not rub the burnt surface. If available, apply creams/ ointments meant for burns on the burnt area.

(vii) Swallowing poison : If someone has consumed some poisonous or toxic substance, the person should be given large amounts of salt water to consume, even forcibly, in order to induce vomiting.

(viii) Snake bite : One should quickly squeeze out some blood from the wound; tie a tourniquet above the site of the wound to prevent the venom from spreading to the rest of the body.

(ix) Stinging : If one has been stung by a bee or wasp, extricate the sting if it is still embedded in the body, squeeze out some blood to expel the venom. It would help to apply to the site of the wound some alkaline substance like lime or baking soda.

(x) Artificial respiration : When due to accidents like drowning, electric shock or a head injury someone stops breathing, it is vital that his respiratory system be stimulated to help him breathe. In this case breathing is usually induced through artificial means.

In a drowning mishap, the victim may have swallowed a lot of water which may enter the victim's lungs and cause suffocation. One needs to place the victim with his front facing downwards and tilt his head to either side. Compress the back repeatedly to expel the water from the system. When most of the water has been removed, begin artificial respiration at once.

While performing artificial respiration the steps below need to be followed :

(1) Carefully place person on their back, and place a towel if available underneath their shoulders in order to raise the chest and throw back the head.

(2) Extend the victims hands upwards and backwards. This will make his chest expand and draw in air.

(3) Next, cross the victim's arms and press them against the ribcage. The air will now be expelled.

(4) Repeat these two steps at least 15 times per minute. Continue till the victim begins breathing naturally or till medical aid arrives.

Studies have shown that people who lack humor in their lives tend to have less protective immune responses.

EXERCISE

A. VERY SHORT ANSWER TYPE

(I) Multiple Choice Questions

(Choose the most suitable option)

1. Streptomycin is :
   (a) a disinfectant (b) an antiseptic
   (c) an antibiotic (d) an antitoxin
2. Lymphocytes produce :
   (a) antitoxins (b) antibodies
   (c) antivenins (d) disinfectants
3. Who discovered Penicillin?
   (a) Spencer Lister (b) Paul Ehrlich
   (c) Louis Pasteur (d) Alexander Fleming

(II) State the Following

1. The full form of WBC.
2. The name of the mould which produced Alexander Fleming's Penicillin.
3. The immunity developed by an individual due to previous infection or antigen.
4. Give the names of three antiseptics and four disinfectants.
5. The antibiotic that was discovered first.
6. The treatment given to a person who has stopped breathing.
7. Introduction of weakened or dead pathogens in the body to produce resistance against disease.

(III) Give the Full Form of

1. WHO
2. AIDS
3. DTP vaccine
4. Give the technical term for chemical substances produced within the body which possess the facility to defuse a specific toxin from entering inside the body.

B. SHORT ANSWER TYPE

(I) State Whether True (T) or False (F)

1. Phenol is an antitoxin.
2. Antivenins are produced inside animals like horses.
3. Antibodies are only made through culturing micro-organisms and never synthetically.
4. BCG is a vaccine against typhoid.
5. Vaccines used against diphtheria and tetanus are examples of toxoids.
6. Chickenpox is the first disease for which a vaccine was developed in the eighteenth century.

(II) State the Differences between

1. Active immunity and Passive immunity
2. Disinfectant and Antiseptic
3. Innate immunity and Acquired immunity
4. Antibiotic and Antiseptic

(III) Pick out the Odd Example in the Group Given Below and State Why it is Odd.

1. Hydrogen peroxide, surgical alcohol, penicillin, sodium bicarbonate
2. HCl, thymol, peracetic acid, lime
3. Sneezing, antibodies, vomiting, diarrhea.
4. Streptomycin, Havrix, cowpox virus, toxoids

(IV) Complete the Table

Vaccine	Disease	Nature of Vaccine
	Tuberculosis	....
Salk vaccine		
....	Polio	Inactivated dead virus
....	Tuberculosis	....
....	Tetanus	Extracts of toxins

(V) Answer the Following Questions

1. Give the name of three vaccines and the diseases against which they offer immunity.
2. Give the merits of the local defense system.
3. State four uses of antibiotics.
4. In case someone has been bitten by a poisonous snake describe the principle of the treatment he should receive.
5. Which first aid steps should one take in the emergency situations mentioned below?
   (a) Particles entering the eye
   (b) A heart attack
   (c) Consumption of poison

C. LONG ANSWER TYPE

1. Explain in brief the Local Defense System.
2. Vaccines have been developed to provide immunity against diseases. Elucidate.
3. State in short the function of the following health aids.
   (a) Antibiotics
   (b) Disinfectants
   (c) Sulphonamides
4. What is First Aid? State briefly which first aid treatment one must carry out in the following cases :
   (a) A little girl's fingers are scalded with boiling water.
   (b) An old man loses consciousness in a crowded train.
   (c) A college student has been hit by a van and has fractured her foot.
   (d) A lady is drowning in the sea.

DO YOU KNOW ?

- Sleeping for less 5 hours a night has been shown to greatly depress immune function in your body.
- Toxins such as air pollution, pesticides and even second-hand cigarette smoke can affect your body's natural defense system.
- There are around 50 billion white cells in the blood whose only function is to keep your body's natural defenses in good condition; so don't worry if you lose 5 billion when you donate blood, you still have a few left.
- When your catecholamine and CD8 levels change, these levels can suppress the immune system.
- Dieting decreases natural killer cell functionality, therefore weakening the immune system.
- Regular massages have been shown to increase the number and aggressiveness of NK cells and protective antibodies, thereby giving the immune system a boost.
- Though the body needs some sunlight to produce vitamin D, too much sunshine can suppress the immune system.
- Even just a month after quitting smoking, smokers can strengthen the immune system - experiencing an increase in immune cell activity and a decrease in the stress hormone cortisol.
- The number one way to boost the immune system is to reduce stress.

14

HEALTH AND HEALTH ORGANIZATIONS

CHAPTER HIGHLIGHTS
14.1. Introduction
14.2. Common Health Problems in India
14.3. Health Organizations
14.3.1. Local Bodies
14.3.2. National Organizations
14.3.3. International Organizations

14.1. INTRODUCTION

Health is defind by World Health Organization (WHO), it is a "State of a complete physical, mental and social well being and not merely the absence of disease or infirmity'. It is derived from the Greek words heuexia, meaning 'a good habit of body' and hygeiea meaning 'a good way of living'. The Greeks considered health to be a holistic entity. An unhealthy lifestyle leads to diseases. Habits like lack of physical movement, a diet that is not conducive to good health, overeating, over-consumption of alcohol and smoking all lead to ill health. Thus health is a positive and enjoyable feeling of well-being reflected in both mental and physical fitness of the mind and body.

14.2. COMMON HEALTH PROBLEMS IN INDIA

In our country, population is widely spread over the following geographical entities :

(a) Big cities : Numerous high-rise buildings, too many public and private vehicles, inadequate potable water supply and lack of sewage facilities are some of the many problems ailing our major cities. Many of our major cities have industries located in populated areas.

(b) Towns : These are not as densely populated as the big cities and life here is laid-back and not as busy. But here also, recent years have seen the pace of life becoming more hectic.

(c) Villages : Villages have a small population. Agriculture, poultry-farming, dairy-farming and cottage industries are the principal occupations here.

(d) Remote areas : Primarily tribals live in remote areas. They usually subsist on forests and forest products. These areas usually lack in proper civic amenities as well as medical facilities.

(e) Slum-dwellings : Slums usually comprise of shanties, huts and small ramshackle houses which generally have unhealthy living conditions. You can easily find them on the outskirts of big cities.

(i) Health problems

Food and water-borne diseases : Food borne diseases are caused by consuming contaminated food or beverages. There are many different types of food borne infections which result in a large number of casualties every year. Water borne diseases are caused by pathogenic micro-organisms that most commonly are transmitted in contaminated water. Water from hand pumps may be contaminated and unfit for bathing and lead to infections of various types.

Washing, drinking and using this water in preparation of food or the consumption of food thus infected can result in various diseases such as diarrhea, gastroenteritis, typhoid and dysentery to name a few. The main causes of food and water borne diseases include inadequate water supply, contaminated water, water with harmful mineral content, water that is fed with untreated sewage, effluents from industries, etc.

(i) Insect and air-borne diseases : Insect-borne diseases include dysentery, cholera, diarrhea and typhoid which are caused by houseflies and malaria, dengue and filariasis are caused by mosquitoes and plague which is caused by rat fleas. Air-borne diseases include tuberculosis, whooping cough, pneumonia and diarrhea (air coming in contact with food). These diseases are caused when we do not live in clean surroundings.

(ii) Medical facilities : *Immunization* is a major means by which we can stop the spread of these diseases. But, our country is still at a nascent stage in the implementation of immunization. Lack of knowledge and superstitious beliefs also play a major role in the spread of these diseases and may lead to serious consequences. The scarcity of medical facilities, primarily in the rural areas also leads to deaths and health problems.

(iii) Professional or occupational hazards : The government is also often concerned about the health of its citizens who may suffer from these diseases because of inhalation of harmful gases and dust. Problems related with people working in carpet industry, glass making units, the fireworks industry etc. still remain serious issues which need to be tackled.

(iv) Diseases due to pollution : Diseases caused due to air, water and soil pollution such as tuberculosis, asthma are very common in cities and towns.

PROGRESS CHECK

ANSWER THE FOLLOWING
1. Name any two common water borne diseases.
2. Name any two disease caused by pollution.

14.3. HEALTH ORGANIZATIONS

14.3.1. Local Bodies

Local bodies work in cities, towns and large villages and cater to the health and sanitation of the inhabitants. These include municipal corporations, municipalities, town area committees etc. They appoint regular staff and maintain equipment to cater to:

(a) Sanitation : Elimination and proper disposal of wastes, garbage, sewage and elimination of breeding places of flies and mosquitoes.

(b) Supply of safe drinking water : Supply clean water for drinking, farming, sanitation and hygiene.

(c) Vaccinations : Immunization is conducted among babies and adults so that they are protected from the onset of diseases like tetanus, pertusis (whooping cough), diphtheria, tuberculosis, polio-myelitis, measles, etc. If there is a risk of outbreak of an epidemic, these programmes are intensified and carried out on a war footing.

(d) Maintaining statistical records : Local bodies compulsorily register births, deaths and statistics of health and diseases in their respective areas. Local bodies have family planning centers to educate the people about the benefits of a small family, medical care centers, community health education to sensitize the people about healthy habits, maternity and child health centers to give guidance to mothers.

14.3.2. National Organisations

There are a number of agencies, institutes and research centers that are involved in the study of the health problems ailing the country. Regular surveys are conducted, disease transmitting agents and their breeding places are recognized and prophylactic immunization is organized. National bodies are particularly working on the following diseases :

(a) Malaria   (b) Dengue
(c) Tuberculosis   (d) Leprosy
(e) Cholera

National Institute of Communicable Diseases, located in Delhi is one such example.

14.3.3. International Organisations

(a) World Health Organization (Fig. 14.1) : It has its headquarters in Geneva and has 193 member countries. WHO is a specialized agency of the United Nations (UN) that is concerned with international public health. It was established on 7 April 1948. WHO has some great achievements in the betterment of health conditions to its credit, especially in third world countries of the tropical regions where there exist grave health problems because of climatic (tropical climates are the infecting grounds of many dangerous organisms) and economic reasons (rapidly growing population poses many health problems). WHO has six regional offices in the world including one in New Delhi. Each regional office works for its member states. Following are the functions of WHO :

Fig. 14.1 : Logo of the world health organization (WHO)

(i) It collects and supplies information about the origin of epidemic diseases like *Cholera, Plague, Typhus, Yellow fever, Small pox*, etc.
(ii) It promotes projects for research on diseases like *Cancer* and *Tuberculosis* by providing finance to such projects.
(iii) It supplies information to the countries on latest *vaccines, antibiotics* and other medicines.
(iv) It regulates quarantine conditions to prevent spread of diseases.
(v) It also fixes pharmaceutical standards for certain group of drugs in order to ensure the purity and size of dose.
(vi) It organizes campaigns for the control of epidemic and endemic diseases.

(b) Red Cross : The Red Cross is a voluntary health organization. It was set up in 1864 by **Henry Dunant**, a native of Switzerland. The organization has its headquarters in Switzerland. The symbol of this society is a red-coloured cross emblazoned on a white background (Fig. 14.2). The Red Cross society is an international non-political organization. It promotes fundamental principles and humanitarian values. Red Cross day is celebrated on 8th of May each year. Following are the functions of Red Cross :

Fig. 14.2 : Symbol of the Red Cross

(i) The organization caters to people's health during war and natural calamities like famine, drought, floods, earthquakes, etc.
(ii) It educates the general public about the importance of learning first aid and other such skills, helps us with ambulances during emergencies and other health care in times of need.
(iii) It looks after maternal and child welfare centers.
(iv) To extend support in case of any accident.
(v) To arrange for supply of blood to needy victims of any calamity.

(c) National Health Programmes : The Government of India has taken up cudgels against common diseases like *malaria, tuberculosis, cholera* and *leprosy*. Following are the activities involved in each of the below mentioned national programmes against diseases :

(i) Malaria : Undertakes survey of malaria-hit areas, controls mosquitoes by using insecticides and distributes anti-malarial drugs.

(ii) Tuberculosis : *Tuberculosis* is detected and treated in its early stages. Also administers the BCG vaccination in healthy population.

(iii) Cholera : This disease is rife mainly in tropical countries. The spread of cholera is controlled by improving sanitation, providing safe drinking water, and removing sewage and garbage. There are mobile medical units that also cater to victims of cholera.

(iv) Leprosy : Leprosy is a skin disorder which is diagnosed and treated. Rehabilitation centers are established for lepers. In our country, the disease still faces ostracism in many places because of superstition.

EXERCISE

A. VERY SHORT ANSWER TYPE

(I) Multiple Choice Questions

Select the most appropriate option in each case :
1. An example of an insect-borne disease is :
   (a) Diarrhoea (b) Typhoid
   (c) Gastroenteritis
2. Leprosy is a :
   (a) Skin disorder (b) blood disorder
   (c) heart disorder
3. The World Health Organization was set up in the year :
   (a) 1957 (b) 1948
   (c) 1962

HEALTH AND HEALTH ORGANIZATIONS

4. Red cross day is celebrated on :
   (a) May 8 (b) June 21
   (c) 18 September (d) 14 November

(II) Name the Following

1. An organization whose one function is to procure and supply blood to needy victims of a natural calamity.
2. An organization which supports projects for research on disease.
3. Year in which Red Cross Organization was founded.
4. Disease spreads by rats.
5. WHO headquarter is located in................

B. SHORT ANSWER TYPE

1. List any three health problems in India.
2. Mention the functions of local bodies.
3. State any four Major activities of the Red Cross Society.

C. LONG ANSWER TYPE

1. State the main functions of World Health Organization.
2. How does the Red Cross work?
3. How do local bodies work to maintain health?
4. What are external health aids?
5. Categorize the following activities as per the functions of the Red Cross Society and the WHO.
   (a) To suggest quarantine measures to prevent spread of disease.
   (b) Humanitarian services to victims of war
   (c) To educate people in accident prevention
   (d) To promote projects for research on disease

DO YOU KNOW ?

➤ 1.8 million persons die every year from diarrhoeal diseases, 90% are children under 5, mostly in developing countries.
➤ Almost, two billion people were affected by natural disasters in the last decade of the 20th century, 86% of them by floods and droughts.

15

POLLUTION : AN INCREASING ENVIRONMENTAL HAZARD

CHAPTER HIGHLIGHTS
- 15.1. Introduction
- 15.2. Pollution
- 15.3. Pollutants
  - 15.3.1. Major Pollutants
- 15.4. Types of Pollution
  - 15.4.1. Air Pollution
  - 15.4.2. Water Pollution
  - 15.4.3. Soil Pollution
  - 15.4.4. Radiation/Nuclear Pollution
  - 15.4.5. Noise Pollution
- 15.5. Environmental Issues
  - 15.5.1. Global Warming
  - 15.5.2. Acid Rain
  - 15.5.3. Ozone Layer Depletion

15.1. INTRODUCTION

Pollution is the introduction of contaminants into the natural environment that cause adverse changes. Pollution can take the form of chemical substances or energy, such as noise, heat or light. Pollutants, the components of pollution, can be either foreign substances/energies or naturally occurring contaminants.

Environment may be defined as the physical and biological world around us. Our natural environment comprises all living and non-living things occurring naturally on earth as a whole or in specific regions.

15.2. POLLUTION

Pollution is defined as an undesirable change in the physical, chemical, or biological characteristics of air, water, and soil that may harmfully affect life or create a potential health hazard for any living organism. In simple terms, pollution is the contamination of the environment as a result of human activities. Nearly everyone causes pollution. The sources of contamination that pollute the environment are known as pollutants. Pollutants are the components of pollution, which can be either foreign substances or naturally occurring environmental contaminants. The sources of pollution or the types of pollutants can be further classified as air, water, soil, radiation, and noise pollutants.

15.3. POLLUTANTS

Pollutants are substances or chemicals, which change the natural balance of the environment, thus, causing pollution. In simple terms, a pollutant is a waste material that pollutes air, water or soil. Pollutants stimulate, initiate or terminate the vital metabolic reactions of the organisms.

15.3.1. Major Pollutants

There are many different kinds of pollutants, but major problems arise from the following :

(a) Gases : Carbon monoxide (CO), Sulphur dioxide (SO_2), Hydrogen sulphide (H_2S), Oxides of Nitrogen (NO, NO_2), Halogens (chlorine, bromine, iodine etc.), and to a lesser extent, Carbon dioxide (CO_2).

(b) Particulate matter : Dust, soot, grit, etc.

(c) Acid droplets : Sulphuric and nitric acid.

POPULATION : AN INCREASING ENVIRONMENTAL HAZARD

(d) Metals : Chromium, lead, zinc, mercury, nickel, cadmium, etc.

(e) Agrochemicals : Insecticides, pesticides, herbicides, weedicides etc.

(f) Organic substances : Benzene, benzpyrene, alkyl benzene sulphonates (ABs)

(g) Fluorides

(h) Photochemical-oxidants : Ozone, peroxyacetyl nitrate (PAN), ethylene etc.

(i) Radioactive substances : Uranium, plutonium, strontium, iodine, etc.

(j) Noise : TV, Loudspeakers, Car Horn, Loud music.

15.4. TYPES OF POLLUTION

The increase in man-made activities over the years has caused severe damage to the earth's ecosystem. It is responsible for global warming, adversely affecting the lives of everyone on earth. Over the years there has been an exponential increase in casualties due to pollution related diseases in both plants and animals on earth. Pollution on earth can be broadly classified into five major types: air, water, soil, radiation, and noise pollution. A brief discussion of each of these five categories of pollution follows.

15.4.1. Air Pollution

Air pollution can be defined as the presence of one or more contaminants in the atmosphere, which may be harmful to the environment. It is perhaps the most common and the most dangerous type of pollution. It involves the direct release of chemicals into the environment.

Sources of air pollution : The sources of air pollution may be both natural and man-made.

(a) Natural sources

(i) These are ash from volcanic eruptions, forest fires, sea-salt sprays, biological decay, photochemical oxidation of terpenes, marshes, extra-terrestrial bodies, pollen-grains of flowers, spores etc.

(ii) Radio-active minerals present in the earth's crust may be the source of radioactivity in the air.

(b) Vehicular sources

(i) The toxic vehicular exhausts are a source of considerable air pollution.

(ii) In big cities about 60% of atmospheric pollution is caused by internal combustion engines like scooter, cars, buses, trucks, etc.

(iii) The two-wheelers and three-wheelers contribute about 60% of total CO and 80% of total hydrocarbons.

(iv) Jet aeroplanes, air conditioners, cleaning solvents and refrigerators release aerosols. These are chlorofluoro carbons (CFCs) and are known to cause serious damage to the environment.

(c) Industrial sources

(i) These may include Thermal power plants, industrial units, vehicular emissions, burning of fossil fuels, agricultural activities etc.

(ii) Thermal power plants, the major source of generating electricity, emit pollutants like fly ash and gases like sulphur dioxide.

(iii) Fertilizer plants, smelters, textile mills, tanneries, refineries, chemical industries, paper and pulp mills are also the sources of air pollution.

(d) Indoor air pollution

(i) In the underdeveloped and developing countries like India commonly used kitchen fuels like coal, dung-cakes, wood and kerosene in their kitchens are a source of indoor smoke.

(ii) Complete combustion of fuels produces CO_2 which may not be toxic but incomplete combustion by badly tuned engines produces toxic CO gas.

(iii) Burning of coal produces sulphur dioxide.

Common pollutants : Most air pollutants cannot be seen or smelled but they still exist in dangerous proportions and can be a serious health hazard. The key polluting gases in the air include :

(1) Sulfur dioxide
(2) Nitrogen oxides
(3) Ammonia
(4) Carbon dioxide
(5) Carbon monoxide
(6) Volatile Organic Compounds (VOCs)
(7) Ozone
(8) Persistent Organic Pollutants (POPs)
(9) Airborne particles
(10) Toxic metals
(11) Radioactive pollutants

Effects of air pollution : Air pollution has a negative impact on human health, crops, forests, fisheries, semi-natural ecosystems, and materials (e.g. corrosion), etc. Air pollution is responsible for major health related issues in humans, can kill plants and trees by destroying their leaves, and can kill animals, especially fish in highly polluted rivers. Some major effects of air pollution on environment are listed below :

Effects on Human Health

➤ High amount of CO in the air causes difficulty in breathing, suffocation, dizziness, unconsciousness and even death.

- Air pollutants, like cigarette smoke cause lung cancer, asthma, chronic bronchitis and emphysema.
- SO_2 causes constriction of the respiratory passage.
- Ozone causes eye inflammation and burning sensation in the chest of humans. It also breaks down molecules of DNA causing skin cancer and cataract.
- Many other air pollutants like benzene (from unleaded petrol), formaldehyde, toxic metals and dioxins (from burning of polythene) may cause mutations, reproductive failure and even cancer.

Effects on Plants
- Hydrocarbons cause premature leaf fall, flower bud shedding, curling of petals and discolouration of sepals.
- Sensitive plants like alfalfa, barley, cotton, wheat, apple etc. are affected by SO_2.
- Ozone is harmful to tobacco, tomato, bean, and pine plants.
- Peroxyacetyl Nitrate (PAN), a secondary pollutant affects Hill reaction in plants by blocking photolysis of water and inhibiting photosystem-II.
- High concentration of fluoride causes 'chlorosis' and 'necrosis' of leaf tips and leaf margins.
- Air pollutants enter through stomata of leaves, destroy chlorophyll thereby affecting photosynthesis.

Effects on aquatic life : Air pollutants combine with rain water causing high acidity in fresh water lakes. This condition affects aquatic life especially fish communities.

Control : Air pollution prevention efforts generally focus on both source and waste reduction, and on reuse and recycling of materials. The following measures can help prevent air pollution:
- Reuse and recycle articles such as paper and plastic bags, paper etc. This will contribute towards reducing air pollution and global warming since fewer trees would be cut and the ecosystem can be preserved.
- Barium compounds should be added to the fuel to control the amount and quality of exhaust gasses.
- Industries should be setup in specific areas.
- Nitrogen oxides should be removed from the combustion process.
- Vehicular pollution may be checked by regular tune-up of engines, replacement of old vehicles, use of fuel efficient engines (to reduce CO and hydrocarbon emission).
- Maximum number of trees should be planted (plants absorb particulate pollutants).

PROGRESS CHECK

FILL IN THE BLANKS

1. The sources of contamination that pollute the environment are known as......................
2. Pollutants stimulate, ...or ....the vital metabolic reactions of the organisms.
3. Air pollutants, like .... cause lung cancer.
4. High concentration of fluoride causes .... and necrosis of leaf tips.

15.4.2. Water Pollution

Around 75% of the earth's surface is covered with water and more than half of the total population of earth's species resides in water. Moreover, our lives are dependent on water and life without water is impossible. Water pollution is contamination of water by foreign matter that deteriorates the quality of the water.

Fresh water pollution : Water pollution not only affects the fish and animals living in it but also affects the entire food chain by transmitting the contaminants and pollutants present in it to the consumers which depend on these aquatic animals for their dietary requirements. The pollution of water has far reaching effects. It not only affects the availability of safe drinking water but also harms the environment.

Marine pollution : Many toxic pollutants enter the sea as a result of rapid industrialization. Oil in sea water due to oil spills can spread over a large area of the sea and remain dispersed or get adsorbed on sediments. Oil spills can be caused by overturned or damaged oil tankers, offshore oil mining, oil refineries etc. They have an adverse effect on marine life like sea birds, fish etc.

Sources : Just like air pollution, water pollution is caused by the direct incorporation of hazardous pollutants. The sources of these pollutants are yet again large industries that dispose of their waste in lakes and ponds (Fig. 15.1). Some common sources are listed below :

Fig. 15.1 : Water pollution

(a) Sewage and other wastes : Sewage is the water borne waste derived from homes (domestic waste) and animal and food processing plants. It includes human excreta, paper, cloth, soap, detergents etc. There is uncontrolled dumping of wastes of rural areas, towns, cities into ponds, lakes and rivers.

(b) Household detergents : Household detergents are released into drains and ultimately carried into lakes, rivers etc. The major constituents of detergents include phosphates, nitrates and ammonium and Alkyl Benzene Sulphonates (ABS).

(c) Oil spills : An oil spill is the release of a liquid petroleum hydrocarbon into the environment, especially marine areas, due to human activity. Oil spills may be due to releases of crude oil from tankers, offshore platforms, drilling rigs and wells, spills of refined petroleum products (such as gasoline, diesel) and their by-products, heavier fuels used by large ships such as bunker fuel, or the spill of any oily refuse or waste oil.

Common pollutants : Below is the list of most common water pollutants, both organic and inorganic:

Organic Water Pollutants

(i) Insecticides and herbicides, a range of organohalides
(ii) Bacteria from livestock operations
(iii) Food processing waste including pathogens
(iv) Tree debris from logging operations
(v) Detergents and chemical compounds found in cosmetics products

Inorganic Water Pollutants

(i) Heavy metals
(ii) Acidity caused by industrial discharges such as sulfur dioxide by power plants
(iii) Chemical waste
(iv) Fertilizers from agricultural use
(v) Silt from construction sites, logging, slash and burn operation

> **Thermal pollution :** Thermal pollution is the degradation of water quality by any process that changes ambient water temperature. A common cause of thermal pollution is the use of water as a coolant by power plants and industrial manufacturers.

Effects of water pollution : The pollution of the water bodies available to humans makes their water unfit for drinking and other uses. Polluted water also breeds viruses, bacteria, intestinal parasites and other harmful microorganisms, which can cause waterborne diseases like diarrhea, dysentery, and typhoid. Some other hazardous effects of water pollution are :

(1) Water pollution not only affects land animals like humans, but also marine animals.
(2) Polluted water is likely to cause water borne diseases like typhoid, dysentery, gastroenteritis, hepatitis etc.
(3) Pollutants like heavy metals, pesticides, cyanides and many other organic and inorganic compounds reaching the water bodies are harmful to aquatic life.
(4) Mercury released by chlorine and caustic soda factories reaches man through the food chain. It affects nervous system leading to death. In 1953, Japan suffered *Minamata disease* (Minamata Bay of Japan) due to Mercury poisoning.
(5) Lead is highly toxic to plants and animals.
(6) Liver and kidney damage, mental disorders, gastrointestinal trouble, residual paralysis are some important problems due to presence of excess lead in water bodies.
(7) Fluorides also destroy the leaf tissues.

Control of water pollution : There are several methods by which water pollution can be prevented or checked.

➢ The waste water should be treated before its discharge into lakes or rivers.
➢ Primary treatment of sewage should be done, which includes physical processes like sedimentation, floatation, etc.
➢ Secondary treatment using microorganisms in oxidation ponds or activated sludge (soft mud) process is also very helpful.
➢ Algal blooms should be removed from time to time.

- Advanced treatment for nitrates and phosphate may prevent eutrophication.
- Judicious use of agrochemicals like pesticides and fertilizers may reduce their surface run-off and leaching.

15.4.3. Soil Pollution

Soil is the upper layer of the earth's crust which is formed by weathering of rocks. Organic matter in the soil makes it suitable for living organisms. Dumping of various types of materials especially domestic and industrial wastes causes soil pollution. Soil pollution involves the contamination of soil by the release of harmful substances into the soil.

Sources of Soil Pollution

(a) Domestic wastes include garbage, rubbish like glass, plastics, metallic cans, paper, fibre, cloth rags, containers, paints, varnishes, etc.

(b) Sewage tanks are harmful and toxic, which pollute the soil. The sewage sludge contains many pathogenic organisms, bacteria, viruses and intestinal worms, which cause pollution in the soil.

(c) Thermal power plants generate a large quantity of 'fly ash'. Huge quantities of these wastes are dumped on soils, thus contaminating them.

(d) Industrial wastes also contain some organic and inorganic compounds that are refractory and *non-biodegradable*.

(e) Soil also receives excreta from animals and humans.

Wastes are substances or objects which are disposed due to our day-to day activities. The waste material can be categorized into two types :

(i) Biodegradable waste

Those waste materials which can be broken down to non-poisonous substances in nature in due course of time by the action of micro-organisms like certain bacteria, are called biodegradable waste. Cattle dung and compost are common examples of biodegradable waste. Other examples are animal bones, leather, tea leaves, wool, paper and wheat.

(ii) Non-biodegradable waste

The waste materials which cannot be broken down into non-poisonous or harmless substances in nature are called non-biodegradable waste. Examples are plastics, polythene bags, ball-point pen refills, synthetic fibres, and glass objects, metal articles like aluminium cans, iron nails, silver foil and radioactive wastes.

Effects of Soil Pollution

(1) Sewage and industrial effluents which pollute the soil ultimately affect human health.

(2) Various types of chemicals like acids, alkalis, pesticides, insecticides etc., in the industrial discharges affect soil fertility by causing changes in physical, chemical, and biological properties.

(3) Some of the persistent toxic chemicals accumulate in food chain and ultimately affect human health.

(4) Pesticide persistence is toxic and causes bioaccumulation in food chain.

Control of Soil Pollution

- Effluents should be properly treated before discharging them into the soil.
- Solid wastes should be properly collected and disposed of by appropriate methods. Biodegradable organic waste should be used for generation of biogas.
- Recovery of useful products from the waste should be done.
- Alternative non-chemical strategies of pest disease and weed control should be adopted by which environmental problems may be alleviated.

15.4.4. Radiation/Nuclear Pollution

Radioactive substances are present in nature. They undergo natural radioactive decay in which unstable isotopes spontaneously give out fast moving particles, high energy radiations or both, at a fixed rate until a new stable isotope is formed. These particles and their rays pass through paper and wood but can be stopped by a concrete wall, lead slabs or water. Damage caused by different types of radiations depends on the penetration power and presence of the source inside or outside the body.

Sources of radioactive pollution : Damage caused by different types of radiations depends on the penetration power and the presence of the sources inside or outside the body.

(a) Natural sources

(i) Cosmic rays from outer space

(ii) Presence of Radio nucleotides in the earth such as Radium-224, Uranium- 235, 238, Thorium-232, Carbon-14, and potassium-40.

(b) Man-made sources

(i) Nuclear Power Plants

(ii) Nuclear weapons

(iii) Disposal of nuclear waste

(iv) Uranium mining

Effects of Radioactive Pollution

(1) Both ionising and non-ionising radiations break the backbone of chain(s) of DNA molecules.

(2) Chromosomes are also affected by radiation.

Single break or two or more breaks in chromosomes, or chromatin may occur. Stickiness or dumping of the chromosomes is another effect of radiation.

(3) Due to effect radiation, the cell may die before it divides or there may be delay in cell division.
(4) Miscarriages, cataract, congenital abnormalities in birth, cancer of bone, thyroid, and breast are some of the effects of radiation.
(5) Non-ionizing radiations i.e. Ultraviolet rays are also harmful to organisms. UV-rays break DNA, RNA and Proteins.
(6) Longer exposure of skin to UV radiations causes a skin disease called *Xeroderma Pigmentosum*.

Control of Radioactive Pollution

➤ Setting up of new nuclear power plants should be carefully done after considering the long and short term effects of doing so.
➤ Proper and careful disposal of wastes from laboratory involving the use of radio isotopes should be done.
➤ Competition for acquiring nuclear weapons should be prohibited.
➤ Radioactive materials may be used for peaceful purposes.

15.4.5. Noise Pollution

Noise is defined as an unpleasant sound that has an adverse effect on the human ear. Noise pollution is the increase in the rate of noise in the environment. Noise can penetrate into the human mind and control it. Too much noise leads to severe psychological illnesses and seriously affects behavior. It leads to hypertension, stress, aggression and annoyance. Noise levels can be measured by the decibel method (decibel is the unit of sound) :

Sources of Noise Pollution

(a) Road, rail and air traffic
(b) Neighborhood and domestic noise
(c) Incompatible land use
(d) Industrial noise

Common Pollutants

(i) Moving vehicles
(ii) Man-made machines
(iii) Loud music

Effects of noise pollution : Noise pollution has the following hazardous effects :

(1) Interferes with human communication since communication is severely affected in noisy surroundings.
(2) Noise can cause temporary or permanent hearing loss. It depends on intensity and duration of sound level.
(3) Continuous exposure to noise affects the functioning of various systems of the body. It may result in hypertension, insomnia (sleeplessness), gastro-intestinal and digestive disorders, etc.

Control of noise pollution : Following measures can be adopted to reduce pollution caused by noise.

(1) Noise making machines should be kept in containers with sound absorbing media. The noise path will be interrupted and less noise will reach the workers.
(2) Proper oiling will reduce the noise from machinery.
(3) Use of sound absorbing silencers in transportation vehicles can reduce noise by absorbing sound. For this purpose various types of fibrous material could be used.
(4) Prohibit use of power horns in cars.
(5) Use of loud speakers, especially at night should be banned.

FILL IN THE BLANKS

1. A common cause of thermal pollution is the use of water as a ....by power plants and industrial manufacturers.
2. Polluted water is likely to cause water borne diseases like .... and............
3. Thermal power plants generate a large quantity of ....
4. Noise levels can be measured by......... method.
5. Noise can cause temporary or permanent ....

15.5. ENVIRONMENTAL ISSUES

As early as 1896, the Swedish scientist **Santé Arrhenius** had predicted that human activities would interfere with the way the sun interacts with the earth, resulting in global warming and climate change. His prediction has become true and climate change is now disrupting global environmental stability. Few examples of environmental issues of global significance are :

(a) Global warming and Greenhouse effect
(b) Ozone layer depletion

15.5.1. Global Warming

Global Warming is an average increase in the temperature of the atmosphere near the Earth's surface and in the troposphere, which can contribute to changes in global climate patterns. It can occur from a variety of causes, both natural and human induced. In common usage, *"global warming"* often refers to the warming that can occur as a result of increased emissions of greenhouse gases from human activities. Therefore, it is closely linked to the enhanced greenhouse effect, which is an increase in the concentration of greenhouse gases in the atmosphere leading to an increase in the amount of infrared or thermal radiation near the surface.

Most scientists agree that enhanced greenhouse effect leads to rising temperatures, referred to as global warming. The results of global warming do not limit themselves to a mere warmer weather, but also to an *erratic* climate that, if left unchecked, could cause pervasive natural disasters and species extinction.

Causes of global warming : The causes for the existence of global warming are not limited to natural causes only, but comprise man-made or anthropogenic causes too.

(a) Greenhouse effect : The major natural greenhouse gases are water vapor, which causes about 36-70% of the greenhouse effect on Earth; carbon dioxide (CO_2), which causes 9-26%; methane, which causes 4-9% and ozone, which causes 3-7%. Other greenhouse gases include nitrous oxide, sulfur hexafluoride, hydro-fluorocarbons, per-fluorocarbons and chlorofluorocarbons (CFCs).

Greenhouse gases in the atmosphere act like a mirror and reflect back to the Earth a part of the heat radiation, which would otherwise be lost to space. The higher the concentration of greenhouse gases like carbon dioxide in the atmosphere, the more heat energy is being reflected back to the Earth. The emission of carbon dioxide into the environment mainly from burning of fossil fuels (oil, gas, petrol, kerosene, etc.) has increased dramatically over the past five decades.

The increase of greenhouse gas concentration (mainly carbon dioxide) led to a substantial warming of the Earth and the sea, called global warming. In other words, it can be said that the increase in the man-made emission of greenhouse gases is the cause for global warming

(b) Pollution : This is one of the biggest man-made problems. Pollution comes in many shapes and sizes. Burning fossil fuels is one thing that causes pollution. Fossil fuels are fuels made of organic matter such as coal, or oil. When fossil fuels are burned, they give off carbon dioxide (CO_2).

(c) Population : Since CO_2 contributes to global warming, the increase in population makes the problem worse because we breathe out CO_2. Also, the trees that convert CO_2 to O_2 are being demolished at an ever faster rate to use the land as property for our homes and buildings.

(d) Deforestation : Clearing away of forests and forest ecosystems on a large-scale has posed several dangers to life on Earth. Trees are essential for absorbing excess carbon dioxide in air. However, deforestation is also a natural cause of global warming because forest fires can occur naturally and these are responsible for tearing through huge areas of forest and woodland.

Effects of global warming : Global warming is already affecting mankind, plants and animals in a number of ways such as increased ocean levels, droughts and changed weather patterns. It is well recognized by scientists around the world as a serious public health and environmental concern. Below is the list of effects that global warming has on the environment, climate and human kind.

(i) Melting of glaciers : The melting of glaciers will create an excess of problems for human kind and the animals living on the Earth. Due to increased global warming, the level of the seas will rise, leading to flooding of coastal areas and this will in turn create havoc in human life.

(ii) Climate change : Warming of atmosphere will considerably increase its moisture-carrying capacity. While the troposphere warms up, the stratosphere will cool down. This would cause widespread changes in rainfall patterns due to changed pattern of air-mass movements. More global warming will lead to more evaporation, which will cause more rains. Animals and plants cannot easily adapt to increased rainfall. Plants may die and animals may migrate to other areas, which can cause entire ecosystem to become off-balance and finally collapse.

(iii) Diseases : As the temperature rises, it will have an effect on the health of humans and the diseases they are exposed to. With the increase in rainfall, water-borne diseases like malaria are likely to spread. With global temperatures rising, disease-carrying insects will migrate to populous regions. The Earth will become warmer and result in major problems for its inhabitants.

(iv) Health problems: One of the serious effects of global warming is the health issues that are caused by many of the contributing factors. It is not healthy to breathe dirty air everyday as it can lead to a decline in the immune system and the onset of health problems such as asthma and bronchitis. This could be common in many big cities across the world as the population tries to fight against global warming effects.

15.5.2. Acid Rain

Acid rain is rain consisting of water droplets that are unusually acidic because of atmospheric pollution

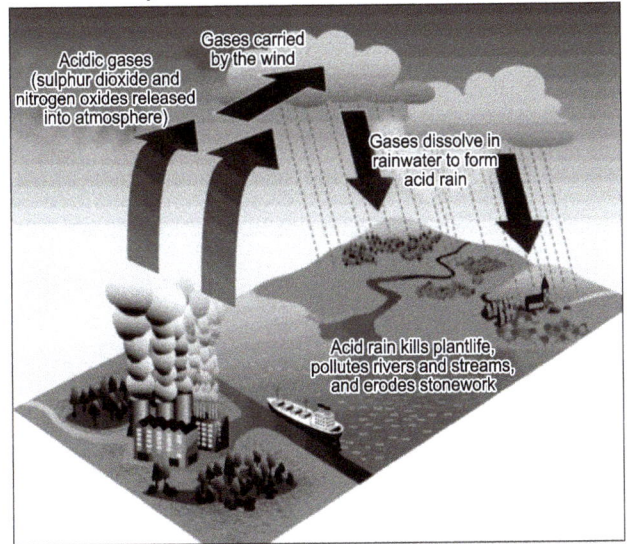

Fig. 15.2 : Acid rain formation

most notably the excessive amounts of sulfur and nitrogen released by cars and industrial processes. Acid rain is also called acid deposition because this term includes other forms of acidic precipitation such as snow.

Acidic deposition occurs in two ways: wet and dry. Wet deposition is any form of precipitation that removes acids from the atmosphere and deposits them on the Earth's surface (Fig. 15.2). Dry deposition polluting particles and gases stick to the ground via dust and smoke in the absence of precipitation. This form of deposition is dangerous however because precipitation can eventually wash pollutants into streams, lakes, and rivers.

Causes of acid rain : Acid rain is caused by a chemical reaction that begins when compounds like sulfur dioxide and nitrogen oxides are released into the air. These substances can rise very high into the atmosphere, where they mix and react with water, oxygen, and other chemicals to form more acidic pollutants, known as *acid rain*. Sulfur dioxide and nitrogen oxides dissolve very easily in water and can be carried very far by the wind. As a result, the two compounds can travel long distances where they become part of the rain, sleet, snow, and fog that we experience on certain days.

Human activities are the main cause of acid rain. Over the past few decades, humans have released so many different chemicals into the air that they have changed the mix of gases in the atmosphere. Power plants release the majority of sulfur dioxide and much of the nitrogen oxides when they burn fossil fuels, such as coal, to produce electricity. In addition, the exhaust from cars, trucks, and buses releases nitrogen oxides and sulfur dioxide into the air. These pollutants cause acid rain.

Effects of acid rain : Acid rain causes acidification of lakes and streams and contributes to damage of trees at high elevations and many sensitive forest soils. In addition, acid rain accelerates the decay of building materials and paints, including irreplaceable buildings, statues, and sculptures that are part of our nation's cultural heritage. Prior to falling to the earth, SO_2 and NO_2 gases and their particulate matter derivatives, sulfates and nitrates, contribute to visibility degradation and harm public health.

15.5.3. Ozone Layer Depletion

Earth's atmosphere is divided into three regions, namely troposphere, stratosphere and mesosphere. The stratosphere extends from 10 to 50 kms from the Earth's surface. This region is concentrated with slightly pungent smelling, light bluish ozone gas. The ozone molecule contains three atoms of oxygen; its chemical formula is O_3. The ozone layer in the stratosphere acts as an efficient filter for harmful solar ultraviolet B (UV-B) rays.

Ozone is produced and destroyed naturally in the atmosphere and un-til recently, this resulted in a well balanced equilibrium. Ozone is formed when oxygen molecules absorb ultraviolet radiation with wavelengths less than 240 nanometers and is destroyed when it absorbs ultraviolet radia-tion with wavelengths greater than 290 nanometers. In recent years, scien-tists have measured a seasonal thinning of the ozone layer primarily at the South Pole. This phenomenon results in the formation of 'ozone hole'.

Effects of Ozone Layer Depletion

(a) Effects on human and animal health : Increased penetration of solar UV-B radiation is likely to have high impact on human health with potential risks of eye diseases, skin cancer and other infectious diseases.

(b) Effects on terrestrial plants : In forests and grasslands, increased radiation is likely to change species composition thus altering the bio-diversity in different ecosystems. It could also affect the plant community indirectly resulting in changes in plant form, secondary metabolism, etc.

(c) Effects on aquatic ecosystems : High levels of radiation exposure in tropics and subtropics may affect the distribution of phytoplankton, which form the foundation of aquatic food webs. It can also cause damage to early development stages of fish, shrimp, crab, amphibians and other animals, the most severe effects being decreased reproductive capacity and impaired larval development.

(d) Effects on bio-geo-chemical Cycles : Increased solar UV radiation could affect terrestrial

and aquatic bio-geo-chemical cycles thus altering both sources and sinks of greenhouse and important trace gases, e.g. carbon dioxide (CO_2), carbon monoxide (CO), carbonyl sulfide (COS), etc.

EXERCISE

A. VERY SHORT ANSWER TYPE

(I) Fill in the Blanks

1. Radio-active minerals present in the earth's crust may be the sources of _____ in the air.
2. The two - wheelers and three-wheelers contribute about _____ of total CO.
3. Burning of coal produces _____ dioxide.
4. Sewage is the water borne waste derived from home and _____ and _____ plants.
5. An _____ is the release of a liquid petroleum hydrocarbon into the environment.
6. _____ is the degradation of water quality by any process that changes ambient water temperature.
7. UV-rays break DNA, _____ and _____.
8. Silencers can reduce noise by _____ sound.
9. _____ is an average increase in the temperature of the atmosphere.
10. Acidic deposition occurs in two ways _____ and _____.
11. The ozone layer, in the stratosphere acts as an efficient filter for harmful solar _____ rays.

(II) Define the Following Terms

1. Sewage
2. Eutrophication
3. Urban and Industrial wastes
4. Nuclear fallout
5. Decibel
6. Oil spill
7. Pollutant
8. Ecosystem
9. Global Warming
10. Greenhouse Effect
11. CFCs

(III) Distinguish between the Following

1. Pollution and pollutant.
2. Natural and man-made sources.
3. Indoor pollution and outdoor pollution.
4. Physical effects of pollution and biological effects of pollution.
5. Water pollution and soil pollution.

(IV) Discuss the Following Statements

1. Pollution destroys the purity of the ecosystem.
2. Pollutants affect the vital metabolic reactions of the organisms.
3. Population growth is a fundamental pollution cause.
4. Water pollution affects the fish communities.
5. Soil pollution decreases the yield of crops.
6. Oil ballast should not be dumped into the sea.
7. More and more trees should be planted.

B. SHORT ANSWER TYPE

1. Define pollution? Name the different kinds of pollution?
2. What are the causative agents of pollution?
3. What do you mean by pollutant? Name some common environmental pollutants.
4. What is Smog? How is it harmful?
5. What is thermal pollution? How does it cause pollution?
6. Define marine pollution.
7. Describe nuclear fallout.
8. Write a note on oil spills
9. Explain the Greenhouse Effect.
10. What is meant by Ozone Hole?
11. What is meant by Global Warming?
12. What is Ozone Layer?

C. LONG ANSWER TYPE

1. Describe the main types of pollution.
2. Describe air pollution and its causative agents.
3. What is water pollution? Describe its various types.
4. What is soil pollution? Describe its control measures.
5. Describe noise pollution? What are the main sources of noise pollution?
6. What preventive measures would you adopt to control noise pollution?
7. What is radioactive pollution? Describe its effects on environment.
8. What are the causes responsible for the depletion of the ozone layer?
9. What are the effects of the Ozone Depletion?

DO YOU KNOW ?

➢ 14 billion pounds of garbage are dumped into the ocean every year. Most of it is plastic.
➢ Over 1 million sea birds and 100,000 sea mammals are killed by pollution every year.
➢ An estimated 1,000 children in India die every day due to diseases caused by polluted water.
➢ 5000 people die every day as a result of drinking unclean water.
➢ More than 100 pesticides in any medium- air, water or soil can cause birth defects, gene mutation and cancer.

www.ingramcontent.com/pod-product-compliance
Ingram Content Group UK Ltd.
Pitfield, Milton Keynes, MK11 3LW, UK
UKHW050418240426
12048UKWH00014B/701